PRIVATE PRISONS AND THE PUBLIC INTEREST

PRIVATE PRISONS
AND THE
PUBLIC INTEREST

DOUGLAS C. McDONALD, Editor

RUTGERS UNIVERSITY PRESS

New Brunswick and London

A Joint Project of the Vera Institute of Justice and
the Institute for Court Management of the
National Center for State Courts, Supported by the
Florence V. Burden and Edna McConnell Clark Foundations

Library of Congress Cataloging-in-Publication Data

Private prisons and the public interest / Douglas C. McDonald, editor.
    p. cm. — (Crime, law, and deviance series)
    Includes bibliographical references.
    ISBN 0-8135-1574-2
    1. Corrections—United States—Contracting out. 2. Prisons—
United States—Overcrowding. 3. Privatization—United States.
I. McDonald, Douglas, 1946–   . II. Series.
HV9469.P75   1990
365'.973—dc20   90-30616
              CIP

British Cataloging-in-Publication information available

To JULIA and NANCY

Contents

List of Figures and Tables

Preface

This collection of essays on the emerging "privatization" of prisons and jails—a phenomenon that encompasses the operation (and sometimes the ownership) of correctional facilities by private for-profit firms contracting with governments, and also the private ownership and financing of facilities that are operated by public employees—is the product of work that began in late 1986. At that time, the Vera Institute of Justice and the Institute for Court Management of the National Center of State Courts commissioned papers on several aspects of this phenomenon that were thought to be poorly understood.

Those invited to write the essays in this book convened on two occasions in New York City, in December 1986 and again four months later, to review early drafts of papers and to discuss the issues. A number of people joined us at these meetings to explore what this phenomenon meant not only for the corrections field but also for social services more generally. We value their contributions. They include Thomas Gilmore, director of the Wharton Applied Social Research Center; Stephanie R. Lewis, vice-president of Government Finance Associates, Inc.; Alfred Kahn, professor of Social Policy and Planning at Columbia University's School of Social Work; Geof Gallas, director of research and special projects at the National Center for State Courts; Edward Loughran, commissioner of the Massachusetts Department of Youth Services; David Nee, then director of the Florence V. Burden Foundation (now of the Ittleson Foundation); Kenneth Schoen, director of the Justice Program of the Edna McConnell Clark Foundation; David Rothman, director of the Center for the Study of Society and Medicine at Columbia University's College of Physicians and Surgeons and also professor of social medicine and of history at Columbia University; Robert Schmidt, then supervisor of detention operations at the U.S. Immigration and Naturalization Service; J. David Seay, vice-president and counsel for the United Hospital Fund of New York; Michael Smith, director of the Vera Institute of Justice; and Larry R. Meachum, director of the Connecticut Department of Corrections.

I especially wish to thank Michael Smith for his collegial

assistance and for the support provided this project; Kenneth Schoen, Barbara Greenberg, David Nee, and the trustees of the Florence V. Burden Foundation and the Edna McConnell Clark Foundation for their generous support and advice; and Barry Mahoney, director of research at the Institute for Court Management of the National Center for State Courts, who served as a codirector of the project. Gail Carmichael and Sarah Lyon of the Vera Institute of Justice devoted much energy and time to clerical and administrative assistance, and their help is much appreciated.

Finally, the opinions expressed and the positions taken in these essays do not represent the policies of any of the organizations involved. The aim of the foundations and of the two organizations carrying out the project has been to explore the issues in a way that enriches the debate and helps public policymakers. By having several writers address the important issues, and by not forcing them to develop a consensus, we hope we have served this purpose.

Douglas C. McDonald
Cambridge, Massachusetts
November 1989

PRIVATE PRISONS AND THE PUBLIC INTEREST

Introduction

DOUGLAS C. MCDONALD

In 1986, the Nashville-based Corrections Corporation of America proposed to take over Tennessee's entire and very troubled prison system, with a ninety-nine-year lease from the state, for which it would pay $250 million. It would then use the prisons to house the state's convicted criminals, charging the state a negotiated daily rate for each prisoner, and would do so in a way that met the standards set by a federal judge who had found the state's prison system to be in violation of the U.S. Constitution. This small group of entrepreneurs, backed by wealthy investors who had previously created a chain of proprietary hospitals, claimed that private management would perform more efficiently than had the governmental agencies, thereby saving taxpayers' money, and that it could make a profit to boot.[1] Although smaller, privately owned or operated facilities had sprung up earlier in different parts of the country, the boldness of this proposal focused attention on an emerging phenomenon and set off some alarms. The state of Tennessee ultimately declined the offer, but this firm and others are acquiring and building prison facilities throughout the country. Correctional facilities are even being built "on spec," on the assumption that the demand for imprisonment cells will outpace the supply and thus create a market for private jailers.[2]

By the end of 1988, private correctional firms were operating approximately two dozen major facilities, including three medium- or maximum-security adult correctional institutions. In addition, they operated five detention centers under contract with the U.S. Immigration and Naturalization Service, which held about 800 of the approximately 2,600 detained aliens being held. They also operated a larger number of low-security or nonsecure institutions for adult offenders, including penal farms, work release facilities, and residential halfway houses, as well as juvenile detention facilities. Several states have changed their laws or are considering passage of legislation to enable private imprisonment. State governments are also leasing prisons built and owned by private corporations and staffing them with public employees, largely to avoid the various restrictions on issuing public debt for construction of publicly owned facilities.

The essays in this book explore this emerging phenomenon and address several questions that seem paramount. What are these new forms of private ownership, financing, and operation? Can privately operated jails and prisons be better managed? If so, is there something about the intrinsic nature of the public and private sectors that determines or contributes to this result? Can private firms deliver equal or better services for lower costs? If so, why? Is the marketplace better suited to provision of cost-effective "imprisonment services" than the public bureaucracies? If so, what is it about that marketplace that generates economizing? Will the structure of the market continue to stimulate economizing as the industry matures, or will the market become less competitive, inducing less pressure for cost cutting? Beyond cost reduction, does drawing the line differently between the public and private sectors yield other important benefits? Other costs? Will, for example, private firms develop an unhealthy relationship with lawmakers so that the public policymaking process is distorted to the benefit of those who have a material stake in a high demand for prisoners? How do the new "creative financing" procedures differ from the more conventional methods of public finance? How do their costs and benefits compare with those of conventional financing, and what are the implications for public accountability and control?

Beyond these practical questions lie moral ones. Is it just and proper that prisons and jails be run like businesses? Should business executives be permitted to harvest a profit from running or owning them? Even if the private sector can do so for a lower cost, is this reason enough to warrant the delegation of authority over individuals' liberty—certainly one of the most sensitive forms of power in a society that cherishes personal liberty?

In large measure, privatization has emerged as a means of alleviating a crisis in the nation's prisons and jails. Private investors are paying for the creation of new or upgraded cell space, thereby helping to accommodate the rising tide of prisoners. But is privatization the best way to resolve the current penal crisis?

Because privatization involves questions of ownership, contracting, and delegation of authority, a number of legal issues are raised by these new developments. Indeed, the American Bar Association's House of Delegates proclaimed in a 1986 resolution that the constitutional, statutory, and contractual questions are so complex that any further moves toward correctional privatization should be forestalled until such questions are clarified.[3] My own view is that many of the legal issues are important but that the threshold issues are broader in that they involve legal, ethical, and empirical considerations. In its most distilled form, the central issue, in my view, is whether it is good public policy to permit and encourage private entities to own and operate places of incarceration. The essays in this book tend to focus, consequently, on the subject as a public policy matter rather than as a strictly legal one, although legal questions are obviously involved.

To some, it may seem too early to give private correctional facilities an extended examination because the private imprisonment industry is still in its infancy and relatively few private prisons and jails exist. (Private correctional institutions did exist for extended periods in the eighteenth and nineteenth centuries in this country, and a few remnants of this practice survived until a few decades ago, as John DiIulio, Jr., discusses in his essay in this volume.) For this reason, it is difficult, if not impossible, to find definitive answers to many of the questions being asked.

That the questions are difficult to answer should not be a reason for avoiding them, however. This nation's federal system of government is a fragmented one, with literally thousands of different governments, and important changes in practice can occur in an incremental fashion almost without being noticed until they become too well entrenched either to stop or to control effectively. For example, private security forces grew to the point where they outnumbered public police before the implications of this change were fully recognized and before the matter was even raised to the status of an "issue."[4] Because the questions posed by the emergence of the private prison and jail are so important from a public policy perspective, it is prudent to devote thoughtful consideration to them early, so that the choices we face may be resolved in ways that advance the public interest.

Why Private Prisons and Jails Now?

Private jails and prisons owe their emergence to forces that show few, if any, signs of abating in the coming years. One is a pervasive reconsideration of the kinds of services that governments and markets are best suited to provide. Faced with a public unwilling to have taxes raised further and to have public debt increased, public officials have begun to explore ways to delegate to the private sector many responsibilities that have until recently been shouldered largely by government.[5] At the federal level, the Reagan administration led the way by encouraging privatization of a wide variety of government services; although the Bush administration has been somewhat less enthusiastic, this policy preference has not been reversed.

This privatization movement has become international, with many governments moving to denationalize and deregulate entire industries. Opportunities for privatization by denationalization have been greatest on the other side of the Atlantic in those societies that have, under various labor, social democratic, or communist governments, brought a wider range of industries under national ownership and control.[6] In the industrially developed noncommunist nations, the privatization movement has been fueled by a reaction against the ideology of welfare capitalism (though not its practice; for the demand for social services remains high), as well as by the need of public administrators to resolve the conflicting pressures of a growing demand for public services and more pronounced taxpayer resistance to paying for them. (A 1987 poll of city and county governments in the United States found these to be the two most commonly cited reasons for being interested in exploring privatization of public services.[7]) Faced with stagnating or slowly growing economies since the early 1970s, several governments have sought to strengthen free market mechanisms by denationalization, deregulation, and more extensive contracting, in hopes of spurring greater productivity and, by extension, lowering costs.

Other dynamics have also been at work within the criminal justice system to stimulate interest in privatized correctional services. Since the mid-1970s, demand for cell space has outstripped supply, creating opportunities for entrepreneurs who can quickly bring private capital and talent into the correctional field. Throughout the 1960s and up to the early 1970s, the numbers of inmates in federal and state prisons had been declining. In 1973, however, they began to increase. Between 1972 and 1986, the nation's state and federal prison population grew 179 percent, more than fifteen times faster than the general population.[8] By the end of that period, 546,659 persons were behind bars in these prisons, an all-time record.[9] To accommodate the increase from 1985 to 1986 alone (43,000 additional prisoners), seven new medium-sized (500-bed) prisons were needed *each month*.

The demand for bed space in the nation's local jails, which number approximately thirty-five hundred, also rose substantially during this period. Reliable estimates of the number of inmates in jail in the early 1970s are not available, but surveys between 1978 and 1986 found that the average daily jail population increased 68 percent, from 157,930 to 265,517.[10]

It is not that there were significantly more crimes and arrests during these years, thus increasing incrementally the number of prisoners behind bars. The annual number of arrests nationwide rose only slightly during this period. For example, in 1985 there were only 8 percent more arrests for "index" crimes (the most serious offenses tracked by the F.B.I. and police) than in 1976.[11] What made the difference was that penal policies became much tougher, partly because public officials felt pressed to do something about crime for their constituents and because they (especially the elected officials) discovered that being tough on crime could be beneficial for their political careers. Beginning in the early 1970s and for about ten years, lawmakers in state after state passed laws mandating imprisonment for many different crimes, most frequently for gun and drug law violations and for violent crimes.[12] Judges' discretion in sentencing was thereby curtailed, parole boards followed suit by becoming more restrictive, and parole release was even abolished in some states.

Federal, state, and local governments have not been able to build new prisons and jails quickly enough to meet the rising demand, and severe crowding has become the norm. Jurisdictions with larger jails (100-plus beds) were running them at about 108 percent of capacity at last count.[13] In 1986, all but seven states were operating their prisons in excess of 95 percent capacity; thirty-eight were operating 100 percent above capacity; and seven states exceeded capacity by more than 50 percent. On average, the nation's state prisons in 1986 had 6 percent more bodies than they had places for, and the federal prison system was operating between 27 percent and 59 percent above capacity.[14] Prisoners were doubled up in small cells and sleeping in hallways, day rooms, gymnasiums, and sometimes even in bathrooms.

This only worsens an already bad situation, because a large proportion of this country's penal facilities are outmoded and even obsolete by contemporary standards. According to a government survey conducted in 1983, half of all state and federal prisons were more than thirty-five years old and a substantial number had existed for more than a century.[15] Furthermore, only a dozen of the nation's 3,500 or so jails and 21 percent of all state and federal prisons have been accredited by the Commission on Accreditation for Corrections as meeting established standards.[16]

In response to lawsuits brought by inmates challenging the conditions of their confinement, federal judges have stepped in and ordered states and localities to improve their prisons and jails. As of mid-1988, thirty-nine states, the District of Columbia, Puerto Rico, and the Virgin Islands were operating prisons and jails under court orders to remedy their conditions.[17] One-third of the jails surveyed in a nationwide survey in mid-1986 were operating under court orders, usually because of crowding and substandard conditions of confinement. Half had lawsuits pending against them.[18] Prisoners were being released on an emergency basis to alleviate crowding; in 1985, over 18,000 prisoners were so released.[19]

In an attempt to meet the short-run demand, the federal government and several state governments were building or planning to build, as of mid-1988, 140 new prisons and to renovate 437 others, which will add 63,800 beds to these prison systems. These projects were budgeted to cost $4.4 billion, $2.5 billion of which has been raised on the bond market.[20] (Equivalent figures for jail construction and renovation by local governments are not available.)

Spending for corrections has been increasing substantially throughout the better part of the past two decades. Between 1971 and 1985, the cost of operating correctional institutions in the United States rose by 122 percent in constant dollars (470 percent, unadjusted for inflation), and all levels of government spent large sums—a total of about $10.5 billion—to increase the physical resources of their correctional systems.[21] During this period, corrections costs rose faster than any other category of state and local government spending—and 50 percent faster than all state and local expenditures.[22]

Precarious Public Finances

Had this demand for additional resources posed no strain on government budgets, the business opportunities for private correctional firms would have been less inviting. Unfortunately, these rapid increases in correctional spending came at a time when state and local governments were suffering several blows to their fiscal health.

Within a few years of the passage of Proposition Thirteen in California in 1978, fifty-one new expenditure controls or revenue restrictions were placed on state and local governments' spending powers. Personal income taxes were decreased in thirty-five states and sales taxes were reduced in nineteen. Federal aid to these governments also began to shrink in 1980. The ratio of federal aid to state and local revenues had been rising for at least twenty-five years, peaking at 32 percent in 1978 (a level three times higher than twenty-five years before). But the federal government's general revenue-sharing program took several deep cuts, first at President Carter's behest and then at President Reagan's.[23] By 1986, the general revenue sharing program was dead, and many local governments were left for the first time without any direct federal assistance.[24]

In the early years of the Reagan administration, many state and local governments were cutting budgets, incurring general fund deficits, and laying off workers. Ironically, this was happening at the same time that the demand for local assistance was increasing because so many people were being thrown out of work. Higher levels of spending for corrections were met by funneling money from other types of services and by raising local taxes. The trend toward reducing taxes was reversed and a scramble for revenue ensued at both state and local levels.[25]

Unfortunately, the ability to raise revenues locally depends upon the health of the state's or locality's tax base. Many regions have not fared well in the recent economic recovery. Indeed, their economic growth has been sluggish, with quite high unemployment rates (and, consequently, high demands for a variety of state and local services and assistance). Pain has therefore been sharpest in those states that have high incarceration rates, large poor populations relative to the rest of the country, and, by extension, weaker tax bases.

Moreover, local governments fare worse than state governments because their revenue bases are narrower. Locally supported corrections will thus face even harsher conditions than state-supported corrections. According to the National Association of Counties' estimates, county-funded justice and public safety programs received approximately one-third of all general revenue-sharing dollars during 1987.[26] With the decline of federal assistance, continued increases in local correctional costs will have to be covered by cuts in other services or parallel increases in tax revenues, or both. In the poorer states, the limits on raising tax revenues are such that increased corrections spending will probably come at the expense of other services.

Future Opportunities for Privatization

There is no indication that pressure on state and local government budgets is going to be eased by a slackening demand for expensive correctional resources. In 1984, Rich and Barnett produced estimates of future state prison populations using a mathematical model that extrapolated crime, incarceration, and demographic patterns found in eight sample states during the early 1980s to Bureau of Census projections of population growth between the late 1980s and the year 2020. They concluded that prison populations would continue to rise into the early 1990s. The "birth dearth" that followed the post-war baby boom would then begin to show its effect on prison admissions, and the number of persons behind bars would decline slightly for about a decade. Around the turn of the century, prison population levels would rise again and would then continue upward through 2020.[27] This forecast paralleled and extended Blumstein, Cohen, and Miller's projections for Pennsylvania, which anticipated a similar decline starting around 1990. (Blumstein and his colleagues made no guesses about what would happen in the twenty-first century.)[28]

The number of persons behind bars has grown at a much faster rate than projected, however. For example, Rich and Barnett forecast a slightly less than 10 percent increase between 1983 and the point in the early 1990s when they expected a downturn to occur. By 1985, only two years later, state prison populations had increased by almost 17 percent.[29] Similarly, Blumstein, Cohen, and Miller's earlier projection of Pennsylvania prison populations, based on models that fit 1970–1977 data quite well, badly underestimated subsequent growth. Whereas they forecast a population level of about 9,500 in 1985, there were actually 14,227 persons in prison by the end of that year—approximately 50 percent more than estimated.[30]

The projections were inaccurate partly because they did not take into account changes in sentencing policy (in the case of Blumstein et al.) and also because the underlying models did not take into account the subtle and changing interactions of age, race, crime, and criminal justice processing. It may be that

Figure 1.1.

**Rich and Barnett's Projection of National State Prison
Population Growth**

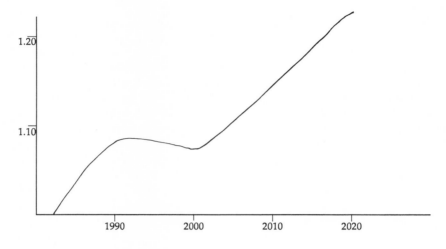

the prison population will indeed taper off in the 1990s, but
other forces are at work that were not included in the projections. These forces may continue to raise population levels without any downturn.

For example, young black and Hispanic men have higher arrest and incarceration rates than young white men. Because the
postwar baby boom never really stopped in the black and Hispanic communities, members of these ethnic groups will constitute an increasingly large proportion of the young male cohort
at risk of imprisonment in the coming decades. The number of
white non-Hispanic men in their twenties began to drop in
1984, but the cohort of black men in their twenties will continue to grow until 1989, and will then diminish very slowly. In
2005, for example, that cohort will be only slightly smaller than
it is currently—about the same size as it was in 1982.[31] (Projections of Hispanic populations were not available at the time of
writing, but Hispanic birth rates have been higher than those of
white non-Hispanics.) Moreover, there is some evidence that the
arrest and incarceration rates of young black and Hispanic men
are increasing—probably as a result of their worsening socioeconomic conditions—which may compound the overrepresenta-
tion of minority prisoners still further.[32] Consequently, the

slowdown in prison population growth that has been forecast by some may not come to pass.

It is safe to conclude, therefore, that the demand for prison and jail cells will continue to put a strain on state and local governments and that the opportunities for private imprisonment firms will continue to exist. Even if the legislatures and the courts were to adopt a zero-growth policy for prisons, and to revise sentencing and parole laws to implement it, there would still be an enormous need for capital investment in corrections. Existing prisons and jails are old and in need of replacement or renovation; overcrowding is pervasive; and the federal courts are demanding that either populations be reduced substantially or more resources be added.

The Issues

The growth of the private corrections industry has been somewhat slower than many expected, in part because public officials have many questions. These questions are both empirical, turning on matters of fact, and normative, involving matters of principle. Are, for example, privately operated facilities more efficient—and thus less costly for a given level of service—than publicly operated ones? Whether they are more or less costly, do we think it proper and just to delegate the punishment of individuals to private firms dedicated to turning a profit for such services? Does this make a difference if the firms are not-for-profit agencies? On what basis do we decide?

If privately operated correctional facilities are more efficient, to what are the efficiencies due? According to one line of theorizing, public agencies have few incentives, if any, to discover and implement ways of improving productivity. In the private sector, competition in the marketplace, and the threat of losing money or going out of business, are seen as the key to efficiency. Shielded from these imperatives, public managers are thought to strive instead to maintain their positions by avoiding risks.[33] But has the private sector really developed a repertoire of more sophisticated management techniques and an expertise better suited to cost control and productivity gains in corrections? If competition is seen as the key to the benefits of privatization, how competitive an industry can corrections be? There are approximately four thousand counties in this country; about thirty-five hundred of them can support only one jail, and most of the inmates have been sent to jail by a single source: the local courts. Is the competition among contractors at the single point of bidding for a multiyear contract—a point at which the winner obtains a monopoly position—sufficient to engender the kinds of cost-controlling innovations expected of privatization? And if this time-delimited competition does indeed result in lower costs, is that result worth the risks of diminishing control over a highly volatile service system and becoming dependent upon a private provider? It is certainly possible that private firms can deliver equal services at lower cost not because of superior managerial talent but simply because they pay their employees lower wages and provide less costly benefits, which can make a large difference because watching, counting, and escorting prisoners are highly labor-intensive activities. To what extent are the lower relative costs—if any—due to this single factor rather than to other efficiencies? And if this is the case, are there disadvantages, such as higher staff turnover or lower-quality personnel? If private firms enjoy a competitive advantage over the public sector largely because of lower labor costs, is this advantage likely to be short-lived?

Moreover, to what extent are the efficiencies of the private sector due to the greater power management has over labor in the absence of civil service and public sector union protections? Does this alone permit a more productive deployment of workers? City and county government managers, when asked in an opinion poll to rank the advantages of contracting, ranked cost savings first and "solving labor problems" second.[34]

If greater cost consciousness flows from having one's eyes on the bottom line (especially on profits), do not the private firms also have incentives to shave costs by reducing service levels? Will this not compound a problem already pervasive in this country's corrections? As discussed earlier, many state and local governments are under court orders to remedy conditions in their prisons and jails. Prisons and jails, whether public or private, are especially vulnerable to substandard services because they are difficult institutions to monitor, and because the ultimate clients—the prisoners—have virtually no choice about where they will be kept and under what conditions, little access to those having authority to enforce standards, little power to compel the allocation of resources required for adequate services (except by means of riots, strikes, and the like), and little ability to create widespread concern for their plight.

Does privatization offer an effective means of *upgrading* the

conditions of confinement? Does privatization permit localities
to comply with federal courts' orders more quickly and reliably,
simply because compliance with court-ordered standards can be
written into a contract with a private firm, and thereby made a
condition of the business agreement? Might this be a method of
achieving compliance more swiftly and economically than by
leaving it to the correctional officials whose management was
responsible in part for the substandard conditions? The experience of the Bay County (Florida) jail, taken over by the Corrections Corporation of America, seems to support this conclusion.
(See Aric Press's essay in this volume.)

What does our experience with the public sector's administration of jails and prisons tell us about the monitoring procedures
best suited to ensuring that services are delivered competently
and in conformity with standards? Would the same procedures
be as effective after privatizing the management of correctional
facilities? Would accountability be enhanced or diminished?

Can privatizing yield other benefits besides cost reduction? In
a White House press conference announcing formation of the
President's Commission on Privatization, the commission's
chairman, David Linowes, was asked what privatization might
accomplish in the federal prison system. He replied, "We know
our prisons are not performing. We know—I think the last sta-
tistic I saw was an 80 percent recidivism rate. We cannot, in a
successful democratic society, tolerate that kind of an arrangement."[35] The rate of recidivism is not quite that high. Several
studies conducted in different states have found that between
one-half and three-quarters of those released from state prisons
are rearrested within a few years, but Linowes's general point
poses a critical question.[36] For what purposes do we incarcerate,
and does the public or private nature of the correctional facility
make a difference with regard to these purposes? Since the collapse of faith in prisoner rehabilitation in the mid-1970s, imprisonment has been embraced largely because it is a means to
"warehouse" (incapacitate) convicted offenders, which may in
and of itself yield the added benefits of punishing criminals and
deterring other would-be lawbreakers. But if prisoner rehabilitation or other goals are sought, might private correctional
firms be better suited to achieving them? To date, those engaged in the controversy surrounding privatization have been
strangely silent about the purposes of imprisonment. Imprisonment is seen as both the objective and the means, and the key
question has become whether method X or method Y of delivering this service is less costly. Should not the question be: What

do we want prisons and jails to accomplish, and what mix of public and private responsibilities is best suited to achieving these ends?

The new combinations of private ownership and financing raise other questions, whether facility operations are placed in public or in private hands. The chief advantage of creative financing arrangements is that they are not subject to the traditional checks and balances of conventional public financing; thus they permit public officials to increase more speedily the number of available cells. To avoid the ever-present temptation to spend more now and pay later by going into debt, most state governments require that voting taxpayers approve of bond issues (i.e., of increasing the government's debt), and many have ceilings on the amount of debt that can be incurred. Such opportunities to approve bond issues are infrequent because they must be scheduled with general elections, and a high percentage of proposed bond issues for jail and prison construction have been defeated in recent years.[37] One "solution" that is becoming quite common is to have a private firm raise the capital, construct a facility that it owns, and then lease it to the government for use by its correctional agency. The lease payments by the government come from operating funds rather than the capital budget, even though a portion of the lease payment goes to pay off the debt, and no voter approval of such expenditures is required.[38]

Should such innovative arrangements be encouraged as a matter of public policy, or should the normal checks and balances of government be adhered to? Does this de facto increase in public debt constitute "fiscal child abuse" (because we pass our debts to our children)? Or is it a laudable way of answering those who demand tougher measures against criminals, and more cells, while taxpayers are resisting higher government debt for prison construction?

Both private financing and private operation of corrections have emerged as a response to the need for more cell space. How the boundary between public and private responsibility is drawn is not necessarily tied up the expansion of correctional resources, for a jurisdiction could choose a zero-growth option and privatize its jails or prisons (or even, as Michael O'Hare, Robert Leone, and Marc Zegans discuss in their essay in this volume, privatization could be used as a means for shrinking institutionalized corrections, as happened in Massachusetts). Nonetheless, the context of the current interest in privatization is one in which public officials are scrambling to build new correctional facilities in order to manage growing prisoner populations.

Is this expansion of prisons and jails necessary? Spending for institutional corrections is constituting an increasingly large proportion of state and local budgets, and continued growth will be at the expense of other kinds of public services unless tax revenues are increased. (Correctional expenditures are growing faster than the gross national product; consequently, these increases cannot be covered by the overall increase in national wealth.) Should the demand for cell space and the forces that generate that demand be taken for granted, or can penal objectives, available resources, and other demands for those resources be managed in a way that requires a lower expenditure for corrections? Are there less expensive ways of achieving our penal goals, aside from locking larger numbers of people behind hardened concrete and steel for longer stretches of time? If so, what are the implications for the various ways in which private firms might be involved in corrections, in either institutional or noninstitutional settings?

A related worry is that public policymaking might be affected in unexpected and possibly undesirable ways by the growth of a private correctional industry. Will private operators, whose business opportunities derive from the shortfall of cell space relative to demand, push for sentencing laws that maintain or even heighten this demand?[39] Will this situation be any different than the pressures exerted now by public employee unions? Will public officials permit their decisions to be influenced by such lobbying? And will those government agencies charged with regulating the private correctional industry be captured by that industry? Given what we know about "regulatory capture" and the dynamics of policymaking in penal matters, how likely is such a distortion of public policy?

The Structure of the Book

In this book we examine the new mix of public and private roles mainly in the context of highly guarded penal institutions for adult inmates—the "hard" end of the correctional continuum—although some attention is given to the "softer" end that includes halfway houses, residential treatment centers, group homes for delinquent juveniles, and work release facilities. The institutions we are most interested in are those operated by private firms and owned by private investors.

Consequently, three broad classes of penal institutions are studied here. The purest type, the most completely private facilities, are those operated and owned by private firms, and financed by private investors ("cocos"—or contractor owned and contractor operated, in the current argot of the industry). A second type includes prisons and jails operated by public authorities but owned and financed by private entities (facilities that Herman Leonard, in his essay, calls "nominally private"). The third type is the government-owned facility that is operated by a private firm ("go-cos," or government owned and contractor operated).

We are excluding the many other institutionalized arrangements by which private organizations provide services in correctional settings. There is a relatively long history of private firms providing specific services to public prisons and jails under contract, such as medical services, health and food services, counseling, vocational training and education, recreational programs, maintenance, and even security.[40] During the past decade, there has also been heightened interest and experience in expanding private sector participation in prison industry programs.[41] Although several of the following essays address the contracting of auxiliary services, the central focus is on contracting for the operation of entire penal facilities because the public policy questions posed by such management contracts are more difficult and in greater need of extended consideration.

It is important to recognize that the financing, ownership, and operation need not be bundled together, and that the term "privatization" has been applied in a relatively indiscriminate way either to one of several different forms of private involvement (ownership, financing, or operational responsibility) or to several combinations of these forms. Different questions are posed by each type of activity.

The first two essays document recent developments in the United States and Britain. Aric Press's "The Good, the Bad, and the Ugly: Private Prisons in the 1980s" focuses on the latest developments in the new proprietary corrections industry in the United States. Because most of the other essays address relatively specific questions about privatization, Press's essay was intended to provide a broad introduction to the subject.

In "British Penal Policy and the Idea of Prison Privatization," Andrew Rutherford reports that, because privatization of government services in general has been the centerpiece of the

Thatcher administration's domestic policy, the transfer of many once-nationalized industries to the private sector has been proceeding apace. In this respect, the British experience with privatization has been richer and deeper than that of the United States, largely because the British have more to denationalize. In the area of corrections, however, privatization has been restricted largely to weighing the arguments pro and con (with a watchful eye on the U.S. experience); the British government has not yet contracted for the management of an adult penal facility. Rutherford examines this debate and the experience of two institutions that have been largely ignored but have considerable relevance to the question of privatization: private immigrant detention centers and private institutions for juvenile offenders, which have a history stretching back to the nineteenth century.

Herman B. Leonard's essay, "Private Time: The Political Economy of Private Prison Finance," details the different combinations of construction, financing, operation, and ownership that have emerged in recent years and that involve private parties in new ways. These include what he calls "nominal privatization," involving public ownership and legally private ownership, and "operational privatization," in which private sector firms operate the prison. Each of the different forms has implications for costs, for how risks are distributed, and for the nature and extent of public and private involvement in the decision-making process. In delineating these implications, he points to several of the central policy issues that are posed by the decision to consider private financing and operation of correctional facilities.

In my essay, "The Costs of Operating Public and Private Correctional Facilities," I examine what it costs to run imprisonment facilities in both sectors. Unfortunately, very few cost analyses exist in the published literature, and most analysts of comparative costs fail to realize that what counts as a cost in the public sector is quite different from the costs in private firms' calculations. Public sector accounting practices are less rigorous than those in the private sector; several real costs tend to be ignored in the typically reported costs of incarceration. The end result is that imprisonment by public agencies is generally more costly than is commonly thought, which makes the private sector's advantage look even greater. The reasons for this are explored in comparisons of public and private alien detention centers, and of public and private work release facilities in the Illinois state prison system, as well as analyses of public savings obtained by contracting with a private firm for a minimum-security work camp in Tennessee.

The emphasis on reducing costs has taken center stage in the debate over privatization, but as Michael O'Hare, Robert Leone, and Marc Zegans argue, privatization can produce other important benefits. In their essay, entitled "The Privatization of Imprisonment: A Managerial Perspective," they analyze several ways that drawing a different boundary between the public and private sectors in corrections might yield improved services. These include creating new organizational cultures and enlarging management's opportunities to focus on the organization's primary goals rather than being absorbed in the soup to nuts of a correctional service. (This point was made by Dalton Roberts, the executive of Tennessee's Hamilton County, in citing efficiency as one of his principal reasons for contracting with the Corrections Corporation of American to run the county's medium-security adult facility. Managing the facility "was taking a toll on my entire administrative staff, and on me. Since they've run it, I haven't spent one-tenth the time on it."[42]) In addition, the authors examine how greater private involvement may be harnessed to speed innovation, developing new approaches to achieving penal objectives.

Perhaps the greatest worry about privatizing correctional facilities is that prisoners will suffer more at the hand of dollar-minded keepers. J. Michael Keating, Jr., in his essay, "Public over Private: Monitoring the Performance of Privately Operated Prisons and Jails," examines the procedures by which accountability is maintained in prisons and jails and the special problems imposed by privately operated facilities. He reviews the history of various methods of monitoring correctional facilities, including the court-appointed masters charged with monitoring institutions that have been found to be in violation of the Constitution, and proposes an approach for ensuring the accountability of privately operated facilities to government and to the public.

John J. DiIulio, Jr., in "The Duty to Govern: A Critical Perspective on the Private Management of Prisons and Jails," reviews U.S. experience with privately contracted prisons and jails in the nineteenth and twentieth centuries and concludes that the answer to badly operated facilities is not to shed responsibility for them by delegating it to private firms but to strengthen public management. According to him, the private sector has no monopoly on competent management; model correctional systems exist in the public sector. Moreover, he argues that there is something distinctive about the criminal justice system (and imprisonment) that makes it unlike many of the other government services that are considered ripe for privatization. In his view, administration of the criminal sanction is a central function of government; to hand it over to private firms deprives the sanction of its symbolic and moral significance.

In the last essay, "When Government Fails: Going Private as a Last Resort," I consider the desirability of delegating correctional authority but come to a different conclusion than DiIulio. After examining the questions of private facilities' constitutionality, propriety, utility, and cost, I am led to conclude that private delegation is a legitimate and, indeed, sensible response when governments have failed to provide adequate conditions of confinement. I see no reason for a wholesale conversion of the now-public correctional system to operation by market-oriented private firms, but I find no compelling reason to ban privately operated prisons if they can provide better services at equal or lower cost to the public. With respect to the private ownership of facilities leased to the government, however, I am more troubled. Creative financing risks loosening too much the discipline of the process of incuring public debt.

The Good, the Bad, and the Ugly: Private Prisons in the 1980s

ARIC PRESS

After he finished a master's degree in public health at Columbia University, J. Clifford Todd returned to his native Kentucky and went into the real estate business. He teamed up with a local architect and bought a large old hospital. But he could not sell any development projects for the site. "There I was sitting with 130 acres and not knowing what to do with them," Todd recalled later. Then he had his epiphany on the road to Louisville. "I'm riding down the highway one day listening to the news about the need for prison space. Just like that, a light bulb went off." His white elephant could be transformed into a jail.[1]

Light bulbs were going off all over the United States in the mid-1980s. The point here is not the importance of Todd's project, about which more will be said later, but the prevailing zeitgeist; the idea of private prisons was in the air, and entrepreneurs with sufficient daring were attempting to seize promising opportunities.[2] A half dozen fledgling private prison operators established franchises throughout the country, and at least that many more were out looking for business. The new industry attracted serious money men from, among others: a division of Bechtel, the giant defense contractor; Wackenhut, the nation's largest private security firm; and the Corrections Corporation of America, the industry leader, which was financed in part by some of the same investors that had helped launch both the Hospital Corporation of America and Kentucky Fried Chicken.

All of these operators were lured by the prospect of an enormous market. For nearly two decades, the prison population in the United States had grown dramatically. Several factors were at work. Crime had become a major political issue. The body politic demanded both retribution and incapacitation, and judges and legislators responded with more severe prison sentences. And the baby boom generation—the same population bulge that had swollen the coffers of blue jeans makers and record companies—was old enough to go to jail. The public sector simply could not keep pace with demand. Between 1979 and 1984, total inmate living space in state prisons grew by 29 percent; in the same period, the number of prisoners grew by 45 percent.[3] There was little reason to suspect that the growth would stop.

The advent of private prisons was not merely a result of market opportunity, although that was a necessary factor. At roughly the same time, the private sector came to occupy a place of honor in the public imagination, whereas government was vilified as awkward at best, and at worst as an evil empire. "Public agencies are held in such low regard," a Massachusetts legislative study reported, "that private companies' ability to outperform them has assumed axiomatic proportions in many people's minds."[4] The movement toward privatizing public responsibilities that began in Margaret Thatcher's Great Britain continued in Ronald Reagan's America.[5] In a climate where the sale of national parks to private operators can be discussed, a proposal for a private prison does not seem so strange.

Prisons were not the only parts of the justice business threatening to go private. The thin blue line had long since snapped: Today those who can afford private security buy it; there are now twice as many private guards as public police.[6] They patrol the country's new main street—the shopping mall—and it's toughest streets—embattled neighborhoods desperate for some law and order. Private courts continue to open. California's rent-a-retired judge is merely the most famous; private "dispute resolution centers" have become a mini-industry.[7] In one sense these developments do not represent a radical departure from state-dispensed justice. It has been argued that private guards are merely an extension of the citizen arrest power.[8] And private courts are but another mechanism for settlement negotiations between the parties. In both situations, one could contend that the state is not relinquishing power but that private citizens are just reordering their affairs. That argument misses the larger point: These forays into private justice are not merely matters of convenience; they also signify a crisis of confidence in the public dispensers of justice and in the corrections system.

The idea of private prisons is not new in the United States. Private workhouses and labor gangs of inmates flourished in the nineteenth and early twentieth centuries. "In the early years of the United States," writes David Wecht, "private jailers fulfill[ed] a task that the young nation was initially unable to perform."[9] Typically, inmates were leased out as a source of labor to businessmen. Those arrangements were ripe for abuse and became the subject of legislative and journalistic investigations. The practice was effectively derailed during the Great Depression when legislatures passed "state use" laws limiting products produced by prisoners to "use" only by the state; hence the advent of the proverbial license plate factory behind bars. According to a recent study,

> An attorney general's survey of prisons found that in 1935–36, only 51,000 of the nation's 106,800 prisoners were working at jobs or prison maintenance. The other 55,800—60 percent—had nothing to do. Chronic idleness had become an entrenched problem of American prisons, one that plagues them to this day. It was in those Depression years that Congress nailed down the legal lid on the commercial use of prison labor. The Hawes-Cooper Act, which took effect in 1934, said that prison-made goods from one state couldn't be sold in another that barred the sale of goods manufactured in its own prisons. The next year, the Ashurst-Sumners Act barred interstate carriers from hauling goods that might violate Hawes-Cooper. In 1940, the Sumners-Ashurst Act imposed a total ban on interstate transportation of prison-made products intended for the private market. That left open the possibility of prison labor for products purchased by state and federal governments. But the Walsh-Healy Act put a $10,000 ceiling on such contracts."[10]

The private sector did not leave the corrections field entirely. Labor gang bosses disappeared only to be replaced by not-for-profit operators who opened juvenile treatment centers and, later, adult halfway houses. According to a federal survey conducted in 1982, forty-nine states—all but Delaware—contracted with 1,877 privately managed firms to establish centers for juveniles. Collectively they housed about 31,000 youngsters, about one-third of whom were delinquents.[11] A 1985 survey found that twenty-eight states used privately managed prerelease, work release, or halfway house facilities for adults.[12] The private sector also provided discrete services to departments of correction. According to one survey, thirty-nine states had contracted with private companies to provide at least one service or program—typically medical, education, training, or food.[13] In 1983, those contracts were worth about $200 million.[14] The camel's nose was under the tent, but it was a very big tent. In 1983 the total federal and state expenditure on private corrections was $6.9 billion.[15] The private involvement was small, but the opportunity was large.

For a while, in the early 1980s, interest in private corrections was stimulated by changes in tax laws. Local governments were

caught between a need for more prison space and an unwillingness on the part of the electorate to approve bond issues for new
jails. Changes in the federal tax laws in 1981 suggested a way to
break through that stalemate: creation of a "quasi-public body"
that would sell shares to investors in order to finance the building of a correctional center. The facility would then be leased
back to the governmental entity. Over the life of the lease, the
rental payments would be used to pay off the investors; at the
end of the term, the facility would revert to the government.[16]
There were two substantial advantages for participants in such
arrangements. First, the bonds would be tax exempt for investors. Second, the local political leadership would not have to
worry about obtaining special authorization for a capital expense; the rent for the new jail (think of it as a disguised mort-
gage payment) would come out of the annual operating budget, a
document over which voters have no direct control. These lease-
purchase arrangements were promoted by three major Wall
Street firms—Merrill Lynch, E. F. Hutton, and Shearson Leh-
man; but despite some initial ballyhoo, they never swept the
nation.[17] Now, the opportunity for pushing these intricate financing schemes may have passed. According to an article by two
accountants, in *The Privatization Review,* the tax reform legislation of 1986 "sharply limits the availability of tax-exempt financing for any private purpose including privatization." They
conclude: "As tax benefits become less important, other benefits
become correspondingly more important. Privatization projects
that depend heavily for their viability on the tax benefits will be
carried out differently—or not at all—after tax reform."[18]

It was, then, an unusual confluence of factors—changing political attitudes, rising incarceration rates, fickle historical trends,
and uncertain tax laws—that contributed to the new atmosphere
in which private prisons could be placed on the public agenda
and actively discussed. In reality, private prisons became the
subject of heated debate. Partisan experts dueled on editorial
pages.[19] The talented publicists from the Corrections Corporation
of America battled the able operatives from the American Federation of State, County, and Municipal Employees (AFSCME) in
any forum they could find. Congress held hearings.[20] The National Institute of Justice convened a conference and produced
widely cited reports, as did state officials in Massachusetts, New
Mexico, Pennsylvania, and Virginia.[21] Professional associations
weighed in with their verdicts. The National Sheriffs' Association (no), the American Correctional Association (a guarded yes),
and the American Bar Association (needs more study).

The continuing debate brings to mind an old story about a conference of football coaches. Each in turn went up to a chalkboard and drew a diagram for a play or a defense that was guaranteed either to score a touchdown or to throw the opposition for a loss. There was no strategy anyone could advance that the next fellow could not overcome at the board. The moral of the story: The last fellow with the chalk in his hand always wins. But there is a difference between chalkboards and actual games. So it is with the debate over private prisons. "Until private prison operators are given an opportunity to succeed or fail," a Massachusetts legislative report concluded, "debate will continue to be clouded by claims, counter-claims and vested interests."[22] Every point had a counterpoint. Consider the following pros and cons.

- Pro: The private sector's management will be more streamlined and professional.
- Con: The personnel who will actually manage the private sector facility are the same individuals who have already failed in the public sector.
- Pro: The private sector can cut labor costs and can schedule, motivate, and discipline its staff more effectively.
- Con: A unionized work force in the public sector tends to be more skillful and better paid; lower pay and benefit packages hurt morale.
- Pro: The private sector can take advantage of its corporate purchasing power and better bids.
- Con: Public bidding rules decrease the likelihood of corruption, the public sector can, with some planning, also take advantage of economies of scale.

Now, like our football coaches, let's change sides.

- Con: Private operators will operate like innkeepers, always trying to keep their beds full. Therefore, they will lobby against and always defeat early release programs or alternatives to incarceration.
- Pro: The demand for prison beds so outstrips supply that private prison operators never have to worry about filling their space.
- Con: Delegating the punishment of criminals to a private operator does not send the right societal message to inmates.
- Pro: The symbolic quality of incarceration is the same no matter what insignia the guards are wearing. The clear moral message—

that the prisoner has been deprived of freedom because of his deeds—becomes diffused, however, if the conditions of confinement are brutal, filthy, or arbitrary. In such cases (and federal courts have found them in more than forty state systems operated by the public sector) the wrong message is sent to inmates.

- Con: Government officials cannot contract out their liability. They have the worst of all situations: They give up day-to-day control over the jail, but ultimately they remain responsible.
- Pro: Government officials will have even greater incentive to carefully select skillful and prudent private operators. And the private companies, if they expect to have their contracts renewed, will have every incentive to run safe and secure institutions.

The debate is vigorous, thoughtful, endless—and in some sense pointless. Because for all the talk—and nary a doubt was expressed by either side—the pontificating experts had very little knowledge on which to base their opinions. Fortunately, while this clash was spilling out in print, a small body of experience was developing from which judgments could be made (tentatively, to be sure) about the nature and quality of private prison operations. The data did not immediately change anyone's mind. (How could it in a climate in which self-interest masquerades as good judgment?)

A Few Generalizations

A few generalizations can be made about the private prison experience. First, the publicly traded private prison companies have yet to show that they can make money in the business. Company leaders and stock analysts predicted that the larger firms were on the verge of breaking into the black, but as of early 1988, that has not happened.[23] In part, all the red ink may be the natural result of starting a new business—indeed, a new industry. Nonetheless, impressive prospectuses and business plans that seem to make sense will impress investors for only so long; at some point these firms must either turn profits or get out of the business.

Second, it is not clear that municipalities are saving money (or spending more, for that matter) on the private centers. All claims remain suspect; further study is needed.

Third, as a National Institute of Justice report suggests, private prisons appear to be legal unless they have been specifically prohibited within a jurisdiction.[24] The question of whether a state can delegate the task of imprisonment has been raised occasionally, but thus far no authoritative court ruling or constitutional provision has been cited to prevent such delegation.[25] If the power to delegate is assumed, there seems to be little doubt that the governmental entity remains liable for the actions of the private contractor. The various avenues of legal analysis lead to the same conclusion: The conduct of a government contractor is a form of state action for which the public entity itself can be held responsible.[26]

Fourth, and perhaps most important, there is reason to believe that the private facilities that are open have performed well, or at least adequately. No scandals, riots, or court battles have occurred to mar the reputation of the industry. So what we know is this: Based on a small number of cases, governments can purchase satisfactory care for some of their inmates. Given the history of prison administration, that is no small feat; whether it makes economic sense remains an open question.

Reality Tests

The recent history of adult private jails begins with a series of federal initiatives. In 1979, the U.S. Immigration and Naturalization Service (INS) did not have enough room in its own facilities to hold all of the detained illegal aliens it was preparing to deport. At about that time, federal agents were approached by Ted Nissen, a former California parole and corrections officer who had gone into business for himself. Nissen, through a not-for-profit corporation, was running a halfway house for state inmates that had empty beds; he offered to take in some of the excess INS population. The INS agreed to transfer "soft, unlikely to escape cases" and signed a cost-plus contract.[27] The arrangement worked well for both sides. The INS began ordering more beds and Nissen converted his firm into a profit-making operation now known as Behavioral Systems Southwest. Under federal law, INS was forced to publish announcements of the proposed contracts and for a while, Nissen was the only bidder. According to Robert Schmidt, former supervisor of INS detention operations, Nissen "layered in an eight per cent profit" that cost the government about $2.00 per day for each inmate.

From that rudimentary beginning, a growth industry was born. By fiscal 1986, fully one-fourth of the INS detention facilities were in private hands. In that year, the government paid an average per diem of $26.25 to the private operators; 550,000 man-days of incarceration cost the INS $14.5 million. On its own facilities, the INS spent $22 million, or $26.42 per diem for 868,000 man-days of incarceration.[28] The Corrections Corporation of America and Wackenhut have both won major contracts from the INS; CCA's contracts are for facilities in Lardo and Houston, Texas, and Wackenhut's are in Denver. Nissen no longer has contracts with the INS, though he has claimed a success that still eludes the industry giants: In 1985, Nissen reported that his company's six small minimum-security prisons and two detention facilities for illegal aliens turned a total profit that year of $160,000 on revenues of $4.5 million.*

In 1981, the federal Bureau of Prisons began relying "solely" on private operators "to provide pre-release housing through its community treatment centers."[29] As of fall 1986, the bureau had contracted for 330 community centers that housed over 3,000 inmates at a cost of more than $29 million annually. These beds cost about $31.00 per day rather than the average of $39.50 at the bureau's other institutions.[30] Most of the private centers are run by not-for-profit groups. In addition, the Bureau of Prisons briefly contracted out the operation of a 60-bed facility in La Honda, California, which held low-security Youth Corrections Act prisoners. (It had expensive beds, costing about $92 per day, compared with $55 per day in similar federally run penitentiaries.) After the repeal of the act, that contract was allowed to lapse in January 1986. The Bureau of Prisons also housed 60 to 80 illegal aliens who had been convicted of federal crimes in an INS detention center in Houston that was managed by the Corrections Corporation of America.

These were the starting points for the new industry, they are worth some reflection. All the ventures had some common factors. They are small; they hold only a small fraction of the total inmate population for which the INS and the Bureau of Prisons are responsible. They are monitored; the INS has an overseer in place at each center.[31] They can be opened and closed more quickly than a traditional federal institution; officials at both federal agencies report that the private contractors offer advan-

*Editor's note: At the end of 1988, both the CCA and one of its rivals, Pricor Incorporated, reported making a profit as well. Wackenhut's corrections division reportedly began making money in mid-1989.

tages of speed and flexibility. When Congress repealed the Youth Corrections Act, the bureau simply phased out the La Honda center: it was a turn-key operation, first opening the door and then closing it.[32] The INS reports that the private contractors can get a new facility up and running faster than the federal bureaucracy. And the INS has twice ceased dealing with contractors who failed to meet contract specifications. This is a particularly important point. According to one INS official, in at least one instance a contract had been let to a firm he suspected of "lowballing" its bid, that is, setting it artificially low in order to get the contract. When his suspicions were proven correct, the INS refused to renew the contract and invited new bidders.[33]

Lowballing is a charge often raised by critics of private jails who fear that unscrupulous contractors will take a loss in the early years of a relationship with an agency in order to establish themselves. They claim that once the public agency has grown dependent upon the relationship, the private operator will sharply raise prices and the community will be powerless to stop such a prison rape. The INS was able to avert that problem because (1) it was spotted before it was time to renew the contract; and (2) the INS was not entirely dependent on the operator for all inmate services. What this teaches us is that the worst fears of the critics are half right; some contractors will try to take advantage of governments. But there is an obvious remedy. The public official responsible for the contract must pay attention to its administration and must be prepared to act when the terms are not being met. That is not an entirely riskless task in a jurisdiction that has only one facility—hence all the more reason to select a contractor carefully. But for larger agencies, as the INS experience demonstrates, lowballing should not be a fatal problem.

The States as Laboratories

Having begun with the federal systems, private prison operators increasingly focused on the states. As noted earlier, a variety of companies quickly tried to enter the field, and none gained more attention than the Corrections Corporation of America, headquartered in Nashville, Tennessee. Its dashing chief executive officer, Thomas Beasley, a West Point graduate turned businessman, has been profiled extensively in print and

on television programs.[34] Incorporated in 1983, the CCA is now
the industry leader. It runs two INS facilities in Texas with 558
beds, two Memphis juvenile facilities with 198 beds, one Chattanooga workhouse with 360 beds, the Bay County, Florida, jail
with 370 beds, the Santa Fe County jail with 133 beds, and a
federal Bureau of Prisons halfway house with 24 beds. It also
has tentative contracts for two 500-bed facilities in Texas.

The seed money for the CCA came from a venture capital
company called Massey Burch, which also helped start the Hospital Corporation of America and Kentucky Fried Chicken. Par-
odying Colonel Sanders's famous slogan, Beasley says "we have
the incentive to do prisons right." They also had, the connec-
tions. Beasley is the former Republican state chairman of Tennessee and ran former Governor Lamar Alexander's first
election campaign. The CCA's first group of private investors
included Alexander's wife and Ned McWherter, a Democrat who
was speaker of the House of the state of Tennessee and is now
himself governor.

The CCA's reputation and that of the entire corrections industry have been inextricably bound up with events in Tennessee. In 1982, a federal judge declared the state prison system an
affront to the Constitution; three years later, having lost pa-
tience, he threatened to start releasing inmates if the state did
not relieve the overcrowding. What happened next did not follow the usual script: The Corrections Corporation of America
came forward and offered to take over the state's seventeen
prisons.

It was a breathtaking proposal. The company offered to put
up $100 million in cash—$50 million immediately—and invest
an additional $150 million in improvements, including the
building of two 500-inmate prisons. In exchange, it wanted the
state's entire $200 million budget. Initially, the governor was
interested and planned to convene a special legislative session
to ask for authority to negotiate a deal with the CCA. Then he
pulled back; the deal was simply too big. "I think we may have
overwhelmed them," venture capitalist Lucius Burch III said
later. In addition, the American Federation of State, County,
and Municipal Employees strongly lobbied against the measure.
The union represented only 150 prison guards in the state but
took the position that what happened on the CCA's home turf
was "of great moment to the rest of the country," according to
union lobbyist Mark Neimeiser.[35]

When the legislature reconvened in 1986, the private prison
plan had been scaled back to a transfer of just two prisons, one

medium-security and one work farm, to a private firm. Once again, AFSCME and CCA went at each other, battling to a draw. The compromise bill that finally emerged and was signed by Governor Alexander allowed only the transfer of the Carter County work farm, provided that the contractor guaranteed a 5 percent saving to the state and agreed to pay all the monitoring costs. When the state put out a Request for Proposals, only the U.S. Corrections Corporation (USCC) responded. The Corrections Department withdrew the contract offer and waited for further direction from the legislature. In the meantime, AFSCME filed suit in state court challenging the constitutionality of the private prison act.

One issue raised during the legislative sessions was the manner in which the CCA operated the Hamilton County (Chattanooga) workhouse. The company took over the 412-bed farm in the fall of 1985. The contract set a per diem rate for inmates of $21, but there was no guaranteed ceiling. That proved to be a mistake. When the CCA took over, the workhouse population was approximately 240. Almost immediately, and coincidentally, the county began to take a sterner line on drunk-driving cases; the workhouse population jumped to 340, and CCA's billings were far higher than anyone expected. By May 1985, the county was running $200,000 over budget. Also contributing to the population increase was the slowing of intake by the state prisons. With their population limit reached, the overflow backed up in local jails.

That series of events was the basis for AFSCME's charge that the CCA was guilty of serious cost overruns, an allegation its lobbyists used effectively in the legislature. Also, AFSCME pointed to the CCA's failure to carry $25 million in liability insurance as the contract stipulated. Instead, the CCA carried one $5 million policy for all of its facilities, a provision that the county later accepted as adequate.

For its part, the CCA emphasized improvements in operations. The company improved security, safety, and medical and training programs, all of which had previously been cited as inadequate by state inspectors. It also built a new kitchen and dormitory, disarmed the guards, and created an inmate grievance board. There were local dustups over an occasional felon CCA put out to work the fields, but for the most part the neighbors did not complain. Nonetheless, problems continued. For one thing, the CCA and the county could not agree on emergency procedures. During a disturbance in August 1986, the CCA called in city, state, and county police, and no one knew who had jurisdiction. For another, contract renewals were handled curiously. According to the *Chattanooga Times,* two of the county commissioners who voted to retain the CCA had private business contracts with it.[36] Finally, the larger crisis in the state prisons has continued to cause a backup in the local jails. The CCA, like Hamilton County before it, cannot solve that problem locally, and is left to reshuffle its programs in an attempt to deal with state-sentenced inmates. In that sense, if not in others, the private operators have no special advantages over the public sector.

As suggested earlier, the events in Tennessee have assumed unusual importance for the image of the industry. The CCA's bid for the statewide system was, in the words of Hubert L. McCullough, chairman of a competing firm called Pricor, a "defining event."[37] Since then, the debate over private prisons has proceeded as though the private companies wanted to assume control over maximum security prisons. That is not the case. The point to keep in mind here is that not only have the firms not sought those big houses, but no state has seriously entertained the notion of turning one over to a private firm. The corrections industry remains at the margin: local jails, minimum-security state facilities, and federal holding penitentiaries. Attica and San Quentin are not in danger of going private. Someday, perhaps, attitudes may change again; some private operators are unwilling to close off any options. George Zoley, vice-president for government services of Wackenhut, Inc., the security firm that has gone into the private prison business, has said:

> There's a logical basis for allowing the private sector to begin at the minimum security stage until we test ourselves and achieve a track record. There's no inherent reason why the private sector could not operate a maximum security facility. We are former public officials ourselves and we draw from a similar labor pool. The only thing that changes is management but there's no technical limitation for the private sector to manage any type of facility.[38]

While the CCA was organizing in Tennessee, the Fenton brothers were attempting to make inroads in Pennsylvania. Joseph was a businessman and Charles was no stranger to prisons. He had been a career warden in the federal system and had run, among other institutions, the prisons in Marion, Illinois, and Lewisburg, Pennsylvania. Their efforts in the private prison business began in the fall of 1985 when they signed a contract with Butler County commissioners to take over the local jail, an institution that all agreed was in poor shape.

Having established a local beachhead, the Fentons tried to go regional. Brother Charles saw a need that could be filled—a regional prison to hold inmates who needed protective custody. Such prisoners tend to be difficult for administrators; either they need protection from other inmates because of the nature of their crimes (the classic example being a child molester), or they are informers who have enemies, known or unknown. Often a prison can hold only a few such prisoners; Charles's marketing scheme was to put them all in one place. Brother Joseph recalls they had no trouble attracting interest from neighboring states, nor did they have a problem finding a site. Beaver County was holding onto a 68-acre plot left behind by a division of Textron that had moved South. Maintenance alone was costing the county $12,000 a month so it sold the industrial site to the Fentons for $1.00. With that purchase price came the "privilege" of cleaning up Textron's toxic wastes. Still, the Fentons said they were pleased. They had 130,000 square feet already built, readily convertible into classes and workshops. They said they planned to add a 720-cell dormitory and, in all, sunk $500,000 into the project.[39]

Unbeknownst to the Fentons or state officials, Philip E. Tack had plans for a private prison of his own in Cowansville, another town in western Pennsylvania that had fallen on hard times with the collapse of heavy industry. Tack apparently thought the town could use guard jobs, among other things. His plans came to the attention of Senator Arlen Specter, who at the time (March 1986) was chairman of the Senate Appropriations Subcommittee on the District of Columbia. Specter wrote Washington's Mayor Marion S. Barry, Jr., advising him of Tack's projected center and inquiring whether it might help relieve the overcrowding at the District of Columbia jail. In the early hours of March 15, 1986, fifty-five D.C. jail inmates arrived at what had become known as the 268 center. They were all black and Cowansville was all white. The neighbors were literally up in arms; they patrolled their neighborhoods carrying shotguns, fearing an escape.[40] But that turned out to be an unreasonable fear. The inmates reportedly were delighted to be out of the D.C. jail and had even gone so far as to clean the cafeteria after breakfast.

Inmate morale was not the issue. (It seldom is, of course.) When news of the 268 center reached Allen Hornblum, the chief lobbyist of the Pennsylvania Prison Society, he sat straight up in his bed.[41] At last, he thought (the *Philadelphia Inquirer Magazine* later reported), he could dramatize the private prison issue and, at the very least, wrest a moratorium from the legislature.[42] Hornblum was right; politicians fell over themselves to join him, and he saw his bill passed within one week. The inmates were returned to the tender mercies of the District of Columbia, proving once again that Pennsylvania was not its brothers' keeper. It is worth noting here that in all the discussion of abstract principles one point was overlooked—namely that the fifty-five inmates from the District of Columbia jail were being taken from a decent setting in Pennsylvania and returned to a poor one in Washington. It was nothing personal. Putting the best light on the situation, Pennsylvania's legislators did not want to house another jurisdiction's criminals. The Pennsylvania Prison Society did not want to see private operators gain a foothold. And if fifty-five small-time crooks were discomfited in the process, to use the vernacular, no big deal. But the unspoken message here is that stopping the spread of private prisons was more important than trying to improve the lot of a few prisoners. (This is the reform movement?)

The moratorium legislation had the effect of killing the Fentons' Beaver County project. But it specifically grandfathered in the Butler County jail, on the condition that the jail not accept out-of-state inmates. That was the least of the Fentons' problems. When the Fentons took over the jail, they planned to fire the entire staff and bring in their own people. The guards' union won an injunction barring that plan so, the Fentons were left with the task of managing a decrepit jail with a hostile staff. Despite that handicap, they have done fairly well. Even William G. Babcock of the Pennsylvania Prison Society credits them: "Charlie knows how to run a jail."[43]

He also knows how to fire people. Stuck with the union members, he made the most of the situation and, immediately laid off the *nonunion* part-timers. The jail was tacitly divided into inmate and staff areas. According to Joe Fenton, the part-timers were burly men who patrolled the tiers warily. With the fifteen part-timers gone, all of the twenty-five union members were reassigned to patrol duty. They received more training, had more programs, to offer, and reasserted control over the entire jail. Using some county money, and some of their own, the Fentons repaired recreation equipment, reopened the commissary, and relit the library to levels at which an inmate could read. At present, the Butler County jail is a success. As a bonus, the U.S. Marshal's Service has resumed using it to house traveling federal prisoners, a practice that has brought a little unexpected income to the county.

Although Pennsylvania resisted the idea of private prisons, the state of Kentucky thought the idea worth an experiment. According to Cheryl Roberts of the state Corrections Cabinet, in 1985 "we had 1,000 people backed up in county jails, waiting for transfers. The governor appointed a task force to develop options. [A privately run prison] was one of them."[44] Five companies bid for the contract in the fall of 1985. It offered the opportunity to run a "community correctional center," which Roberts described as more than a halfway house and not quite a minimum-security facility. The state used a point system when it considered the bids, weighing program ideas and price, and awarded the three-year contract to the U.S. Corrections Corporations, a local company that had never run a prison before. The per diem charge was $25; the state guaranteed a minimum of 175 people and an average annual population of 200. The inmates were drawn from those eligible for minimum security and within three years of appearing before the parole board.

The USCC's strongest selling point was its site. The company had bought a former Catholic seminary that was set on 115 acres in the middle of the state. The Roman Catholic Church had orginially sold it to a group called the Living Love Church; after six years, the group had moved to Oregon, leaving behind a 300-bed dorm, a gym, classrooms, and a fair piece of farmland. The USCC's Cliff Todd liked the facilities and the fact that Marion County might be receptive to a prison because the unemployment rate there was about 20 percent. Although the prison meant jobs—most of the staff was to be hired locally—there was local opposition that was crushed in a manner only a lawyer could love. According to Todd, his site was in the incorporated village of St. Mary's; when the mayor sued on behalf of his town, Todd's counsel discovered that St. Mary's had never bothered to collect local taxes. Therefore, under the state constitution, the town could be dissolved by a state judge. Todd says his lawyer used that technicality to countersue and then stood back to watch St. Mary's disappear. Since then, Todd has invited a citizen advisory counsel to the prison and has begun assigning inmate labor to odd jobs (chopping firewood and maintaining streets) around the community.[45]

Both the state and the USCC declare that Marion is the state's nicest prison. And although there has been trouble on the campus—contraband and occasional fights—both state and USCC officials say they think most inmates would prefer to stay there and will not break the rules. There are no perimeter walls or fences and seven men have walked away. Four have been caught and the local judge has dealt severely with three of them thus far, adding between five and sixteen years to their sentences.

Escape is the most serious of infractions, but more routine offenses are also subject to prison discipline. According to Mary Beth Smith of the state Corrections Cabinet, the procedures at Marion are similar to those followed throughout the state system. Charges against inmates are lodged in Disciplinary Incident Reports, which are sent to an adjustment committee at Marion that decides what action should be taken. The committee consists of USCC employees, just as at other centers where prison staffers serve on local review boards. The warden must approve the verdict and it is then sent to the state capital for a final review by a state official. Among other punishments, the panels can recommend loss of "good time" (time off for good behavior) or other privileges.[46]

There is no reason to assume that Marion's disciplinary board is any better, or worse, than those at other facilities. Presumably, its members are as sensitive—or insensitive—to due process concerns as any other group of prison workers. But two serious questions are raised by this arrangement. The first is whether a private company should be in the business of adjudicating charges against inmates. The second is whether the private company might not abuse disciplinary proceedings to keep its inmate head count high.

The first question is more serious, and again, there are powerful arguments on both sides. If the firm can hold the inmates in custody, why can its employees not also sit in judgment on their acts? Maintaining discipline is an inherent part of the task of managing any jail, and punishing offenders, the argument goes, is just part of that task. Furthermore, private judges have a long history in the United States and play important roles. Labor arbitrators, for instance, regularly decide the fate of workers' careers, decisions that are as serious as the loss of some period of good time.

The counter argument asserts that holding prisoners in custody is a mainly administrative task that follows a public verdict on the defendants' guilt. But it is another matter to turn the process of judgment itself over to the private sector. In practical terms, that is a distinction without a difference. The public pays no attention to prison disciplinary actions now, and citizens could rarely be admitted to such sessions even if they demanded access. But that fact does not resolve the symbolic, moral issue. The state does have an interest in retaining exclusive control over the power to order punishment. Delegating that power is an act of abdication that the state cannot commit. Simply put, sitting in judgment is a core public function.

There are at least two ways to deal with this problem. One is to have the disciplinary committee of the private prison serve only as a fact-finding body. The description of events submitted by the private firm's employees could then be sent to a state officer who would determine the appropriate punishment. Alternatively, the state could supply a disciplinary officer to the private facility who would both find facts and fix punishments. But neither of these plans can completely eliminate the role private employees will play in disciplining inmates. They will continue to exercise discretion—concerning what they ignore, what they file, and what they resolve by themselves.

> Correctional officers, who work in a hostile environment under constant pressure, are required to be part policeman and part social worker. Their ability to perform this dual role is intimately connected with their participation in disciplinary decisions. . . . Some of the infractions which can result in disciplinary actions permit a considerable degree of employee discretion. This discretion extends from the decision to cite an inmate for a particular offense to the choice of whether to handle the matter in a formal or informal manner. Inmates' awareness of correctional officers' influence over disciplinary decisions plays a large role in enabling the officers to maintain control of the facility and, short of using force, compel prisoner compliance with institutional regulation. If private correctional officers are relegated to a mere administrative or housekeeping role, they are likely to encounter substantial problems in dealing with inmates.[47]

The second question is less troublesome. There is the possibility that a private company will abuse the disciplinary system to keep its inmate head count high. But at the moment, given the almost standing-room-only status of most jails, it is unnecessary to fret very much about that prospect. Also, if the state retains the power of judgment, the opportunities for the private operator to use the system to achieve inappropriate ends will be limited.

Another part of the discipline issue is the use of force. It should be stated at the outset that this is a very important problem but one that is unlikely to arise often in its most extreme and dangerous form. Prison guards seldom use deadly force and never carry weapons when routinely patrolling cellblocks. In minimum-security institutions, such as the one in Kentucky, the guards on the perimeter patrols are not armed either. In county jails, however, which are often regarded as maximum-security facilities, they may be. Should an employee of a private security firm be empowered to shoot an escapee? In New Mexico, for instance, local jail employees who work for private firms are designated as peace officers within the confines of the jail, outside the institution while transporting prisoners, or while pursuing an escapee. They become, in effect, dual appointees, working for the private sector while also carrying public sector license and responsibility. As Charles Ring argues in his report for the Massachusetts legislature, this situation strongly suggests that private guards should receive the same training as public guards, perhaps at the same academy. That is a reasonable compromise but it does not fully resolve the symbolic issue. We would deny a private guard the right to sit in judgment on eligibility for good time, yet allow a private guard to pull the trigger on a fleeing felon climbing over razor wire? Such a prospect is made tolerable only by the unlikelihood of its repeated occurrence. A better situation would be the patrolling of perimeter areas by public officers, if the facility required armed guards to keep its population inside.[48]

One of the selling points of private prisons has been the claim that they can be more innovative. It is not at all clear that the operators have in fact developed any new population management techniques, but they have shown some ability to be flexible in the conduct of their operations so that they can take advantage of business opportunities. The best example is the new county jail that opened in May 1985 in Santa Fe, New Mexico.

State of the art and paid for with a $5 million bond issue, it attracted visitors from all over the West. There was just one catch: the county could not afford to operate it. It was budgeted to cost $1.2 million annually; analysts projected that after three months it would cost twice that. The county started making cuts but could not stop the hemorrhage. "The adjustments we made weren't significant enough to give us any hope that we could afford to run the jail," recalls Nancy Rodriguez, the county manager. "We started looking for options, including the private sector."[49]

A year earlier the state legislature had authorized two private jails for the state but no locality had taken up the offer.

Then Santa Fe did, put out its Request for Proposals, and five companies bid. Rodriguez brought in two National Institute of Corrections advisers who helped rate the proposals. The county awarded the three-year contract to the CCA in August 1986.

She was well advised; the contract clearly benefits Santa Fe County. Rodriguez estimates that the county per diem charge would have been $100 per head under public management; the CCA agreed to a per diem rate of $44.90, with a cap of $3.9 million on county payments for the life of the contract. Note the contrast: The budget analysts had estimated the county's runaway cost at $7.5 million over the next three years. Also as part of the deal, the CCA agreed to keep all sixty-three of the jail employees who wanted to stay. They would no longer be protected by civil service, but they would retain all their salary and benefits. Fifty-seven stayed on.

The contract also worked to the CCA's advantage. Santa Fe was operating its jail at half capacity. In return for charging the county bargain prices, the CCA won the right in the contract to fill the prison with inmates from other counties, as well as those sent by the INS and the U.S. Marshals Service, each of which would pay a premium per diem of rate of between $50 and $70. The overhead was roughly the same for the CCA, and the out-of-towners would pay the CCA's profit. This has not been a perfect meshing of needs because a handful of Cuban aliens the INS had deposited in Santa Fe promptly escaped—right over the state-of-the-art walls, made of specially reinforced concrete able to withstand four thousand pounds of pressure and fortified with internal bars. Santa Fe told the CCA not to take any more Cubans and the INS agreed. Nevertheless, Nancy Rodriguez is positively ebullient. "We want this to work," she says.

Of all the private jails that have been opened, none has received more public attention than the one in Bay County, Florida. Representatives from European governments, reporters for national publications, and curious local officials have all trooped through the private jail that works. Part of its appeal is the fact that it was once a public jail that *did not* work.

The Bay County jail, a six-story concrete structure in downtown Panama City, opened in 1977. There were problems almost from the beginning. State overseers had found fire code violations, overcrowded conditions, and serious understaffing. During one state inspection, guards were found to have left the inmates in charge, preferring to congregate by themselves in the jail basement. Medical care was erratic, the halls were dirty, and the plastic windows resembled Swiss cheese—the result of inmates' handiwork with lighted cigarettes. "We were running a shoestring operation," recalls Sheriff LaVelle Pitts.[50]

But it was a situation that the state would not tolerate indefinitely. The state sued the county, demanding repairs to the jailhouse and changes in its operations. At a meeting of the Board of County Commissioners in January 1985, Sheriff Pitts offered his solutions. To solve the staffing problem, he needed to hire twenty-five more people. To deal with the overpopulation there were, he said, only three choices. First, build a new jail that would cost at least $8 million. Second, limit the jail population to 196 and release prisoners whenever the jail exceeded that limit. Third, build a work camp nearby that would hold inmates sentenced to less than one year in jail. None of these alternatives pleased the five-member board, which over the past three years had seen the budget for the jail increase by 59 percent, without any reduction in problems. County Commissioner John Hutt reported that he had been informed about an outfit in Tennessee called the Corrections Corporation of America. The CCA was willing to send down one of its consultants to survey Bay County's situation and offer some solutions. Sheriff Pitts said that private jails were a complicated matter with lots of tricky questions but that ultimately "he did not care who ran the county jail." The board then passed a resolution inviting the CCA to come to town.[51]

Nine days later, on January 31, the county board held a "workshop" meeting to listen to a presentation from the CCA. Ever mindful that all politics is local, Tom Beasley came accompanied by one Mr. Bobby Brantley, who is identified in the minutes as "facility marketing representative" for the CCA. He was also a member of the Florida legislature and had chaired a subcommittee on overcrowding in prisons and jails. (Brantley is now lieutenant governor of Florida.) Brantley pitched the CCA's case. He said that CCA could "bring the financing to the table to build a new jail, operate the facility, and contract with the county on a per diem basis." It would custom design the facility and build it faster because it would not have to bother with competitive bids. Finally, he guaranteed the board that the facility would be safe and secure, and would comply with the standards of the American Correctional Association. The board asked a host of questions about private jails and then adjourned to solicit proposals from various other companies.[52]

On May 7, representatives from the CCA and three other firms appeared; the board voted to turn the management of the jail over to the CCA effective October 1, 1985.[53] The county leased the jail rent free to the CCA for twenty years. The CCA agreed to build a work camp for $4.5 million on ten acres of wooded land north of Panama City. The CCA would be paid on a per diem basis for inmates, with increases capped at 5 percent each year and computed on the basis of increases in the rate of inflation. It promised to indemnify the county against all litigation and agreed to carry a $15 million liability policy. Ultimately, the CCA was able to obtain only $5 million in coverage.

The changes that followed were quite remarkable. According to a report of a state inspection that took place February 19–20, 1986, the facility was clean and orderly, and an adequate staff was on duty. The overcrowding problem was still acute, but the work camp promised to alleviate that stress. Within nine months, the state had dropped its lawsuits because conditions in the jail had improved so dramatically.

All of this was accomplished with much of the same staff. The CCA offered to retain the corrections officers who wanted to stay. "There were very good people there," said David Myers, CCA's first administrator at the Bay County jail. "They just weren't being allowed to do their jobs." One could speculate endlessly on the effects of private sector corporate culture on job performance but the CCA's impact was clearly positive. Instead of considering their job at the jail as punishment duty for sheriff's deputies, employees were encouraged to take pride in their work. They were enrolled in a stock ownership program. Their suggestions were welcomed. "They went from the bottom of the totem pole to number one," says Myers. "They understand that if the company does well, they do well, too." One must not be naive here. There is no magic formula that turns the Keystone Kops into a benevolent tier patrol. But reasonable, rational employees often react positively to new and favorable opportunities. By appealing to both self-interest and pride, the CCA helped change employee performance at the Bay County jail. Given the previously existing climate, it is hard to imagine how that could have been accomplished from within.

The effects have not been lost on the inmates. "My clients are much better off and much happier today than they were three or four years ago," said Randall Berg, executive director of the Florida Justice Institute. But how can all this be possible? More programs, more recreation, a law library that is open, a happier staff—all for less money than the county used to spend? County officials say that in the first year of the CCA's operation alone, they saved $750,000. And once the work camp opened, the value of the inmate labor was effectively a savings of another $600,000. "The damn thing works and it's working cheaper," says County Commissioner Hutt. "Nobody can get around that or explain why."

Some have tried. Berg, for one, thinks the Bay County jail is a "loss leader," a superb demonstration project the CCA is running to attract more business. But Myers denies that, pointing to streamlined management and sharper purchasing practices as reasons for the CCA's success. Indeed, he says the Bay County jail's operation actually turns a small profit, albeit one that does not yet offset the overall corporate losses. An independent observer, Charles Thomas of the University of Florida, who is studying private jails for the Florida legislature, thinks the CCA may be benefiting from economies of scale. "Huge amounts of money are lost on local procurement," he says. "If you can get a paper clip cheaper in Nashville, there's not a whole lot of thought that has to go into it." He also says it is very hard to measure just how much the county is actually saving on the CCA's per diem rate of $30.62. The problem, says Thomas, is that most local government budgets do not break down the costs of amortization, utilities, or legal services that are provided by different public agencies. "Nobody," he concludes, "knows what the comparison figures are. They haven't the foggiest notion of what their costs were."[54]

As of this writing (May 1988), we end with an expert declaring that the past practices of public jails are as shrouded in mystery as are the future prospects of the private sector; the industry is poised to take off. But will it? Last year, a consortium composed of Bechtel Construction, the Daewoo Corporation (the Korean conglomerate), and some local operatives constructed a private jail in Ault, Colorado. It was a great idea, but the jail is still empty.

The next great "defining" event will probably occur in Texas, where the legislature has authorized and contracts have been let for construction of four 500-bed prerelease centers. Two contracts were awarded to the CCA and two to a new firm formed by Bechtel Construction and the Wackenhut Corporation. Pricor, which operates the jail in Tuscaloosa, Alabama, came in third. The final contracts have not yet been signed. The Texas Department of Corrections is attempting to drive a hard bargain, according to one principal in the negotiations, by insisting on a price lower than that authorized by the legislature. Is that because the Department of Corrections wants to prove that it, too, is cost conscious? Or is it because the department is not eager to have private operators in the state? No doubt other explanations are also possible.

I conclude this survey a hopeful agnostic. The entry of new players, motivated by profit but terrified by scandal, can bring about some modest change. For that, we can all be grateful.

British Penal Policy and the Idea of Prison Privatization

ANDREW RUTHERFORD

Since Margaret Thatcher came to power in May 1979, there has been a radical reformulation of the role of the state in the provision of human services, which has during much of the twentieth century, and certainly since 1945, been regarded as a primary, if not exclusive, responsibility of government. The essence of the emerging arrangements is a greatly enhanced role of the private sector in the delivery of services that remain largely supported by public funds. It is not, however, part of the Thatcher agenda to weaken the central government. Indeed, considerable power in a variety of spheres has shifted from local governments and other institutions to the national government. In this essay I first examine the emergence of notions concerning the privatization of prisons in Britain with reference to the political ideology espoused by the Thatcher government and some of its supporters. Unless considered in this particular political context, the very notion of private prisons would be dismissed as unthinkable if not an absurdity. But Mrs. Thatcher's position has been made more powerful by widely shared expectations that she may enjoy a fourth term as prime minister, results in serious consideration being given to the contribution the private sector might make to the prison system. The essay then explores those aspects of the crisis in the prison system that have been linked with the idea of prison privatization. I argue that privatization will not usefully contribute to penal practice in Britain and that it carries the danger of distracting attention from the underlying penal crisis, of which the dire straits of prisons today are the most visible symptom.

The Thatcher Government
and the Free Market Ideology

The Thatcher administrations have gone much further than other postwar Conservative governments in returning nationalized industries to the private sector. The privatization program has included British Gas, British Aerospace, British Telecom, British Airways, and British Petroleum (the remaining portion of which was sold despite the stock market crash of October 1987).[1] First on the agenda in early 1988 were the water authorities, the electricity boards, and possibly the more profitable parts of British Coal and British Rail. The privatization strategy has been carefully coordinated at the Cabinet level and tightly controlled by the Treasury. Stuart Butler of the Heritage Foundation has noted that this has enabled the government to minimize mistakes and to lay the groundwork carefully before a privatization initiative is launched. "In this way," observes the admiring Butler, "the Thatcherites have been able to move swiftly and decisively to build up the necessary coalitions for privatization and to concentrate on the weak points of the potential opponents."[2]

The Thatcher government's privatization agenda also includes a role for the private sector in the delivery of a variety of health, welfare, and other human services. These "partial forms of privatization" do not, as Paul Starr has noted, involve either the sale of assets or the delegation of policy formation, but enable the private sector to be responsible for policy implementation.[3] Already a number of publicly funded services have been contracted out to the private sector, including laundry and cleaning services in the National Health Service and the armed services, testing of trucks and public vehicles, and maintenance and cleaning of public buildings. There is continual speculation in the press about other aspects of the welfare state that might be placed under private management. To a considerable extent, public housing has already gone this route. Since 1979 over one million public housing units have been sold. This has resulted in a sharp rise in homelessness, which has, in part, been relieved by a greatly increased provision of bed and breakfast accommodations, subsidized by public funds, in private hotels.

As a result of the deification of the private sector in Britain since the early 1980s, very little remains that is regarded as being safely out of bounds. The Royal Mail (but not yet the Royal

Family) has been mentioned as a potential target by some supporters of the government. One consequence has been some adjustment in the position of the opposition parties. In December 1987, the leader of the then Social Democratic party suggested that private businesses might compete to provide welfare services. Even the Labour party, although still committed to state ownership and control of basic industries, is displaying some uncertainty in view of the much wider spread of home and stock ownership. It is perhaps not surprising, given the political atmosphere of "anything goes" (one former Conservative prime minister complained that the government was "selling off the family silver"), that prisons and other aspects of corrections have been mentioned as targets for partial privatization.

The Worsening Penal Crisis in Britain

At the crux of the British penal crisis is the trend toward harsher decisions throughout the criminal justice process, resulting in greater use of imprisonment.[4] In particular, there has been an increased use of custody with respect to pretrial and sentencing decisions. Between 1960 and 1987, the average daily prison population in England and Wales increased by 81 percent, with the total reaching a record level of 49,950 in 1988.[5] The prison population rate for England of 96 per 100,000 inhabitants was, in 1988, exceeded the rates of all other countries (outside the United Kingdom) in Western Europe.[6] The pretrial population (i.e., unconvicted and unsentenced prisoners) has experienced especially rapid growth, rising, in the same period, from 8 percent to 22 percent of the total prison population.[7]

During the 1960s, prison population growth to a large extent reflected increased numbers being dealt with by the courts. It was not until the late 1960s that the Home Office, as the responsible department of the central government, began to try to reduce, or at least stabilize, the size of the prison population. The measures had some effect, especially in terms of shortening the average time served for prison sentences. Prison population levels during the 1970s remained generally stable despite a shift by the courts toward more severe sentencing in the middle part of the decade.

During the 1980's, however, the number of prisoners resumed a higher rate of growth, attributable to an increased proportion of convicted persons receiving custodial sentences, imposition of longer prison sentences, and some lengthening of the delays in bringing people to trial. Essentially, the upward trend in prison population reflects the Thatcherite rhetoric on law and order and an unwillingness by the government to check the powers of the court. Although the rate of recorded indictable crime rose by an average of 7 percent per annum between 1980 and 1986, there was a 19 percent decline between 1982 and 1986 in the number of persons sentenced by the courts. The reduced court case load resulted from a decline in police clearance rates, an increased tendency by police and prosecutors to divert more serious offenders by means of a formal caution rather than prosecution, and the demographic effects of a reduced proportion of young people in the population.[8]

Although some emergency steps were taken to stem the tide (e.g., modifications of the rules governing parole eligibility and remission, or good time), the steady rate of growth continued. The overriding government policy since 1980 has been to massively increase the resources of the prison system; expenditures in real terms increased 72 percent between fiscal years 1980 and 1987.[9] In 1988 the prison building program projected a 53 percent increase in capacity between 1980 and 1995.[10]

Despite this greatly increased expenditure, about 40 percent of the total prison population is housed in overcrowded facilities.[11] Most of this crowding (two or three prisoners share an accommodation designed for one person, often for twenty-three hours a day) is in local prisons and remand centers where prisoners in pretrial detention are held. Remand prisoners are also backed up in police cells; this number averaged 530 in 1987, despite government pledges that the practice would be ended.[12] Overcrowded prisons are often squalid, in many instances, because of the lack of access to toilets. "Slopping-out" of chamber pots is still common throughout much of the English prison system. In the early 1980s, Home Office ministers claimed they were "on course" to eliminate overcrowding by the end of the decade. But these claims failed to take account of the continuing rate of prison population growth. Furthermore, the issue was obscured by semantics. In 1985, the Home Office acknowledged that what it meant by eliminating overcrowding was achieving a match of available places with the average prison population.[13] Even when such a match is achieved, considerable crowding may occur in local prisons as a consequence of the Prison Department's procedures for allocating prisoners.[14]

The imbalance of prisoners and cells has left the government with immediate problems of tactical management, sharply exacerbated by upward fluctuations in numbers. Between 1980 and 1987, prison population growth was almost twice that of capacity, resulting in a capacity shortfall in relation to population of 5,800 at the end of 1987.[15] In the period 1988–1990, the situation was expected to deteriorate further, in part because many of the prisons under construction will not be opened until 1991 or later. As of December 1987, the additional capacity in new prisons planned to be available between 1988 and 1990 (assuming no delays in construction) was estimated to be 3,000 cells.[16] The time lag associated with prison construction, typically about ten years, prompted the government to seek advice from the private sector as to how the building program might be accelerated. Regarding the longer term, anxiety existed among Home Office officials that even when the planned additional prisons become operational in 1995, capacity may still be insufficient. This reflects the government's reluctance to undertake a fundamental assessment of sentencing policy and will allow the prison population to continue to rise faster than the provision of new cells. Sir Brian Cubbon, the permanent head of the Home Office, remarked in Australia a few months before he retired, "Can we never contemplate inserting mechanisms of 'demand management' into the sentencing process, so that the volume of demand for imprisonment can be more closely tied to the available supply?"[17]

The Emergence of the Privatization Idea

The notion of privatizing some aspects of the British prison system has gained remarkably rapid acceptance, despite a lack of interest in the idea up to mid-1986. Little attention was given to a report published by the Adam Smith Institute in 1984 that advocated privatization of the prison system.[18] A similar fate befell rather milder proposals published by two academic members of the then Social Democratic party the following year.[19] On February 17, 1986, the following exchange took place during hearings held by the Public Accounts Committee of the House of Commons.

> *Dale Campbell-Savours M.P. (Labour):* Could you give me an assurance that no work is being done at the moment within your

department on the privatization of prisons within the United Kingdom?

Sir Brian Cubbon, permanent undersecretary of the Home Office: I can give you that assurance.

Dale Campbell-Savours: There is no work being done and there are no proposals that you know of for a privatisation programme?

Sir Brian Cubbon: That is so.[20]

Within a few months the Home Affairs Committee of the House of Commons, which has primary parliamentary oversight of the prison system, decided, as part of an inquiry into the state and use of prisons in England and Wales, to examine the privatization experience in the United States. In one of the briefest and most superficial reports ever made by a select committee of Parliament, the impressions of a visit made by some members of the committee to observe two privately operated prisons in the United States were summarized in three pages.[21] The committee (four Conservative members for the proposal and three Labour members against) recommended that "the Home Office should, as an experiment, enable private sector companies to tender for the construction and management of custodial institutions." The committee further recommended that any such contracting should, in particular, be directed at new remand centers, "because it is there that the most overcrowding in the prison system is concentrated."[22]

It is important to note that the committee did not hear any formal testimony in favor of privatization. Indeed, several witnesses argued against this policy direction. In particular, the members of the Prison Officers' Association were vehemently opposed, having carried out their own inquiry into privatization, which included visits to privately run institutions in the United States.[23] The overall conclusion of the POA was that "no civilized society could ever lend credence to the arguments in favour of prison privatization."[24] This observation prompted the following exchange between Jeremy Hanley, M.P. (Conservative) and John Bartell, chairman of the Prison Officers' Association:

Hanley: In the private prisons that I saw—and that means prisons contracted by the state to take on the job of carrying out the role of imprisoning people, those particular facilities were more civilized than the state prisons that I saw. Would you believe therefore that they are not civilized?

Bartell: We would find it somewhat difficult to comprehend that particular statement.[25]

In evidence presented to the committee, an official of the Howard League for Penal Reform stated: "The frightening problems we face as a nation in solving the prison crisis cannot be shirked by hiving it off to private management. . . . Privatisation of prisons is a diversion from the critical policy choices as to who should go to prison and for what offence."[26] A rather similar point was made by Terry Bone, chairman of the Prison Governors' Branch of the Society of Civil Servants following an exchange with John Wheeler, M.P. (Conservative), himself a former assistant prison governor.

Wheeler: I suggest to you that you should not be fearful of resisting an idea until you have explored it very carefully.

Bone: Of course we would want to study very carefully any ideas that might improve the system in which we are working. However, I have to say that on the knowledge that we have about privatization it seems a curious. . .

Wheeler: It is not privatisation. We are not talking about privatisation.

Bone: You are talking about the private running of prisons. That seems to me to be privatisation.

Wheeler: No it is not.

David Winnick, M.P. (Labour): Semantics.

Bone: I have to say that whether you call it privatisation or whether you all it private running of prisons, it seems to us to be a curious irrelevance to the problems that the prison system faces in this country. It is a diversion from the main crisis that we are facing.[27]

The committee's first witness, in November 1986, was the Home Office minister responsible for prisons, Lord Caithness. The committee chairman, Sir Edward Gardner, M.P. (Conservative), told the minister: "When I went out to the United States to look at what are called 'private prisons,' I had in mind the possibility that they were more absurd than realistic. However, those of us who went out to America and saw these private prisons . . . were profoundly impressed by what we saw. Far from thinking that these prisons might be something in fantasy rather than something we could use in practice, I think we all felt that they are in fact institutions of a very high standard indeed." The minister was then asked if the Home Office had any objection in principle to the contract management of prisons. Lord Caithness replied: "We welcome any suggestions of reform of the Prison Service and we will consider the same."[28]

In March 1987 two reports, written from very different vantage points, gave further support to the notion of private prisons. Peter Young of the Adam Smith Institute urged that "an entirely fresh approach is required if we are ever to break out of this depressing cycle of overcrowding, violence and decline. Fundamental reform is necessary. The system needs to be changed, not just tinkered with."[29] At the heart of the problem, according to Young, was "monopoly provision"; he prescribed what he considered the obvious remedy: "By introducing an element of competition into the prison business one should be able to increase supply, improve quality and reduce cost." Drawing from a survey of publications describing experience in the United States (his sources included publications of the National Institute of Justice and the *Reader's Digest*), Young concluded that "the most compelling argument for prison privatization is the humanitarian one." He recommended that five existing prisons be privatized on an experimental basis and that privatization of a new private remand prison in London be the first priority. If the results were satisfactory, the rest of the system should be gradually privatized.[30]

If the proposals of the Adam Smith Institute were little cause for surprise, this was not the case for a report prepared by two liberal academics, Maxwell Taylor of University College, Cork, and Ken Pease of the University of Manchester. They argued that "private prisons can be the springboard for the development of a truly rehabilitative programme, so lacking in our present prisons." Contracts would include a "no reconviction" bonus element—a conviction-free two-year period after release. Taylor and Pease displayed a somewhat unusual faith in the rehabilitative possibilities of prisons. "The provision of a commercial incentive to develop programmes which really change people would be a welcome development."[31] Two months later, the Home Affairs Committee published its majority report. The Labour members, although dissenting, and despite earlier indications, did not produce a minority report.

Following the June 1987 election and commencement of the third Thatcher administration, Lord Caithness left for the United States in September to examine for himself the evidence on prison privatization. Accompanied by three Home Office officials, he was flown by the Corrections Corporation of America, in their company plane, to the jail run by CCA in Panama City,

Florida. Don Hutto, director of CCA International, remarked: "We are the market leaders, so it is appropriate that they should come to see us."[32] During the Caithness visit, two British construction companies announced that they were joining with CCA to form a consortium to promote the privatization of British prisons. Jack Pullin, a member of the consortium's management committee, boasted: "We have done our homework and are ready and raring to go. All we are waiting for is the word from the minister." As to the inmates, Pullin took a somewhat selective approach: "People sent there may not have paid their rates [local taxes] or something like that. Anyone charged with multiple rape would probably be sent elsewhere."[33]

In the government's formal reply to the Home Affairs Committee's proposals on privatization, published in the summer of 1988, it was indicated that contracting out the management of new remand centers to the private sector was a likely policy choice. The government saw no "over-riding difficulty of principle which ought to rule out private sector involvement, provided that sensible practical safeguards are built into the arrangements."[34] Management consultants, appointed by the government, concluded that private sector involvement was feasible and in March 1989 it was announced that investigations would proceed into the private sector's role in operating remand centers and that, in the light of these, legislation would be introduced. By early 1990 there were no signs of political urgency on the issue. A Home Office official was quoted as saying: "The exercise and ministers will take a good deal of time to assess whether the deal is feasible. The program has to be viewed in the light of prison expenditure and would not go ahead independently."[35]

Private Sector Precedents

In July 1970 the Home Office contracted with Securicor Ltd. to to staff and operate its immigrant detention centers at the four major airports in addition to assuming other duties associated with the escort of immigrants. It is curious that this long-standing arrangement has been so rarely mentioned in the debate about the role of the private sector in regard to British prisons.

Securicor was established in 1935, when it was known as Night Watch Services. By the late 1970s it employed 18,000 people in the United Kingdom and 8,000 overseas. Prior to 1970, Securicor and other private security firms were employed by the airline companies to enable them to fulfil their statutory duties for the detention and removal of passengers who had been refused permission to land. Securicor, until it lost its contract in December 1988, was accountable to the Immigration and Nationality Department of the Home Office. Although questions have been raised in Parliament, and during the course of inquiries by parliamentary committees, much less than a full picture has emerged regarding the contract between the Home Office and Securicor and the manner in which it was carried out.

Securicor was responsible for short-term (up to five days' detention) facilities at four airports and for the longer-term detention center at Harmondsworth, adjacent to Heathrow Airport, which has accommodation for sixty-six detainees who have committed no criminal offense.[36] What little is known about the staffing and operation of these facilities has been gained from statements made in Parliament. For example, in October 1970 a Home Office minister, in a Written Answer, stated: "From experience gained in doing similar work for the airline at London airport since 1967, Securicor is well placed to select suitable personnel and to give them adequate training in both the custodial and welfare aspects of their duties."[37] Eight years later a Home Office minister commented that Securicor provided a one-week course for all new employees and an additional one-day training course for staff engaged full time on escort and detention duties. It had not been necessary to require inclusion of screening procedures in the contract with Securicor.[38] A brief description of the situation at Harmondsworth was provided in 1983. "Harmondsworth provides accommodation for both sexes and may also hold children. Detainees are in general free to go where they will within the center, and may spend their time as they choose. Television is provided, and there is a small open-air recreational area. Visiting is permitted daily. Public pay telephones are provided and may be used by detainees at any time. The centre is staffed by employees of Securicor Ltd., whose instructions are to treat all detainees with humanity, kindness, courtesy and understanding."[39]

The facilities operated by Securicor were not subject to close scrutiny by parliamentary committees. The Harmondsworth facility was visited by a House of Commons committee in 1978 and questions were subsequently put to Home Office officials. The committee were assured that the Home Office exercised adequate oversight of the facility, which came "within the purview of the inspector of the Immigration Service who is stationed at Harmondsworth, not in the detention center but in the same area, and he or one of his staff visits the detention center about six times a day."[40] It was also explained to the committee that detailed rules governing behavior of the Securicor staff were set out in a document drawn up in 1970 but have never been part of the contract between the Home Office and Securicor, "because these are not matters which give rise to any difficulties because Securicor have observed these rules of practice since."[41] As to the contract itself, it continues unless terminated by either party and is monitored "from time to time" to take account of increasing costs. With reference to the relatively low level of training provided by Securicor to its staff working in the detention centers, the committee was told that a comparison with prison officers (who receive six week's preservice training) was not appropriate. "They are not dealing at Harmondsworth with the same type of people that the prison officer will be dealing with in a prison. . . . They are not in Harmondsworth for a long time and they are not in conditions of high security."[42]

Representatives of prison governors (called "wardens" or "superintendents" in the United States) expressed concern to the committee about the principle of an involvement by the private sector. The committee stated that it fully shared the concern of the prison governors about that principle and recommended that the arrangements be reviewed by the Home Office.[43] The government replied that there were practical difficulties in the way of providing a suitable alternative and that "the use of private security orderlies should continue for the time being."[44]

The committee's recommendation that the chief inspector of prisons be invited to inspect the detention facilities at Harmondsworth and Heathrow was accepted by the government. Inspections were carried out during 1980 but no reports were published. The new Inspectorate of Prisons, which was set up in 1981, carried out its first inspection of the Harmondsworth center in November 1988.[45]

In an earlier inquiry, the Home Affairs Committee gave only cursory attention to detention facilities and even less to the role of Securicor. It was determined that the cost to hold a detainee in a Prison Department establishment was 34 per day and that the cost for an Immigration Service detainee was three times as much.[46] The committee commented on the absence of adequate complaint procedures. Complaints are investigated only by the immigration authorities. No record of complaints is published and indeed the annual reports of the Immigration and Nationality Department of the Home Office contain very little information about its detention centers. That the lack of public accountability is particularly important, given the role of a private security firm, has been a matter of criticism.[47] Ironically, the very involvement of the private sector has provided the rationale for not releasing detailed information on costs. A Home Office minister revealed that twenty-seven posts charged with escort and detention duties were regularly filled by Securicor in 1982 but refused to supply cost information as this would be "a breach of commercial confidence."[48]

The experience of the immigration detention centers since 1970 provides rather mixed evidence with respect to prison privatization. Certainly there were few known complaints lodged against Securicor. Furthermore, the Joint Committee for the Welfare of Immigrants, along with the Prison Reform Trust, has concluded that "conditions and facilities in Immigration Service detention centers are far better than those prevalent in the prison establishments used to detain those arrested after entry to this country. The day-to-day regime is far more relaxed and easy-going, with longer visiting hours, no real constraints on day-time association, and access to pay phones. Immigration Service detention centers are far preferable to prison establishments given the administrative nature of detention."[49] The abysmally bad conditions of facilities in the prison system may have done much to mute criticisms of immigration detention centers. The operational costs of the detention centers are relatively high, but it is by no means certain that there would be savings if public servants were to be employed as custodial staff. The main reservations that arise concern the quality of staff, the absence of complaint procedures, and the lack of independent inspection or oversight of the facilities.

Certainly the arrangements between the Home Office and Group 4 Total Security, which took over from Securicor, do not provide a model for contracting out a remand center to the private sector. Prisons tend to be closed worlds and governments often appear to seek means of evading close monitoring and accountability. The decision to involve the private sector in the operation of the immigration detention centers may be most explicable in this context.

Institutions for Young Offenders

The emerging idea of prison privatization in Britain has remained largely disconnected from the correctional activities of the voluntary (nonprofit private) sector. In particular, virtually no reference has been made in the debates about privatization to the involvement of voluntary agencies in the management of young offender institutions. The industrial schools and reformatories of the mid-nineteenth century were the inspiration and creation of the private, but noncommercial, sector. From the beginning, costs were met largely by the Home Office and local governments. The history of these institutions in large part records the tensions that arise from the combination of public funding and private management.

In 1894, a recently retired permanent head of the Home Office revealed his doubts about private sector management in evidence presented during a departmental inquiry: "Reformatory managers notoriously keep the boys too long. . . . It is, of course, to the interest of managers to keep their reformatories full, and also to have the profit from the remunerative labour of the older boys."[50] In 1922 an unpublished Home Office report was described as "the most damning indictment of the privately managed, publicly financed Certified School system we have yet seen."[51] Public concerns about the quality of operation and fiscal mismanagement led to the closing of many of these institutions. The Home Office has exercised an increasingly tight grip on those that have survived. The emasculation of the voluntary private sector has been usefully summarized by Julius Carlebach as demonstrating "the shift in over-all authority in all areas of the system from the managers to the Home Office. This shift was based on the transference of financial responsibility for the schools from the voluntary bodies to the State and the simultaneous demands by the State to justify the assumption of financial control by assuming control also over those aspects of the system which in the course of time had been shown to be inadequate."[52]

The voluntary sector still plays a role in the operation of youth institutions, but that role is much diminished. The institutions, now known as community homes (between 1933 and 1969 they were referred to as approved schools), hold not only children adjudicated as offenders but a variety of other children who have been placed in the care of the local authority. Since the early 1970s the number of children in care who are held in all types of institutions has decreased by about one-third; in the same period, the number of children held in institutions managed by the private sector has decreased by more than one-half.[53]

The network of institutional arrangements for children in care has become widely dispersed. Local authorities enjoy considerable discretion as to placement in institutions managed by either the public sector or the private sector. The settings include boarding schools and psychiatric institutions serving a variety of public agencies, as well as fee-paying parents. At least one commercial hospital company is holding young offenders on behalf of local authorities. The underlying dynamic of this "youth in trouble system" may be, as Paul Lerman has suggested, an "increasing incentive to redefine youth in trouble according to diagnostic categories which will legitimate placement in facilities deemed appropriate for reimbursement."[54]

Historical assessments of the private sector's contribution with respect to young offender institutions suggest that there have been occasional instances of innovative and enlightened management, but in general practice differed little from when management was in the hands of the local authority. Carlebach, who is generally supportive of private management, has commented that in the course of time, "the managers who were originally the trend-setters, the idealists, the reformers, the people who conceptualized and activated the various forms of treatment for destitute and delinquent children had been reduced to a position where it was necessary for [them to be told] what the schools they were managing were for."[55] In Gordon Rose's view, the revitalization of private sector initiatives and the tightening of Home Office controls were contradictory. Based on his review of the one-hundred-year history of young offender institutions, Rose was convinced that close Home Office oversight was essential. The logic therefore pointed to both public control and public management.[56] Neither of these studies extends beyond the 1960s; a careful review of the range of private institutional provisions for young people in trouble that exists in the late 1980s is thus long overdue.

The privately managed young offender institutions and the immigration detention centers have had a relatively low level of visibility. Virtually no data have been published about their inmates, staff, or management. The "youth in trouble" system is so complex that, although it is largely publicly funded, the number of children being held is not even known.[57] For detained immigrants, language difficulties and distance from family and friends makes them especially vulnerable. Both these examples suggest that, when institutional management is not vested in public officials, problems of oversight and accountability become especially intractable.

Ideology and Pragmatism

The impetus for the notion of prison privatization in Britain arises from a combination of ideological and pragmatic considerations. Privatization of certain public services is a central part of the Thatcher government's political agenda, reflecting the ideology of some of its supporters, especially policy groups in the Conservative party's right wing. Certainly in the absence of this political context the notion of privatized prisons would almost certainly be dismissed as a fantasy, but as one senior civil servant remarked to the author in 1984, "With this lot, you never know." Not surprisingly, ideological concerns were the focus of a report published by the Adam Smith Institute that castigates state prison system monopoly for its complacency and failure to innovate. In particular, the report seeks to reduce the vested interests of prison officers and other employees. "The prison system is just such a case of a state service being run to benefit the producers of the service, the employees, rather than the inmates and the taxpaying public."[58]

Most proponents of prison privatization, however, have downplayed ideological considerations. In 1987 the Conservative majority of the Home Affairs Committee of the House of Commons took a generally pragmatic stance. "The present state of our prisons, blighted by age, severe overcrowding, insanitary conditions and painfully slow progress in modernisation makes it necessary to consider urgent new ways of dealing with these problems which at present seem almost insoluble."[59] This proposition led the Conservative members to the view that "a new dimension of urgency and flexibility has to be introduced into the prison building programme. This could be achieved by inviting commercial companies to tender for the construction and *management* of custodial institutions" (emphasis added).[60] Standards would be laid down in the contract between the Home Office and the provider, and adherence to them would be mon-

itored by the Home Office. It is of interest to note that the issue
of standards has also been given particular emphasis by John
Wheeler, M.P., one of the leading parliamentary proponents of
prison privatization. During the committee's hearings, Wheeler
observed that "the engine which has driven the authorities in
the United States to contract out the management of their
prison services has been the requirement of the courts, because
there is a minimum standard of conditions of treatment for prisoners."[61] Leaving aside the veracity of this observation, the linkage between prison minimum standards and privatization is of
significance, given the government's refusal to develop such a
code despite calls from pressure groups and parliamentary committees.[62] Proponents of the private prison seem to be saying to
liberal penal reformers that the most viable route to minimum
standards may be the breaking of the public monopoly of provision of prisons. For example, the Home Affairs Committee has
unanimously urged the removal of Crown immunity.[63] This
would open the way for institution of court proceedings when
conditions in Crown (public) buildings failed to meet standards
required by legislation concerning hygiene and safety. The Conservative majority commented, with reference to the phasing
out of Crown immunity for prisons, that "whether or not this is
done we believe that contractually managed prisons should not
enjoy this protection."[64]

Critics of the prison privatization idea have argued that the
difficulties of ensuring greater accountability within the prison
system would become worse, not be eliminated, if management
were to be contracted out to the private sector. Stephen Shaw,
director of the Prison Reform Trust, has suggested that "privatisation may provide a means for the State to further avoid
making prisons publicly accountable."[65] There is considerable
merit to this contention, even if this outcome is unintended.

The Home Affairs Committee also put forward the proposition that "the state should be the sole provider of a service only
when no-one else exists who can provide the same service at
less cost or can provide a better service."[66] This curious and sim-
plistic notion was not developed by the committee. There seems
to be little recognition that in the exercise of coercive power
over prisons (as with some other areas of public administration), the state, to quote Paul Starr, "represents the nation and
seeks to speak with one voice, [thus] it needs public servants
loyal to its highest interests, not private contractors, maximis-
ing their own."[67] The committee dismissed the argument
against the introduction of a profit motive as being "bizarre"

and added that "people are employed in the prison service to gain the benefit of wages and conditions of service. That is simply another profit motive."[68] This extraordinary observation not only equates wages and profits but totally fails to acknowledge the need for a disinterested public service.

The Profit Factor

The argument about prison privatization in Britain has been conducted almost exclusively with the commercial private sector in mind; only scant reference has been made to involvement of voluntary (nonprofit) agencies. As mentioned earlier, little attention has been given to the role of the voluntary private sector in the management of young offender institutions. This is almost certainly because of the particular heritage of these institutions, which were founded as a result of the initiatives of charitable agencies a century or more ago. In recent years, most of the new developments in the voluntary sector have occurred in the area of community-based programs. These activities have included establishment of hostels (group homes), but the main theme has been the provision of a range of support services for young offenders in their homes and communities. Developments of this sort have been encouraged by both Labour and Conservative governments and have received the support of penal reform groups.[69] Some of the local programs that have contributed to a reduction of the number of juveniles in the prison system during the 1980s have been managed by the voluntary sector, often in close collaboration with the local government.

The innovative nature of some of these programs appears to be attributable in part to the nongovernmental status of the agencies.[70] Problems of effective monitoring and implementation of other measures to ensure proper control and accountability do arise, but those facing the nonprofit agencies are much less complex than those existing in the commercial sector, for two main reasons.[71] First, voluntary agencies, for the most part, provide programs that are nonresidential and certainly noncustodial. The power and vulnerability that are associated with the deprivation of liberty are usually absent. Second, the absence of the profit motive promises a more disinterested stance by the voluntary sector. Some caution is, of course, required here as voluntary agencies may, in their search for financial viability, be driven by considerations at variance with the public interest.

The Custody Factor

Many opponents of prison privatization argue that the core issue is the exercise of power that arises in the custodial situation. So awesome is this responsibility that the state should not delegate it. For some observers, the degree of importance attached to this point depends upon the category of prisoner. As noted earlier, there has been general agreement in Britain that the detained immigrant need not be held in the prison system. In the absence of any readily available alternative, the private sector has stepped in and this has prompted little attention or objection. Remand prisoners, especially those of pretrial status, may also be a softer target for privatization. This is clearly the view of Lord Windlesham, who notes: "While there are strong arguments against the state handing over to private enterprise responsibility for the custody of convicted and sentenced prisoners, these objections do not apply with equal force to those individuals, currently numbering one in five of the prison population, who have been charged with a criminal offence and are awaiting trial." Windlesham argues that punishment is the "touchstone" for distinguishing sentenced prisoners from pretrial prisoners. The latter are held in prison for preventive reasons. For these persons to be managed by the private sector "would at once relieve the pressure on the prisons and signify the special status of the inmates."[72]

Pretrial remand prisoners are no less vulnerable in the custodial setting than those who have been sentenced, however. Indeed, in some instances their vulnerability may be greater. For pretrial prisoners there are a variety of pressures that arise in an especially acute form. It may be their first experience of custody. They may also have intense anxiety about the forthcoming court proceedings, family, employment, and other uncertainties. As John Irwin has noted, when persons are arrested and jailed, their ties and arrangements with people outside very often disintegrate.[73] The risk of suicide appears to be higher for pretrial prisoners than for sentenced prisoners. No less than sentenced prisoners, pretrial prisoners are held in prison by order of a court and it is up to the state to provide directly for their security and welfare.

The Position of Prison Officers

The largest employees' union, the Prison Officers' Association, remains a powerful opponent of prison privatization. "Privatisation may, at the moment, excite the minds of businessmen and some politicians but the enormity of the moral, ethical and legal arguments against it will eventually ensure that it remains nothing more than a distasteful experiment"; so concluded the assistant secretary of the POA.[74] As mentioned earlier, the POA conducted its own fact-finding tour of privatized penal facilities in the United States and its officials returned with a largely negative impression. In particular, in the evidence it presented to the Home Affairs Committee, the POA expressed anxiety as to the impact of privatization on its members. Given that salaries and benefits make up the largest part of operational costs, it is feared that this is the area in which savings will be made.

These concerns of the POA should be viewed in the context of a relationship with the Home Office that, especially since the early 1970s, has been characterized by acrimony and distrust. Between 1976 and 1980 an average of seventy-four industrial disputes occurred annually. Through a variety of actions, which included refusing to allow vehicles in and out of prisons and denying prisoners access to bathing and exercise, the POA, at the local and national levels, challenged the authority of the governors and the Home Office to manage the prison system.[75] In the early 1980s a prison governor commented: "The control of prisons had by the mid-seventies to a very large extent passed into the hands of the Prison Officers' Association."[76]

Much of the discord between the Home Office and the POA has concerned overtime arrangements and fringe benefits. In 1979 an official inquiry concluded, with respect to the determination of manning levels, that "over the entire area there appears to rest a pall of uncertainty, if not incomprehension."[77] By 1985 the POA's position on manning levels had become increasingly untenable. In the previous six years, the staff had increased at a rate almost twice as high as that of the prison population; average weekly overtime amounted to sixteen hours and showed no sign of decline. The Home Office began reasserting its authority, and steps were taken to put together a new pay and conditions structure, known as "Fresh Start," which would greatly reduce reliance on overtime earnings. Matters came to a head in the early summer of 1986 when the POA instructed its members not to work overtime. The withdrawal of staff resulted in disturbances at forty prisons over a three-day period. So great was the ensuing physical damage that the POA called off its protest. Since that time the Home Office has moved ahead with its Fresh Start initiative but relations with the POA remain fragile, clouded by threats of further industrial action.

It might be cynically suggested that prison privatization has arisen as a means of bypassing the POA or at least reducing its power. The Adam Smith Institute report referred to the staff's vested interests, but the Thatcher government is far from sympathetic to the trade union movement in Britain. Given the recent history of deepening discord between the Home Office and the POA, it would not be surprising if considerations of this sort had not been raised. It must, however, be concluded that no evidence is available that gives weight to this connection. Certainly the disturbances of 1986 were traumatic for the prison system as a whole and prompted Her Majesty's chief inspector of prisons to question the propriety of industrial action in a prison setting.[78] Although no action has been taken by the Home Office on this issue, it has almost certainly strengthened the voices of those seeking to curb POA power.

The opposition to prison privatization by the POA is based in part on a desire to protect its own interests. But other considerations are also important. For the POA, the administration of punishment must remain the responsibility of the state. "Private industry cannot be allowed to place the maintenance of profits over and above the protection of the public."[79] The POA's opposition to privatization is not confined to issues of management but extends to an increased role for the private sector in prison construction. In 1987 the POA, along with all the penal reform groups, argued against further prison construction, a position that has emerged in the development of a more sophisticated analysis of Britain's penal crisis.

The Home Office is on particularly difficult ground as it charts a plan for prison privatization that does not unduly provoke the POA. Although Home Office ministers (and perhaps some civil servants) might be tempted to regard privatization as a tool for taming the POA, they acknowledge that the crucial task ahead is the successful implementation of Fresh Start as a sound basis for effective management. The government's concerns that any experimentation with privatization will prompt industrial action may deter any initiative in this direction, however.

Likely Developments

In December 1987, the government announced a role for private sector employees in speeding up implementation of the prison building program. A new Prisons Building Board was set up that included three nonexecutive members from the private construction industry. This may be a first step in opening the way for an extended role for the private sector in executing the prison building program. It has already been decided that government departments will retain much closer control of their own building projects and thus will rely less on the Public Services Agency, which in the past has been responsible for all new public construction. Furthermore, since April 1988, government departments have not been obliged to use the PSA for major programs requiring large capital expenditure. Instead, departments will decide whether to use the PSA or directly tender for construction contracts. In the longer term, similar arrangements may become possible for capital expenditure on existing institutions. These measures are intended to meet criticisms by the comptroller and auditor general and by the Public Accounts Committee regarding delays and waste in the prison expansion program.[80] Such difficulties have not arisen because of lack of financial support from the Treasury. By 1988, a capital expenditure of approximately £1500 million had been approved for the prison system in England and Wales, extending through 1995. In the event of a shift of spending priorities away from the prison system, however, there might be an interest in financial arrangements such as lease-back deals, which have been used in the United States to overcome an unwillingness to support bond issues.

In the immediate future, the private sector's role in prison management in Britain is likely to be marginal at most. Tentative steps may be taken to pave the way toward some experimentation, possibly with a remand center. But, legislation would be required to amend the Prison Act of 1952 if management were to be contracted out by the Home Office for responsibilities other than support services such as laundry.[81] The best prospects for growth are those of nonprofit agencies involved in the management of non-custodial programs, as is emphasized in the government's recent emphasis on "punishment in the community."[82]

Conclusion

The early history of prison reform in Britain is, in large part, a chronicle of the private sector giving way to public control. One aspect of the perceived requirement of state intervention has been described by Sean McConville: "So necessary was a good and constant flow of prisoners that some gaolers felt it improvident to trust in the normal workings of the law. Instead they had themselves placed as commissioners of the peace and indicted quite innocent parties who between committal and release paid numerous fees and charges."[83] Much of the impetus for reform during the late eighteenth century was provided by the appalling conditions endured by prisoners held in privately managed institutions. The situation in Britain two hundred years later is not without irony, for advocates of the private sector have highlighted the abysmally bad conditions, found especially in local prisons and remand centers. But there is no reason to assume that involvement of the private sector in the management of parts of the prison system will contribute to an improvement in conditions for either prisoners or staff. The pressure for establishment of minimum prison standards has grown in recent years despite opposition from the Home Office since 1984. In time the position of the Home Office is likely to soften. Although the courts have shifted little from their traditional "hands-off" stance with regard to prison conditions, increased pressure is likely to be brought as a result of cases dealt with under the European Convention of Human Rights.[84] Progress in this direction will probably be impeded rather than encouraged by the involvement of the private sector.

The lack of information about the administration of immigration detention centers strongly suggests that the lack of visibility that commonly characterizes prison administration will be exacerbated. What is known about staff recruitment and training procedures, for example, indicates a more lax approach than is being taken in the public sector. A strong case can be made to bring the immigration detention centers under the direct management of the Home Office (but not as part of the Prison Department). But the grounds are even stronger for resisting any private sector encroachment on management of the prison system itself.

To view the private sector as being able to rescue British prisons from a desperate state of affairs is to confuse prison and penal reform, however. At the heart of the situation confronting the prison system is the direction of penal policy and practice. In particular, the British penal crisis derives from the failure to treat punishment, especially the use of custody, as a scarce resource. Since 1974 the courts of England and Wales have imposed immediate custodial sentences on an increasing proportion of persons judged guilty of indictable offenses.[85] During this period, prison sentences, imposed and served, have become longer.[86] Government policy has been an "open front door" modified by a variety of "back door" strategies. Open front door policy is exemplified in a hands-off stance toward sentencing practice. In March 1982 the Home Secretary stated: "We are determined to ensure that there will be room in the prison system for every person whom the judges and magistrates decide should go there, and we will continue to do whatever is necessary for that purpose."[87] This declaration, which has been repeated with various degrees of emphasis by successive ministers, reflects the powerful prevailing reluctance to place a lid on either prison capacity or population. Spending, especially capital expenditure, on the prison system was an area, among others in the sphere of law and order, which was to be protected from cuts to be applied more generally in the public sector. While penal reform groups, and some academic studies, have criticized the high level of spending on the prison system, perspectives of this kind have only rarely surfaced in official documents. One example was the comments in February 1986 when a specialist adviser to the House of Commons Treasury and Civil Service Committee stated: "Some discussion is required of whether a change in sentencing policy could reduce the cost of the penal system. The White Paper [on the government's expenditure plans 1986–87 to 1988–1989] assumes too uncritically that the aim of the Home Office is to provide prison places for as many convicts as the courts give custodial sentences to on present sentencing policies."[88]

There were some signs, however, toward the end of the 1980s of a shift by the government away from the "open door" stance. The harmful effects of imprisonment were highlighted, together with the need for a shift of emphasis toward "punishment in the community."[89] This message was sharply underlined in a major white paper of Feburary 1990 which specifically sought to reduce the prison population.[90] Legislation is anticipated during 1990–91 but it is possible that discussions about the overuse of imprisonment, both at the public and private level, have had a positive effect on sentencers, with a drop of 1,500 in the prison population occurring between 1988 and the early months of 1990.

Beyond financial limits, there is the fundamental normative issue of viewing punishment in a liberal democratic state as something that must be used with restraint. Given that imprisonment is the most severe penalty in Britain, every effort should be made to ensure that it is rationed prudently. At least since the early 1980s, penal policy appears to have abandoned any such restraint. In this situation, an enlarged role for the private sector seems both irrelevant and a diversion from crucial and urgent penal policy issues. The problem is not that there are insufficient prisons but that there are far too many people in prison. The prison population in England as a proportion of total inhabitants doubled between 1950 and 1990, seemingly out of step with the country's liberal casting and humanistic tradition.[91] Furthermore, presenting the problem in terms of prison management misses the core issue. There is significant room for improvements in the management of British prisons, but it does not follow that they would result from privatization. Indeed, there is every reason to suppose that existing difficulties would become more intractable. The management of prisons is inherently part of the public service. The reforms that are required largely concern areas outside the prison system, affected by decisions that determine the extent and distribution of punishment. These are exclusively public policy issues, and it is in this domain that they must be addressed.

Private Time: The Political Economy of Private Prison Finance

HERMAN B. LEONARD

The movement to privatize some public services—garbage collection, waste water treatment, prisons, and jails, to name but a few—is a legacy of grass-roots "reduce government" movements of a decade ago. The tax and expenditure limitation movements of the late 1970s and early 1980s may be dormant in many jurisdictions, but they are far from dead. They sprang from the frustration of taxpayers who felt that government was too willing to try to meet too many requests for aid from too many quarters. They continue to exert political force to hold down spending, to limit the extent of tax increases, to threaten officials who seem too prone to increase spending. But the demands for public services—for better schools, better quality of life in old age, safer streets, cleaner surroundings, and more prisons and jails—also continue unabated.

These competing forces keep public officials in a perilous political vise. Squeezed on the one side by those who claim that service levels are too low and on the other by those who claim the cost of government is too high, they struggle to defend and maintain essential services, to identify low-priority or inefficient resource use, and, generally, to find ways to do "more with less."

Privatization of public services has been proferred as a promising direction for meeting these conflicting challenges. Part of the tax and expenditure limitation movement is founded on the idea that the public sector is an inherently inefficient producer, procurer, or deliverer of services; moving service provision to the private sector seems a natural way to reduce this alleged inefficiency. Another part of the tax and expenditure limitation movement (following the so-called public choice school of the economics profession) argues that the public sector is inherently self-aggrandizing, that public officials (usually referred to as "bureaucrats") will naturally seek to increase their budgets, providing services beyond the level desired by taxpayers. If services under the control of public officials will tend to grow beyond what is socially desired, then transferring control to the private sector, it is suggested, may be an effective way to combat these incentive problems—though it is not obvious why private contractors, with a profit motive for expanding the public services they provide, would be expected to be a less effective political force than public officials in expanding services under their control.[1]

Depending upon the form of private involvement that is contemplated, the political, managerial, and economic issues and the consequences of privatization may differ markedly. Like most political concepts, "privatization" is used to mean many different things. To some, a project is "privatized" (or has become a public-private partnership) if private sector firms or individuals have been involved in any part of its design, construction, or financing. This would include virtually all public projects, and in this view the concept of privatization ceases to distinguish anything from anything else. Even when private involvement in public services is taken seriously, though, there remains a wide range of forms and degrees of public and private interaction. It can mean as little as private ownership of the facility in which public services are produced by public employees, and as much as complete private ownership, operation, and assumption of risk by a private contractor producing services under contract with the public. In examining proposals to rearrange public and private responsibilities for the production of public services, it is important to specify exactly what changes are contemplated.

For any given service, the decision of whether and how to privatize the provision of public services has several consequences. First, the total cost of providing services may change, and who pays the cost may change as well. For example, when a water treatment facility is sold to and operated by a private entity, the cost of treatment may change. In addition, water services formerly funded partially through property taxes may suddenly be covered entirely by user charges on water bills. Second, the magnitude of risks may change, and who is at risk may also be changed. When a private company signs a long-term, fixed-price contract to collect and dispose of a city's residential garbage, it takes on the risk that changing landfill standards may affect its future costs; this risk would formerly have been borne by taxpayers (who would have faced higher garbage bills or property taxes as the city was forced to pay higher landfill costs). Finally, privatization may affect who is involved at what stage of decision making about the service. The taxpayer may have the right to vote on a bond referendum to finance a public project. The same facility built by a private company and leased to the public can often be financed entirely without public notice or approval.

Forms of Privatization in Corrections

The provision of correctional services has three separable components: construction, finance, and operations. At the outset of a new construction or major rehabilitation program, there is a process of design and construction conventionally carried out by a public organization with assistance from outside architectural, construction, and possibly construction management contractors. This part of the life cycle of correctional facilities has a substantial mixture of public and private actors, whose responsibilities vary according to who will eventually own and manage the facility. Although there has been some debate about changing the mix of public and private actors in this aspect of prison service production, the issues raised have little to do with corrections directly, and this will not be a central focus of discussion in this essay.[2]

The second component of prison services is the ownership of the facilities used for incarceration. Traditionally, prisons and jails have been owned by the public, paid for out of tax revenues or through bond issues supported by future tax revenues, borne by the taxpayer as a necessary cost of the exercise of denying liberty. Since the early 1970s, however, a number of prison facilities have been owned by private firms. No matter who owns the facility, of course, either public or private employees can staff, manage, and operate it; ownership has no necessary or direct operational implication. Prisons, jails, and detention centers have been built and owned by private firms and leased to governments for their use in a number of different states. Nonetheless, the locus of ownership can still have substantial consequences in determining who is involved at what stages of decision-making about the design and construction of a facility.

At one extreme, the entire siting, design, and construction process may be conducted by a private owner under a letter of intent from a public corrections agency, with direct public involvement in decision making at every stage. At the other extreme, facilities may be sited, designed, and built entirely by private organizations "on spec"—that is, in the hopeful expectation that they will be needed, and that a public agency will eventually contract to use them.

This form of privatization—moving the ownership of the capital that makes up the prison facility to private hands—will be referred to here as a *nominal privatization*. Although it is essentially independent of privatization of the actual production of the services, and therefore is less in keeping with the ordinary meaning of the term, it nonetheless has important substantive implications. Indeed, since decisions about design of facilities have some of the longest-lasting consequences of any decisions made about corrections, nominal privatization raises questions whose resolution can leave a particularly deep footprint through time if it involves privatizing design decisions. Moreover, if nominal privatization has an impact on the degree of public awareness of or involvement in correctional policy decisions, then it may change the effectiveness of systems of checks and balances imposed upon the exercise of one of the most sensitive applications of governmental authority. Thus, nominal privatization raises important issues about the governance and accountability of corrections.

The third distinct component is the operation of the correctional facility itself—the staffing, management, and ordinary conduct of the day-to-day activities within the facility's walls. In this phase, too, there has long been private involvement in some prison systems; private contractors provide food services, medical and health care, and so on. Traditionally, though, the function of incarceration itself—as against the ancillary services required as a result of incarceration—has been carried out by public employees supervised by public managers acting under regulations and policies formulated through public processes. Since the early 1980s, control over many of the core central management functions of a variety of facilities (the ordinary staffing, day-to-day management, and, in some cases, some of their policy setting) has been shifted to private firms. This substitution of private for public operation of correctional facilities will be referred to here as *operational privatization*. It is privatization of incarceration in the fullest sense.

The principal purpose of this essay is to frame the distinction between operational and nominal privatization and to examine the differing consequences of the two approaches to privatization in corrections. Many have argued for the potential of privatization of corrections facilities to provide better services at lower cost. Often, the case made for this proposition includes assertions about alleged lower wages and higher productivity of private sector employees—that is, the argument for privatization is an argument for *operational* privatization. In actuality, however, much of the privatization activity in the corrections field involves only a change in ownership—that is, the contemplated change more commonly involves *nominal* privatization.

Nominal Privatization

Many of the discussions about privatizing incarceration facilities are arguments about whether operational privatization would be more effective, less costly, and more in keeping with constitutional norms and social customs about the use of public authority to deny liberty to its transgressors. But much of the actual "privatization" taking place has nothing to do with changing who the guards are, to whom they report, or who signs their paychecks. Rather, it has to do with who owns the walls that separate the free from the imprisoned. Nominal privatization refers to transferring the ownership of the prison facility to private hands.

Cost

Liberal "capital recovery" (depreciation) rules established by the Economic Recovery Tax Act of 1981 generated substantial potential cost advantages for nominal privatization of a variety of public service facilities. From the perspective of state and local corrections officials, the tax advantages provided real savings— in effect, subsidies from the federal Treasury.

Two main forms of nominal privatization developed. In the first, a private firm is the long-term owner of the facility, renting it under contract to a public agency (or, when privatization is both nominal and operational, selling services of incarceration to the public agency). In this form of nominal privatization, the tax advantages to investors came mainly from the timing of depreciation deductions and investment tax credits. Because of the favorable federal tax treatment, state and local governments were able to obtain capital quite inexpensively. If the federal cost were added in, however, the total cost of capital in projects financed in this way would be *higher* than it would have been if the funds had simply been borrowed by the state or local government itself. This form of nominal privatization was thus more expensive to society, but less expensive to state and local governments, which procured a variety of services (most of them in water supply and treatment) through this device. Congress spent a good portion of its tax reform energy between 1981 and 1985 trying to rectify some of the more egregious anomalies this generated. Finally, in the Tax Reform Act of 1986, it eliminated virtually all tax advantages from pure private ownership of public service facilities.

The private return received by investors through this form of privatization was always well above the cost of funds if borrowed directly by a state or local government. The substantial federal tax advantages lowered the charge for capital as seen by state and local agencies through this device to a level generally below or close to their direct borrowing rate. In the absence of the tax advantage, the cost of capital procured this way is substantially higher than the cost of funds borrowed directly by the state or local agency.

In the second form of nominal privatization, a private entity becomes the owner of a prison facility and sells it on an installment basis to a public agency through a "lease purchase." At the end of the lease, the public owns or has an option to buy the facility for well below its market value. The advantages of this form of nominal privatization come from the fact that the interest on the public's borrowing of the facility (through the lease) is exempt from federal taxes. This arrangement, though called a lease purchase, is simply a form of borrowing by the state, and is recognized as such by the Internal Revenue Service. Since interest on borrowing by state and local governments is not taxed by the federal government, the interest rate under such a lease is much lower than it would otherwise be. This form of tax-advantaged borrowing has remained intact through the tax reform debate of 1986.

In this form, too, the cost of borrowing is generally higher than it would be if the state or local government borrowed the funds through a general obligation bond issue. The tax-exempt lease purchase shares the principal feature of the general obligation bond issue, the federal tax advantage of exempting interest from taxation. Nonetheless, interest rates on tax-exempt lease purchases tend to exceed those of general obligation bond issues of the same jursidiction. This interest rate premium can be as much as twenty-five to fifty basic points, or $10 million to $30 million in borrowing costs over the thirty-year financing of a $200 million facility. Typically, the higher interest charge is explained by saying that a lease purchase is somewhat riskier from the perspective of the capital provider because the corrections agency typically reserves the right to cancel the lease. The capital market requires a premium for bearing this extra risk.

Under current tax laws, then, and given the extra risk capital markets ascribe to tax-exempt lease purchases, the cost of capital obtained by public agencies through either form of nominal privatization is higher than the cost would be if the funds were procured directly through a general obligation bond issue.

Risk

Two kinds of risk that would not otherwise exist are created through nominal privatization. First, there is risk because the contract is subject to debate and interpretation; what each party gets may not be what it thought it had agreed to. One party may default, in which case the terms of the contract are changed (even though the outcome may be specified in the contract). Foreseen but improbable contingencies treated in the contract may come to pass, in which case the contract may play out in circumstances quite different from those expected. The agreement may try to deal with many of the most probable contingencies (like bankruptcy of the private owner or default on payments by the public agency), but there is always the chance that the contract will be applied or interpreted or enforced in unexpected ways, even when contingencies have been amply foreseen. And when unforeseen contingencies arise, the results of the contract may be even more unpredictable.

The second risk is introduced by the shift in ownership. The public renter of the facility may ultimately want to make changes in its design or condition or operation that it could easily implement if it owned the property. As a renter, however, it may be constrained in what it can change, and it may not be able to successfully negotiate the changes it wants. There is a risk that the facility will not be as adjustable as it would be if it were publicly owned and the changes did not have to be agreed to by another party.

Good contract design can reduce both risks. It can reduce the risk of surprises and permit the renter to have some influence over desired changes during the term of the contract. Specifying just what influence the renter is to have, however, is a complicated matter, and writing a contract that both foresees much of what the future can bring and specifies clearly what is to be done in various situations is a burdensome task. Mitigation of these risks results in complex and lengthy contracts—and some risks will still remain.

Involvement

The cost of providing incarceration is commonly higher with nominal privatization, and these schemes generally create new risks for both parties. Why, then, are they used? The answer lies in the level of public scrutiny imposed on nominally private actions—and here the conflict of interest between public officials and the public they claim to serve becomes sharpest. The most dramatic changes under nominal privatization are those concerning who is involved at what stages of decision making about the project. Publicly funded capital projects are generally subject to a lengthy and highly public authorization process. Funds must be appropriated. Bonds must be authorized and issued. Project designs must be examined, reviewed, approved. The public gains formal access to the discussion in budget hearings, public hearings on site selection and design approval, and in many states, at the ballot box for a bond referendum. Interested parties can gain informal access to legislators, agency officials, the press, and often the courts. In the case of local projects, there are often state guidelines about public involvement in the process, and many state public finance laws limit the amount of local debt that can be issued or specify additional procedures that must be followed when debt is to be issued for a capital project.

When the owner is a private firm, the story may be entirely different. Private construction and ownership of a facility is subject to local zoning ordinances, but zoning codes specify protections of the property owner from undue intrusion on the right to use private property for private purposes (including, it appears, renting it to the public). Still, the public must eventually enter into a contract to use a private facility. Since this is a public contract, the contract approval process may provide all the access that is needed by a sufficiently strong and motivated lobby opposed to the project. What, then, makes the difference in ownership important?

The principal answer lies in the form of scrutiny applied to public debt issues. Under the system of accountability in public spending, it is important that those who benefit be reasonably related to those who pay. A debt issue provides an opportunity to escape the balancing of benefits against costs by allowing the present generation of taxpayers to authorize projects that benefit only themselves but that are paid for through borrowing that imposes costs on later generations of taxpayers. To avoid this compelling temptation, we have devised elaborate rules that prevent a sitting legislature from binding a future legislature to make payments *except in very special circumstances*. In the case of capital projects with long-term benefits that will be spread across more than one generation of users, borrowing is allowed in many jurisdictions, but extra procedural safeguards are imposed to ensure that the project being financed really is a capital project with long-term benefits. Most states require passage of a special bond resolution by the legislature, and many states require a referendum of taxpayers approving the bond issue. It is precisely these special procedures that increase the visibility of large-scale public capital projects and that have permitted small but strongly motivated groups of taxpayers to stymie the authorization of debt for the construction of public correctional facilities.[3]

Nominal privatization typically avoids this extra scrutiny given programs financed by issues of public debt. The capital is still borrowed, but not directly by the government from investors. If the facility is privately owned and operated, the public agency rents the capital of the facility along with the private operators in the per diem charge it pays for each inmate; the borrowing process is hidden. Even if the facility is operated publicly and is rented directly from the private owner as a landlord, the borrowing of the capital (implicit in the rent payment) is not considered public borrowing; state public finance laws consider the payments as rent, not debt service. Perhaps most surprising, *even in a lease-purchase arrangement*, in which the public winds up owning the facility and is borrowing it while it pays for it on an installment basis, the arrangement is not deemed public borrowing. This has been tested in courts in a variety of jurisdictions. A device is used to make this interpretation more likely: Nearly all leases include a "subject to appropriations" contingency that allows the jurisdiction to end the lease at the end of any fiscal year if it so chooses. This permits the interpretation that the future legislature is not bound to make the payments, and they are therefore mere annual appropriations, not contractual debt obligations. Many leases include substantial penalties for early termination. Moreover, many jurisdictions that lease their correctional facilities have entered into "nonsubstitution" agreements in which they pledge that they will not seek alternative facilities in which to house their inmates. In such jurisdictions, canceling the lease would appear to require turning the inmates loose. Nonetheless, lease contracts with nonappropriation clauses have routinely been upheld as "operating leases," not long-term debt.

This interpretation allows nominally privatized public facilities to be financed without meeting the requirements imposed on public debt issues. For example, when a public bond issue is subject to a state debt limitation, an "operating" lease is simply another expenditure in the operating budget. When a bond issue requires authorization by a vote of a majority of taxpayers in an election, a lease can be approved by the city council or state legislature. Avoiding these accountability devices can dramatically increase the rate at which a project progresses from the drawing board to the ribbon cutting. If nominal privatization permits the project to avoid any of the zoning, public hearing, or facility siting processes required of public projects, its relative speed of travel—as compared with that of a publicly owned project—is all the greater.

This is an enormous advantage in the eyes of many correctional administrators. Indeed, it may be their main reason for relying on it. From the perspective of public accountability, however, this feature of privatization raises the most challenging questions. If the public chooses to impose checks and balances on the issuance of debt and the construction of public facilities (and particularly incarceration facilities), then how can allowing public officials to avoid the level of scrutiny traditionally required for such projects be considered an *advantage* of nominal privatization? It is not surprising that public officials see nominal privatization schemes as highly advantageous precisely because they permit the officials to act more freely, without "intervention" by the public. Such officials are sometimes frustratingly constrained by a public, part of which demands action but the rest of which will not permit it. And the freedom offered by nominal privatization schemes must be very attractive. But when public officials use financing devices to avoid accountability, they court a conflict of interest with the very public they have pledged to serve—and which they claim to be serving.

What is particularly troubling about the accountability problems raised by nominal privatization is that the conflict of interest between officials and their public exists no matter what the cost implications of privatization may be. As argued earlier, nominal privatization is likely to involve *higher* cost than public provision. In spite of its higher cost, the latitude it offers public officials to get the job done may make it very attractive. But from the public's perspective, both the higher cost and the reduction in scrutiny that result from nominal privatization schemes are a distinct disadvantage.

Operational Privatization

In various prison and jail facilities throughout the nation, private sector managers oversee private sector employees who guard publicly incarcerated inmates. At the federal level, the Immigration and Naturalization Service makes extensive use of facilities that are both owned and operated by private employees. (In the language introduced earlier, these facilities are both operationally and nominally private.) What are the implications of operational privatization of prisons with regard to cost, risk, and involvement?

Cost

No definitive data yet exist on the question of whether private sector managers can operate incarceration facilities at lower cost than their public sector counterparts. What does seem clear is that some public managers believe that the *total* value—the benefits from services minus their cost—of incarceration under full privatization (that is, privatization of both ownership and operation) is greater than the value the public will receive if the service is produced using public facilities and employees. This is indicated by the fact that these public managers have opted to contract out for these services. Several uncertainties remain about these impressions, however. First, this choice is not definitive with respect to cost. Proponents argue that operational privatization will reduce the cost to the public, but often they are describing the results of complete privatization, with both ownership and operation moved to the private sector. As described earlier, there are many noneconomic reasons why public officials may prefer nominal privatization. These motivations,

which may account in part for the choice to privatize operationally, make it impossible to separate out the purely economic
influences.

Second, it is difficult to find a situation in which a direct comparison of costs is easy to make. When operations are completely privatized, public officials are typically faced with a
quoted per diem rate for incarceration, with fees fixed for some
contract period. What costs the public will face after that period
(which may be as short as three or five years) are not known.
Moreover, it is not easy to calculate what the comparable costs
would be if the service were provided entirely publicly, and
even harder to figure out what the equivalent public per diem
rate would be. (See Douglas McDonald's essay on costs in this
volume.) Thus, "clean" cost comparisons are difficult to make.

Third, and perhaps most important, it is difficult to assess
whether the service provided is really the same. Observers assert that the service level (amenities, rehabilitation, quality of
life) is higher in operationally privatized facilities, so that in
addition to having (allegedly) lower costs the public enjoys the
benefit of better services. But it is not obvious that all of the
incentives in an operationally privatized prison are appropriate
from society's viewpoint. The potential bargain between inmates and a private, profit-making keeper (you help us keep our
costs down and we'll make your life more comfortable) may not
be seen by all observers as an appropriate approach to punishing offenders through incarceration.[4] If some segment of the
public has more vengeful motives, it may wish to force inmates
to submit to living conditions that are not the least costly to
produce (when inmates' reactions to them—like destruction of
fixtures—are counted as part of the cost).

Indeed, some observers have raised the question of whether
incarceration conducted by employees of a private company can
ever be the same as that conducted by public employees. If incarceration is such an intrinsically governmental function that
it cannot meaningfully be conducted by a private hotelkeeper,
then there is no way to provide the same service in an operationally privatized setting.[5] For example, incarceration may be
intended to communicate public condemnation, and perhaps
this can be done only in public facilities. Still, taxpayers face a
choice between whatever service can be provided by private employees and the service conducted under public auspices by public officials. The fact that the service may be somewhat different
does not necessarily resolve the question of which version to

choose, but it does complicate the question of assessing what value is being received in return for cost under the two alternatives.

Some observers have been concerned that it is inherently inappropriate to have a private enterprise earn profits by providing correctional services. At least three separate issues have been raised. First, some find it objectionable that private profit be earned as a consequence of the public meting out punishment. Why this should be more of a concern when the profit rewards management services than when it comes from producing food services is less than obvious. Private entrepreneurs are more or less deeply involved in every corrections facility, no matter how "public." (No state agency makes its own chain link fence or steel reinforcing rods.) It takes a special philosophical twist to separate out managerial profit as particularly inappropriate.

A second concern about private profit is that it is alleged to raise the public's costs. Again, there is no obvious reason to separate out profit as a problem. Taxpayers should try to assess the overall costs, not the separate components. The cost of capital, as described earlier, is likely to be higher, but if lower salaries or greater productivity results in lower total costs, there would appear to be no obvious reason to forego the cost advantage simply because some of what is paid flows to investors or managers as profit.

Third, some have said that the public and inmates may be defrauded by private contractors who cut costs and services to make extra profits. Incarcerated inmates may not be in a good position to protest these cuts, and public officials may not notice them (or, worse, may be paid not to notice them). This issue is clearly important; a critical responsibility of public officials who contract for incarceration is to ensure that the services provided are appropriate. But there is no reason to believe that fraud is more likely in this area of government service procurement than in any other. Inmates are hardly completely powerless. They have avenues through which to seek redress of grievances. Moreover, it is likely that private service providers will encounter lower costs by keeping inmates relatively satisfied than by squeezing out the last possible dime of short run profits by lowering inmate quality of life. The same things that protect private buyers from being defrauded by private sellers (the value of long-run relationships, larger profits over time than those available as a result of current clipping, and so on) protect the government as a buyer in this setting.

Finally, there is no reason to think that most of the gains from discovering more efficient ways to incarcerate inmates will flow as profits to the private operator of the prison. If the government runs its procurement process efficiently—that is, reasonably competitively—discovery of a lower-cost means of providing incarceration services will result in lower contract bids, and the savings will be in the form of lower public costs, not higher profits. In the short run, the private provider may earn higher profits, but with competitive contract renewals cost savings will be passed to the taxpayers. In a competitive procurement setting, the taxpayer eventually shares gains in efficiency with the entrepreneur.

Many of the arguments for privatization concern operational privatization, and many are made on the basis of presumed lower cost. The notion that the public bureaucracy is inefficient, overpaid, lazy, and lacking in creativity suggests that efficiency-minded private entrepreneurs will be able to produce services more cheaply. This argument has been salient politically, and it may well have a solid foundation, but its empirical basis with regard to operationally privatizing prisons is at present rather thin. There is no inherent reason to believe that public officials and civil servants cannot produce quality services efficiently. Until we have had more long-term experiments with operational privatization in prisons, we will lack the data necessary to know whether what is true in principle is true in fact, or, rather, whether private enterprise as applied to incarceration is truly more efficient.

Risk

As operations are shifted to private hands, who is at risk for what may also be changed. The distribution of risks is an important subject of the contractual arrangement through which operational privatization takes place. Under most contracts, the public pays a per diem rate for incarcerating inmates. It is thus "at risk" for fluctuating costs as the number of inmates varies. By contrast, in a fully public setting, the budget for the institution generally does not vary except as a result of substantial changes in the number of inmates. Thus, operational privatization generally involves some budgetary risk that can be avoided in an all-public setting.

The private contract may impose a discipline that the public has political difficulty imposing upon itself. Contracts generally specify a maximum number of inmates that can be housed in a given facility. If the public relies on an operationally private facility for all of its incarceration, then the public bears the risk that the number of inmates will exceed the contractual capacity. Again, this is potentially a budget risk issue, as the jurisdiction incurs higher costs in finding a facility that will accept its overflow inmates. Alternatively, it is a risk that some inmates will have to be discharged before serving their whole sentences because there is no place to house them. By contrast, when the public runs its own facility, it can decide to stretch the capacity of its prisons—though this is not itself without some risk (either of disturbance or of court intervention). Indeed, although the existence of contractually specified limited capacity changes the risks faced by the public, it may also impose a useful discipline and constraint from the perspective of safeguarding the right of inmates not to be housed in overcrowded facilities.

Involvement

What is most likely to change when a prison facility is operationally privatized is the nature of involvement by public and private officials in various aspects of setting and implementing the operational policies of the institution. In an all-public setting, the public managers who run the facility have relatively broad discretion (within the considerable constraints of law, custom, and court orders) to determine the schedules, activities, and quality of life of the inmates. In an operationally privatized setting, control of the operational details—who does what to whom, when, and under what conditions—are markedly different. The governing agency, of course, plays a strong role. It can specify how the facility should be run as conditions of the contract. It retains the right (indeed, it cannot contractually alienate its responsibility) to conduct general oversight procedures, and it may contractually reserve the right to a voice in the conduct of aspects of operation not specifically treated in the contract. Moreover, the contract establishes only the minimal legal backdrop against which the actual management will be conducted; the private corrections manager often chooses to accommodate requests from the involved public officials in spite of the fact that there may not be a contractual obligation to do so.

Nonetheless, the degree of public control is (or at least can be) markedly different in a facility that is privately owned and managed than in an all-public facility. The governing agency may not, for example, be able to choose unilaterally to upgrade the physical conditions of such a facility. It cannot readily choose to change the maximum number of prisoners that can be held there. Obviously, it may be able to obtain any of these changes, but it can no longer act *on its own*. The existence of a contract and a private management team implies that nearly every change the public wants to make in the conditions and operation of the facility will require some negotiation, and many will require explicit alteration in the terms of the contract. This raises issues of the complexity and, possibly, the expense of making changes; the private contractor must, at a minimum, be convinced of the necessity of, and in some cases compensated for, making the desired change.

An important feature of the negotiation of contract changes is that it involves a one-on-one communication between the contractor and the public manager. In the "procurement" process the corrections department officials may be negotiating with several willing potential contractors, and thus may be able to engender a sense of competition among them, improving the bargain from the standpoint of the public. By contrast, when the time comes to change a particular item in an existing contract, there is only one firm with which the public manager can deal. When the public manager wants to change an existing contract, the private operator is in a much better bargaining position than during the procurement process, before being chosen as the facility manager. The operator becomes a monopoly provider with respect to contract *changes;* this means that, in general, it will be more expensive to make a change than it would have been if the new contract feature had been specified during the procurement process. The relative costliness of contract amendments implies that on average, fewer adjustments will be made in the operation of a facility that is under contract. The two-person bargaining game that is played after the contract is signed has the disadvantage of reducing the flexibility with which the facility is managed.

Perhaps the most critical change in the involvement of the public in the management of a correctional facility under operational privatization is the importance of the procurement process. The public manager knows in advance that it will be more expensive to make changes after the contract signing than before. Two responses during the procurement process will tend to mitigate (though not eliminate) this disadvantage: First, the manager can try to think more carefully about what future changes will be needed and build them into the contract now; or, second, she can reserve the right to make certain changes in the future. Both require more thought about what the future will bring than the manager would have to engage in if she knew she would later be free to make whatever changes she wanted. Both result in a more complicated contract than would be required if she knew what the future would bring. And both increase the uncertainty of the potential contractor about what the future costs will be, making the private side of the enterprise more risky.

From the perspective of the public manager, the prospect of managing the facility over time indirectly—at arm's length and constrained by the relative rigidity of the contract—puts a premium on very careful thought now about future contingencies and exerts a great strain on the procurement process. As the future unfolds—case loads change, the demographics of the prison population change, the mix of offenses for which people are incarcerated evolves, the services needed by (or that society wants to provide to) inmates change, and so on—the manager will be confronted by a myriad of small decisions, and some large ones, about how a facility should be operated. If the public retains control of the facility, it can make those decisions as they come up. If, instead, it enters into a long-term management contract with a private provider, the public must either specify, or retain the right to specify, those changes in advance—or live with the possibility that it will not be able to make some of them as they become appropriate because doing so will be too expensive.

Some aspects of the long-term operational management of a correctional facility, then (those which, if the public operates the facility itself, will be played out and decided about over time), become compressed into the procurement process under operational privatization. Specifying the terms of a complicated bargain about the operation of a corrections facility, and administering a competition among potential suppliers, is a very different procurement problem than most state and local corrections officials or procurement office officials have previously dealt with. If operational privatization of correctional facilities is to evolve successfully, corrections officials will have to realize how important the procurement process is to their eventual success and work effectively to develop procurement methods that are equal to the task.

Conclusion

The push for greater efficiency in government and the push for less government have combined to put considerable pressure on public officials to contract with private firms for the provision of public services formerly provided by public employees using publicly owned facilities and equipment. The two broad forms of "privatization" that have resulted are markedly different. The first, *operational privatization,* involves a substantive shift of operating control of service provision from the public to a private firm and private employees. At the level of the service recipient, this form of privatization is distinctly noticeable in any service where the "client" directly encounters a service provider. In a prison setting, that encounter is constant.

Operational privatization is described as a way for the public to get the benefits of more efficient private management of public service provision. It is too early to tell whether the costs of private provision will really be lower, and it may be a long time before a definitive answer can be rendered, because it is very difficult to figure the costs incurred with either public or private provision and it is even more difficult to assess whether the services provided are the same or even comparable. We do know that there are risks associated with whatever cost gains may be achieved. The nature of management through a contract also implies that the adjustment of a privately managed prison facility in accordance with changing public views of what services should be provided is likely to be slower than if the facility were publicly operated. Moreover, and perhaps most important, it is clear that if operational privatization of prisons proceeds successfully, such success will in large measure be due to effective development of the procurement process through which private corrections operators are selected. Much work is yet to be done on how to conduct such procurement effectively before we can be sure that procurement systems are routinely able to carry this load.

The alternative form of privatization, *nominal privatization,* refers to the location of ownership of the physical property involved in the provision of the public service. Who owns the property at any given instant is irrelevant for all operational purposes. Given the authority to use the existing facility, either public or private operators can provide the services within it; who owns (tax) title to the property is an insignificant matter.

Of course, in time one owner may be more willing or able than another to make investments or other adjustments or to confer authority to use the facility in a particular way. If the owner and the operator are different parties, they may not be able to make as many or as smooth adjustments to the facility as opportunities for improvement arise. Thus, over time the split between ownership and operation may have operational significance. If the rental arrangement is functioning well, however, who owns the facility should be largely transparent to operators, inmates, and the taxpaying public.

In accountability terms, however, nominal privatization can be of dramatic importance. Shifting ownership to the private sector may simplify site selection and issuance of permits, thus avoiding construction delays. It generally will eliminate the need for public bond issuance, thereby substantially reducing the likelihood of delay resulting from debt limitations or failures of bond referenda. It circumvents a considerable portion of the accountability structure designed to provide scrutiny when long-term indebtedness is shouldered.

Whether this feature of nominal privatization is, on the whole, a plus or a minus depends on whether it is easy or hard to construct publicly owned prisons. Voters often voice the view that more criminals should be in jails. Courts say that jails are too crowded. Voters turn down bond referenda on the building of additional facilities. It is not easy to figure out which of these conflicting expressions of the political system we should take as guidance. Voters may be saying they prefer more crowded jails, but they may not have that choice. In that case, should we applaud privatization as a means to permit spending that the public has explicitly demanded? Or should we decry it as a device for conducting spending the public has explicitly voted down? Since we have no perfect test of the public interest, there is no way to know the answer.

We might argue that we should avoid breaking down the accountability system because it is the only way we know to define what the public interest might be. This argument asserts that we should not allow privatization as an end run around debt limitations and taxpayer referenda because those mechanisms are the best answer we have been able to figure out to the question of how to determine what the public really wants. But even that argument may be too facile. If the public knows about privatization and accepts it, is that not enough?

This fundamental question about the accountability of privatization as a financing device—about the use of nominal privatization to avoid restrictions on public action—cannot be resolved without more experience concerning how privatization works and how the public responds to it. Few would argue today that the public is fully aware of the costs imposed upon it for services provided through privatization. We cannot now separate acceptance from lack of knowledge. If privatization develops further, however, we will begin to see either informed acceptance or resistance. That will be the test of whether the privatization of prisons is an accountable response to public demands for more prison services or an unaccountable end run around legitimate scrutiny devices by hard-pressed public managers.

The Costs of Operating Public and Private Correctional Facilities

DOUGLAS C. McDONALD

At the heart of the debate over private prisons and jails lies the question of whether the private sector can operate correctional facilities more efficiently than the government, providing services that are equivalent or even better at lower cost. Arguing on behalf of privately managed facilities, one for-profit correctional firm's spokesman said: "We believe that the private sector can achieve economic efficiencies impossible to achieve working through the government bureaucracies."[1] The private sector's advantages, according to this line of argument, are several. Private firms are more likely to introduce sophisticated management techniques and expertise, are able to deploy their work force more productively because they are not hemmed in by civil service restrictions—or by negotiated work rules, if employees are not unionized—and are able to purchase supplies and materials faster and at lower cost. In addition, if they design and build the facility, they can complete construction more quickly and at lower cost, and, more important, can design a structure that requires a smaller staff.

Not everyone agrees. Some wonder where these sophisticated management techniques come from, noting that most managers in these private firms developed their skills in public correctional agencies.[2] Moreover, governments can hire architects to design labor-conserving facilities just as private firms do, and can create fast-track procurement procedures to speed construction. As one California sheriff pointed out, speaking on behalf of the National Sheriffs' Association, "There is a perception by the public that the private sector can do things better and cheaper than government can. But this is not true. Public servants can run facilities more cheaply because they do not have to make a profit."[3]

The debate over the capabilities of the public and private sectors in corrections has consisted in large part of unsupported or self-interested claims by advocates and opponents of privatization, which have tended to obstruct useful analysis. The important question to ask is not whether private managers are more intelligent or more skilled than public ones, or whether government agencies have the capability to provide services more efficiently, but whether the incentives and disincentives that confront correctional administrators, and the constraints that narrow their freedom of action, tend to elicit more cost-effective performance from private managers than from their public counterparts. Framed in this way, the question draws attention to the conditions that engender economizing—conditions that might be transferred from the private sector to the public if they appear to stimulate or support efficiency.

In this essay I review the findings of the few published studies that compare costs of public and private correctional facilities, and develop some new information on the costs of detention centers operated by the U.S. Immigration and Naturalization Service with and by private firms under contract. Throughout, I am pursuing three different aims. The first is to sift through the available data to determine if there is any good evidence to support the proposition that private correctional facilities are more cost-effective than public ones. The second is to explore the reasons why such differences exist, if it appears that costs do differ. The third is more didactic. Studies of correctional costs are exceedingly difficult to conduct with any precision because the public and private sectors have different accounting practices. By failing to account adequately for these differences, several of the published studies have reported findings that are misleading or, at least, of indeterminable validity. The examination of cost data in this essay both assesses what these data reveal and shows how comparisons between public and private costs might be improved.

The Hazards of Inconsistent Counting Rules

The few existing studies that compare the cost-effectiveness of public and private correctional institutions reach different conclusions; some have found that private facilities are less costly, others have shown the differences to be insignificant, and still others have found public facilities to be *less* expensive. This lack of consensus is to be expected of studies that examine different facilities in different locations. More troubling, however, is that attention has not consistently been given to what counts as a cost in both the public and the private sectors.

Probably the first study of public and private correctional facilities was the short essay by Keon S. Chi, published in 1982, on the Illinois work release centers.[4] In 1975, the Illinois Department of Corrections began contracting with private firms to operate work release facilities (called "community corrections centers") to augment the department's own network of centers, which had been in existence since 1968. At the time of Chi's study, the department operated eleven public centers; another seven centers were operating under contract. Analyzing available data on both types of facilities, Chi concluded that "perhaps the most significant difference between the two types of community correctional centers in Illinois is the fact that it is less expensive to maintain work release programs at privately-run facilities than in state-run centers. In 1982, according to the [Illinois Department of Corrections], per inmate cost per day in private contractual centers is $25, compared to $39.81 in state-run CCCs."[5] This difference, he argued, was due to two major factors. First, the private centers were operated by nonprofit organizations that received private contributions and enjoyed the free labor of volunteers, both of which defrayed costs. "Second and more importantly, there exists a wide gap in salary schedules for corrections staffers between the two types of CCCs: those in private centers are paid 40–60 percent less than state correctional employees in the state-run centers who belong to the union."[6] Unfortunately, one cannot draw such definite conclusions about the relative efficiency of the two types of centers from the data because no attempt was made to determine the private centers' true costs, including the value of the subsidies of volunteered money and time. Nor was there any attempt to examine what was counted (or not counted) as a cost by the Illinois Department of Corrections and the private organizations.

The failure to use similar cost accounting rules—or to question what underlies available cost data—makes less valid the findings of other studies as well. For example, a study by the American Correctional Association examined the transfer of the Florida School for Boys in Okeechobee to the Jack and Ruth Eckerd Foundation in 1982. Two years after the transfer took place, the evaluation team found improved efficiencies in the school's operation (in the purchasing of supplies, for example), but concluded that, overall, no cost savings were realized.[7] Unfortunately, the team did not treat capital spending figures correctly, thereby yielding an inaccurate picture of current operating costs.

In his study of public and private custodial centers for juveniles in the United States, John Donahue relied on reported data and determined that the cost per resident in 1985 was $22,600 in public facilities and $22,845 in private ones, leading him to conclude that the difference was "minuscule."[8] Similarly, the Legislative Budget and Finance Committee of the Pennsylvania General Assembly, in its 1985 study of privately operated detention facilities, examined cost data provided by the U.S. Immigration and Naturalization Service and compared the costs of the detention centers operated directly by the INS with those operated by private firms under contract. It concluded that the average daily cost of private contract centers was 17 percent higher, on a per capita basis, than that of facilities run directly by the INS.[9] The validity of these conclusions is open to question because of several problems, however. Neither study seems to have imposed standardized rules for counting costs in both public and private sectors. Public accounting procedures usually ignore costs that are carried by other agencies or by more general government accounts, which results in undercounting the actual direct costs of government services. Such costs include, in many governing units, the costs of employee retirement fund contributions, fringe benefits, utilities, transportation, maintenance, and legal services. The treatment of capital costs is also deficient in most government accounting, resulting in an entirely undecipherable picture of what it cost to support public services. In contrast, private firms count capital costs as direct costs.[10]

In theory, comparing costs should be relatively straightforward and easy to accomplish, but in practice it has been difficult. Precisely how private firms have structured their facilities and at what cost is hard to learn because the details are often guarded as proprietary information. Governments' expenditure reports are public documents, but the true costs of services are obscured by inadequate public accounting procedures, by the distribution of costs for services to more than one agency or to more than one account, and by the frequently deficient treatment of capital spending (such as failing to count the value of all physical assets used up during any year of operation). It is therefore surprisingly difficult to determine even so basic a cost as the average daily cost of an inmate's imprisonment.

Counting Hidden Costs: The Hamilton County Jail

One of the most rigorous studies published to date, which counts cost in the same manner on both the public and the private sides of the ledger, is Charles Logan and Bill McGriff's analysis of the Corrections Corporation of America's Silverdale Detention Center in Hamilton County, Tennessee.[11] In 1984, the county contracted with the CCA to operate the 350-bed minimum-security work camp for convicted male misdemeanants and a small number of convicted felons (about twenty, on average), as well as some female pretrial detainees.[12]

Every year Bill McGriff, the county auditor, prepares an analysis comparing the total cost of running the prison under the CCA contract with what the county would be paying if it were to resume direct management. In addition to the obvious direct costs, he counts a variety of other costs that the county would incur if it resumed responsibility for operations. These "hidden" costs include property and liability insurance, maintenance, garbage collection, the cost of record clerks, expenditures by the county hospital on prisoners' health care, costs of capital assets, and government overhead for support activities, such as personnel, accounting, data processing, purchasing, and financial management. Because private firms count expenditures for these services as direct costs, Logan and McGriff did also to maximize comparability. The resulting cost comparison is summarized in Table 5.1.

Table 5.1

Estimated Costs of Operating Hamilton County Penal Farm under County Management and under Contract with the Corrections Corporation of America, Fiscal Years 1986–1988

	1985–1986	1986–1987	1987–1988
County operation	$2,853,513	$3,413,741	$3,642,464
(per diem)	($25.05)	($25.71)	($27.49)
CCA contract	2,746,073	3,312,428	3,346,300
(per diem)	($24.10)	($24.95)	($25.25)
Savings	107,440	101,313	296,164
(as %)	(3.8)	(3.0)	(8.1)
Prisoner days	113,928	132,788	132,514
(Avg. daily pop.)	(312)	(364)	(363)

SOURCE: Charles H. Logan and Bill W. McGriff, "Comparing Costs of Public and Private Prisons: A Case Study," *NIJ Reports*, no. 216 (Sept./Oct. 1989), p. 7.

McGriff estimates that the county spends approximately 3 to 8 percent less by contracting than it would if it were to resume management of the facility. He argues that this is a conservative estimate, and that the savings may indeed be larger because the county costs might be higher than his projections show.

The simple comparison of expenditures obscures an important difference, however. Since assuming the management of Silverdale from the county, the CCA has added bed space, hired staff, and improved recreational facilities, medical care, and inmate classification systems. In addition, the firm agreed in its contract to achieve American Correctional Association accreditation for the facility. Guards have been given more training than they would have received were the county-employed Corrections authorities operating the center.[13] According to one report, and to the Hamilton County Commission, the standards that govern the facility's operations are more stringent than they were when the county managed it.[14] Private management has provided better service to the county than it would have gotten from public operation, which makes the cost-benefit comparison even more favorable for the private contracting arrangement than the relatively small cost difference suggests.

Logan and McGriff's comparison points to differences in labor costs as the main reason why direct public administration can be lower. Other ways that private firms may achieve more cost-effective provision of services are ignored because the comparison assumes that there would be no change in the design of the building, the staffing, or other features that may affect costs.

Public and Private Correctional Facilities in Kentucky and Massachusetts

Another rigorous study by Harry Hatry and his associates at the Urban Institute shows that privately operated correctional facilities can deliver services that are as good, or better than, those provided by public facilities without substantially greater costs.[15] Hatry's team examined two correctional facilities in Kentucky—the Marion Adjustment Center, operated by a private firm under contract with the state government to hold convicted minimum-security prisoners, and another minimum-security prison operated directly by the state, the Blackburn Correctional Complex. In addition, they examined two matched pairs of juvenile secure treatment facilities for the most serious offenders placed by the courts in the Massachusetts Department of Youth Services. One facility in each pair was privately operated, the other publicly operated.

The unit cost of the private facility in Kentucky was determined to be 10 percent higher than the public facility during the year studied (1987). In Massachusetts, the public facilities' costs were about one percent less than the private ones. However, capital costs were not included in the tally of public expenditures, whereas they were counted in the private firms' costs. In Kentucky, the study's authors concluded, the public sector's costs would have been about 20 to 28 percent *higher* than the private firm's had the state chosen instead to construct or redesign a public prison.

The study team's analysts undertook a systematic data collection effort to assess the quality of service and effectiveness of the public and private facilities in each state. They concluded that "by and large, both staff and inmates gave better rating to the services and programs at the privately-operated facilities; escape rates were lower, there were fewer disturbances by inmates; and in general, staff and offenders felt more comfortable at the privately-operated ones."[16] The authors speculated that this may be due to the more youthful and less experienced staff in the private facilities. "We conjecture that youthful enthusiasm may combat 'job burnout' of longer-tenured members."[17] (Because the private facility's staff was younger and less experienced, the labor costs were lower than in the public facilities.)

Public and Private Detention Centers for Illegal Aliens

Since 1979, the United States Immigration and Naturalization Service (INS) has contracted with private firms to house detained illegal aliens awaiting deportation hearings or expulsion from this country, thus augmenting the number of detention centers it operates on its own. On any given day during fiscal year 1988, there were an average of 548 illegal aliens held in five privately owned and operated detention facilities. Seven government-run detention centers held an average of 1,722 inmates during that same year. Because the services provided by all facilities are essentially the same, and because they all operate under similar constraints, these detention centers offer a good opportunity to explore the relative costs and benefits of public and private management.

Government-Operated Centers

The seven detention centers operated by the INS were located in El Centro, California; Florence, Arizona; Port Isabel, Texas; Boston; Miami; New York City; and El Paso. The average daily cost of these facilities during fiscal year 1988 was determined by federal auditors and INS officials to be $39.61 per inmate. This was higher than the previous year's average cost ($33.93), as well as the subsequent year's ($29.12).[18]

The costs of operating the seven facilities varied substantially. During fiscal year 1988, for example, the least expensive facility was the one in El Centro, California, which cost $19 per day for each detainee. The most expensive was that in Boston, which cost $130 per day per inmate. This variation resulted from differences in location, size, and utilization. The per capita cost of the Boston facility was higher because it was a small facility, because it was located in a metropolitan area, and because it was not running at full capacity during fiscal year 1988. Although built to hold 50 detainees, it held an average of only 42 on any given day that year. The cost per capita was therefore about 19 percent higher than it would have been had the facility been operating at full capacity. (Because so many of the costs of operating correctional facilities are fixed, the total expenditure is little affected by the numbers of people detained.) In addition, because of its northern location, heating bills were much higher. The El Centro facility, in contrast, was operating in excess of capacity during this period. Built for 344 persons, it held an average of 466 inmates on any given day, or 30 percent more than it was designed to hold.[19] This crowding contributed to a lower per capita operating cost in this facility. Lower costs resulted also from its rural location.

Privately Operated Centers

In 1988, the INS contracted with private firms for five centers. The Nashville-based Corrections Corporation of America operated two detention centers: a 300-bed facility opened in Houston in 1984 (which, since 1987, has had 150 beds available for aliens), and a 175-bed center that opened in 1985 in Laredo, Texas. The Wackenhut Corporation, a private security firm headquartered in Coral Gables, Florida, opened a 150-bed facility near Denver in 1987. Eclectic Communications, Inc., had two facilities: a small 30-bed facility near the INS-operated center at El Centro, California, and a larger 100-bed facility in Los Angeles. In 1986, the INS began contracting with the El Centro facility to hold women and children; in 1988, the contract was changed to hold only unaccompanied minors.

The arrangement between the Los Angeles facility and the INS differs from that of the other four. Rather than initiating the contract, the INS in 1986 assumed a contract from the U.S. Marshals Service. The agreement is year to year, and Eclectic Communications is paid on a cost-plus basis. The regional manager for the INS allocates the money to the facility, and staff at INS headquarters audit the expenditures. The firm consequently lacks the autonomy and control over its operations that the other private firms have in the other facilities. Eclectic Communications is also paid for its El Centro facility on a cost-plus basis, although not according to how many detainees are housed there. Instead, the INS leases the entire block of thirty beds, regardless of how many are filled on any given day.

In the last quarter of 1989, the INS entered into a contract with yet another firm for a 68-bed detention center in Seattle, and in 1990 it contracted with Wackenhut Corporation for a 100-bed center in New York City.

Table 5.2 is a comparison of the combined average daily per capita costs of all INS-operated detention centers, as reported by the INS, with the average daily per capita costs of five private contract detention centers during fiscal years 1984–1989. (Spending for the Seattle facility is not included because it was only open for a few months at the end of 1989.) The contract centers' costs are *estimates* of what was charged to INS during these years. Lacking data on actual billing for all years, the number of bed/days available in each center was used as a proxy for actual bed/days billed. These estimates are probably good indicators of the actual amounts charged in each of the years. In one year (1988), for example, where we do have information on the amounts actually billed to the INS by the private contractors, the cost of the private facilities averaged $33.59 per day per inmate. This is nearly identical to the estimate based upon the number of beds available: $33.63.[20]

As Table 5.2 shows, the estimated average cost per inmate in the contract facilities between 1984 and 1988 was reported to be

Table 5.2

Cost of Alien Detention
in INS-Operated and Contracted Facilities,
Fiscal Years 1981–1989

| | Facilities' Average Daily Cost, Per Capita | | | | | | | | |
	1981	1982	1983	1984	1985	1986	1987	1988	1989
INS-operated facilities	$22.10	$23.28	$25.07	$ 26.91	$ 27.41	$ 30.45	$ 33.93	$ 39.61	$ 29.12
Contracted facilities									
Houston (300/150 beds)				23.37	25.40	26.34	28.16	30.45	31.10
Laredo (175 beds)					26.00	30.00	23.00	23.00	23.46
Denver (150 beds)							24.51	39.63	33.78
Los Angeles (100 beds)						31.11	33.51	37.81	51.88
El Centro (30 beds)						44.07	46.81	67.56	33.60
Est. avg. daily cost per contracted bed				23.37	25.62	29.07	27.59	33.63	55.11
Est. avg. daily contracted cost as % of INS cost				87	93	95	81	82	114

SOURCES: Per diem costs of INS-operated facilities for fiscal years 1981–1989 derived from CADM524 reports of audited expenditures. Per diem costs of Houston, Laredo, and Denver facilities from contract documents; Los Angeles and El Centro facilities' per diem costs from Eclectic Communications, Inc. (private communication, 1989) and from INS officials (private communication, 1990).

7 to 19 percent less than the average cost per bed in the INS-operated facilities. Whereas the average daily per capita cost in the INS facilities ranged between $26.91 and $39.61 during these years, the private facilities charged, on average, between $23.37 and $33.63. In 1989, the public facilities became *less* expensive: $29.12, on average, compared to $33.11 in the private detention centers. This precipitous drop in the public sector's average per capita cost resulted from the sharp increase in the numbers of detainees held that year in the detention centers. During 1988, the average daily population in the INS centers was 1,722 inmates, who occupied 79 percent of the available

beds. In 1989, the average daily population jumped by a thousand to 2,772, and the occupancy rate averaged 27 percent over maximum capacity. Because most of the costs of running a detention center are fixed, holding more people in the same space had the effect of driving down the average per capita cost.

The year-to-year variation in the difference between public and private costs also reflected the way private firms amortized their capital expenses from one year to the next. In some instances, it reflected also a change in service. The cost of the El Centro facility operated by Eclectic Communications increased sharply in fiscal year 1988 because this firm began that year to detain only unaccompanied children who were in violation of immigration laws, and more extensive and expensive psychiatric and educational services were provided to them.

The Private Firms' Cost and Price

It is possible that these cost comparisons are distorted because what is being counted on the private firms' side is a *price* rather than a *cost,* and these prices may not bear a close relationship to true costs. In some circumstances (where little competition for the service exists and demand is strong, for example), the firm may decide that the market will bear a much higher price than the actual cost of the service, thus producing a handsome profit. In other instances, profits may be very slim; price is then a good indicator of cost. In still other instances, the cost of providing the service may be higher than the price charged to consumers, resulting in the firm's taking a loss. The decision to take a loss may reflect a conscious marketing strategy. The firm may, for example, decide to bid a price that is below cost in order to establish a foothold in the industry, with an eye toward raising prices if and when the firm's market position improves. The firm may also choose to price its service at a level that will generate profits only after a certain scale of operations has been achieved; at that point, costs will, it is hoped, be lower than prices.

This last scenario probably describes best what has been happening in the private alien-detention market. Prior to late 1988, the Corrections Corporation of America was posting losses; after this point, the firm began turning a profit. In mid-1989, the Wackenhut Corporation's correctional services division began to contribute to the firm's profits after producing losses for the firm up to that point. Although the prices negotiated with the INS and other governments for its private prisons, jails, and detention centers were not high enough to carry all the costs of the obligations incurred by the firms (or the correctional services division, in Wackenhut's case), once the numbers of beds under contract by these firms increased to a certain threshold, revenues exceeded costs of operations, including the overhead costs of marketing and organizational development—which have been large during the start-up phase. Some critics have read this situation as showing that the existing facilities have been priced as "loss leaders," and that firms will either "have to cut costs, raise prices, or go out of business," but this is probably a misreading of the firms' financial positions.[21]

There is, of course, no guarantee that firms will not offer loss leaders to attract more business. The ability to do so is especially great if the firms are subsidiaries of larger companies that have large amounts of surplus cash, because there are tax advantages to writing off the losses. This possibility has implications for public policy, as it increases the odds of the firm eventually going out of business, or of the parent firm shedding the losing subsidiary.

Although the determination of the actual cost of service delivery in the private sector is important for our understanding of the relative ability of the public and private sectors to control spending, from the taxpaying citizens' point of view this issue is less compelling. The cost to the taxpayer of purchasing the private firms' detention services is not the cost to the firms but the price charged the INS.

Uncounted Costs on the Public Side

The difference between the costs of the government and those of private facilities is actually greater than Table 5.2 shows because the INS expenditures reflect an undercounting of what it really costs to operate the government facilities. This problem is common in government accounting; consequently, most comparisons of public and privately provided services are skewed. If the costs of the private sector are hard to discern because they have an unknown relation to announced prices, they are even more obscure in the public sector. Government accounting methods were designed principally for fund control rather than cost analysis, and the direct costs borne by other agencies or government accounts are not aggregated into a single figure for a particular type of service. Accounting methods used in the private sector, in contrast, include a larger proportion of all direct costs. Costs that are included in private firms' reports (and reflected in their prices) therefore include many different costs not counted by government auditors.

Costs not counted in the INS agency budget include the value of all capital assets consumed, legal services, insurance and other liability costs, administrative overhead, external oversight, and other interagency costs. Moreover, the reported costs of the government-operated detention facilities do not include spending by the higher levels of INS administration. Each of the facilities receives support from the agency's regional headquarters, as well as from its national headquarters in Washington, D.C. These various types of costs are typically captured by private sector accounting practices and are reflected in the private firms' determination of costs. Including these categories of direct expenditure increases the actual cost of the government operations by about 4 or 5 percent. (See the last section of this essay for the assumptions made in developing this estimate.) No attempt is made here to estimate the value of the capital assets owned by the INS in its facilities. An accurate assessment of public costs would include some portion of the cost of those assets in each year of operation, but estimating the current value of the existing capital assests in the government facilities is impossible without very detailed data. Were annualized capital costs included, the cost of operations would be higher by at least a few percent.

Uncounted Costs on the Private Side

In addition to the cost of the private firm's providing imprisonment services, the government incurs costs that are not "internalized" in the firm's cost. These "externalities" consist of the social costs to the government of contracting rather than providing the service directly. For example, government spending for developing and negotiating contracts with private firms is not counted in the firm's cost of doing business, but these transaction costs should be included if the firm's costs are to be compared with those of the government-run facilities. Moreover, if the government takes seriously its role of ensuring that the conditions of confinement are adequate, it must monitor the private vendors, at an additional cost to the taxpayer.

The INS experience indicates that these transaction costs are not large. To be sure, INS managers devoted considerable time and energy to developing the first of the Requests for Proposals and the contracts that followed. Subsequent offerings have been less time-consuming.[22] In each case, the agency's chief of detention operations spends a few weeks specifying the product the agency wants; a contracts specialist then spends a few weeks completing the contract, publishing and distributing it, coordinating the bidding, and managing the award. This contracts officer then spends a small amount of time monitoring the invoices submitted by the contractors. The chief of INS detention operations estimates that about one-eighth of the contract specialist's time each year is devoted to managing the procurement of one new privately operated facility.

This cost would not be avoided entirely if the government operated all facilities. Every substantial purchase involved in the construction and renovation of public facilities has to be bid for competitively. The main difference between the government's procuring an entire build-and-operate package and contracting for the construction of a new public facility is that the former involves a "lumpier" transaction than the latter. When the government undertakes to build a public facility that it will operate, its contract specialists and monitors are occupied on a more continuous basis with smaller purchases and are saddled with the larger task of coordinating these transactions. The private company contracts to manage the details of the entire project. The chief of INS detention operations estimates that the costs of the two processes are approximately the same.

Monitoring the continuing operations of private facilities is, however, slightly more costly for the INS than monitoring its own facilities. The INS employees assigned to monitor each private facility attempt to ensure that its operations meet the standards agreed to in the contract. Monitors devote approximately half their time to this job; each was paid an average of $40,000 a year in 1988. When retirement fund contributions and other fringe benefits are included, the cost of the services of this official adds about 31 cents (or one percent) to the per diem cost to INS of privately operated cell space. Some additional monitoring costs are incurred at the higher levels of management, in the regional and Washington, D.C., offices. The time given to monitoring the private and public facilities is about the same in both cases, according to INS sources. Because they are roughly equal, estimates of these costs have been omitted from both the public and private per capita costs.

Other uncounted costs include the government's cost of having to manage facilities when firms fail to perform adequately. In one instance, the INS contracted for private security guards to augment the staff in one of its own facilities. The contractor went bankrupt and was unable to pay its employees working in the detention center (which was still holding prisoners for the INS). To keep the detention center operating, an INS officer flew there with a strongbox full of cash to make the payroll.[23] The cost of managing the transition to a new contractor is also borne by the government and is not reflected in the negotiated per diem costs shown in Table 5.2. Nor are investment tax credits and depreciation allowances allowed the private firms included, although they are in effect subsidies by the government (or, more precisely, by other taxpayers). How large these costs are depends upon the size of the capital investment made by the firm. No attempt has been made here to estimate these various externalized costs.

Estimating the True Difference between the Costs of Public and Private Detention Centers

If all the uncounted costs on both the public and private sides were included in the reported daily per capita costs, the actual difference between the costs of government and private detention facilities would probably be greater than the spreads shown in Table 5.2 for the years between 1984 and 1988. (Recall that the private contractors' estimated average per diem costs were between 7 and 19 percent lower than the costs reported for the INS-operated facilities during those years.) The public sector's advantage in 1989 would also diminish somewhat (private contractors' estimated costs were about 14 percent than the INS's costs in that year). This is because the uncounted costs of public operation are probably larger than of private operation. As discussed earlier, some readily identifiable off-budget costs increase the cost of public facilities by about 4 to 5 percent above reported levels, and spending for monitoring private facilities increases the cost of private operations by about one percent. The difference between public and private costs would be still larger if spending for regional and national administration were included in the costs of public detention facilities, and if the cost of the physical assets were properly valued. How much larger is impossible to estimate without better data.

The Weakness of the Per Diem Cost as an Indicator

The difficulty of assessing the economic advantages or disadvantages of private detention services relative to publicly provided ones is compounded by the weakness of the per capita cost measure as an indicator. As discussed earlier, most of the costs of imprisonment are fixed. About 70 percent of the cost of operating INS detention centers is for staff salaries and benefits.[24] Due to the way jails and prisons are designed, roughly the same size staff is required to operate them whether they are fully occupied with prisoners or are running at substantially under their designed capacities. One cannot reduce staff by 20 percent if the inmate population is 20 percent below capacity unless entire cellblocks are closed. Moreover, the facilities must be staffed to handle a full house, even if the daily census reaches maximum-capacity levels for no more than brief periods. Consequently, approximately the same amount of money is required to operate a facility that is 60 percent occupied as one that is 100 percent occupied (or even 110 percent). Because the unit cost used here (the average per capita daily cost) is computed by dividing the total expenditure by the average number of prisoners held on any given day during a particular year, the cost appears lower for a facility having a 100 percent occupancy rate than for one with 60 percent occupancy.

Because the apparent cost-efficiency of a facility, measured by per capita expenditure, is so sensitive to variations in occupancy rates, comparisons using per capita costs should take occupancy rates into account. If this is done, the public/private comparison looks quite different. For example, in 1988, the average daily cost of the publicly operated detention centers was $39.61 per prisoner; the per prisoner cost in the private facilities was $33.63. During that year, the average occupancy rate of the public facilities was 79 pecent; occupancy in the private facilities was higher—91 percent. Had the public facilities operated at 91 percent occupancy, the average cost per head would have been quite close to the private facilities' costs—perhaps about $34.50 or less. What may therefore appear to be an indication of superior management or, at least, of greater cost effectiveness, may be a simple result of a difference in facility utilization—or the demand for cell space—which may have little or nothing to do with how talented management is.

Differences in Quality?

One of the critics main fears is that private facilities will achieve lower costs by providing a lower quality of service than is provided in the government facilities.[25] Although a direct comparison of services and conditions was not undertaken here, the INS contracting office reports that services in the private facilities are generally comparable with, and no worse than, those in the public facilities.[26] Standards have been developed for government facilities, and inspection teams are sent out on a periodic basis to audit performance. These standards have been incorporated in the contracts that are written for private contractors. As mentioned, the INS monitors the performance of these contractors to ensure that they comply with the set standards. (They do so using their on-site contract monitors rather than the same inspection team that audits the public facilities, however.)

Labor Costs

There is some evidence that the private sector pays lower wages and provides less costly fringe benefits than does the INS. For example, the private facility in Denver paid its detention officers a median wage of $6.75 an hour in 1988, with a fringe benefit package that cost in the range of 21 percent of salary, yielding a total cost to the firm of $8.17. This was lower than what INS detention officers were paid that year in all government facilities: their median salary was $8.12 per hour, plus a fringe benefit and retirement fund contribution totaling 31.95 percent of salary. The combined salary and benefit package therefore cost the INS $10.71 per hour that year.[27] (It is likely, however, that the private firms pay managers more generously than managers in the public sector.) It is reasonable to expect that some of the other private facilities also paid their detention officers lower wages and less costly benefits, on average, than they could have received at any of the INS-operated facilities. This is not a universal pattern, however. The private detention center under contract with the INS that opened during fiscal year 1990 in New York City reportedly has to pay *higher* salaries than the INS pays in order to recruit competent employees.[28]

This suggests that some of the apparent difference in cost is not due to the superior economizing techniques of the private firms but is simply a result of having located themselves in regions of the country where labor costs are lower. The two most expensive facilities in 1988, on a per capita basis, were both government-run facilities: Boston averaged about $130 per capita, and New York City about $102.[29] (These figures include only those costs in the INS budget, not the additional uncounted costs discussed earlier.) Ignoring these two facilities, and counting only the costs in the five other facilities, the average per capita cost in INS-operated facilities during 1988 was approximately $31, lower than the average per capita cost of the five privately operated facilities ($33.63).[30]

Conclusion

The studies and information reviewed in the preceding sections suggest that the claims of the private sector's superior cost effectiveness (or the public sector's tendency toward waste and inefficiency) are less robust than they might first appear. To the extent that they rely upon apparently simple comparisons of unit costs, which have not been computed by standardized accounting procedures, they are suspect. The exclusion of several categories of off-budget costs probably favors the public sector more than the private, as does the deficient treatment of capital spending. Where there does appear to be a difference between the costs of public and private imprisonment, the limited information suggests that less expensive labor, rather than the superior ingenuity of private management or of the market, is the principal cause.

This does not mean that private imprisonment may make no economic sense. Governments may decide to contract for the operation of its jail because they are unable to overcome the constraints that create inefficiencies and high costs. For example, the Santa Fe County jail was built larger than it needed to be, and the county was losing money to keep it fully staffed. Although the county's commissioners could have chosen to go into the business of renting out its jail space to other jurisdictions (as the Washington State prison system did for a few years until its own home-grown demand was sufficient to fill all its beds), they didn't. Instead, they contracted with a firm that did advertise its unfilled beds to other government agencies, thereby recruiting additional inmates in order to utilize the building more efficiently.[31]

The speed with which the private sector can build facilities also in some places provides a short-run advantage over the public sector. For the INS to build or renovate a new facility, it must first obtain funds appropriated by Congress. This may take a good deal of time. If the INS chooses to contract, however, the private firm puts up the money to build or renovate a facility—which may take only a few months from closing the deal to opening the facility—and then captures a portion of that investment in its per diem "rental" charges to the INS. The INS is able to pay this rental charge out of its operations rather than its capital budget.

The abstract propositions that "contracting is (or is not) cheaper than direct government provision" have power to catch attention, but the few studies that exist do not yet provide us with the data needed to establish their validity. This lack of generalized knowledge does not necessarily pose a problem for government decision makers. In most circumstances, the choice of whether to contract or to operate directly a prison, jail, or detention center does not turn simply on an assessment of whether one or the other has been shown to be less expensive. The more relevant question is whether a contractor is likely to be better able to provide the desired services, within a range of acceptable costs, given specific circumstances and constraints found in a particular jurisdiction. In some circumstances, contracting for private management may seem more promising than trying to reform an existing system. In others, privatization may offer no apparent advantages. Rather than hoping to rely on general knowledge built up from numerous cases (knowledge which does not yet exist), the policy maker should examine the tradeoffs, the potential gains and risks, of specific privatization possibilities. This will provide a surer guide.

A Note on Estimating the Counted Costs of Detailing Illegal Aliens

As discussed earlier, a number of costs of alien detention are not counted in the agency budgets of the U.S. Immigration and

Naturalization Service. They include the following categories of expenditures.

True Cost of Materials and Supplies

In most instances, prices charged to the INS by the federal government's General Services Administration for materials and supplies do not include all the costs of acquisition and storage. The Office of Management and Budget estimates that these costs equal either 5, 11, or 23 percent of the charged cost, depending upon how they are provided.[32] Because data are not available to support a precise cost analysis of all supplies used by the INS, we will assume that approximately 17 percent of the average per diem operations cost was spent for materials and supplies, and that the costs of acquiring and storing them averaged 13 percent (the average of all three figures cited by the Office of Management and Budget). This increases the average per diem operating expenditure slightly, by 2.2 percent.[33]

Insurance

The federal government self-insures for losses and liabilities. The Office of Management and Budget estimates that the cost of this insurance is approximately 0.05 percent of the value of the capital assets used for any particular service. Again, the data needed to analyze this kind of estimation are not available, but a conservative estimate is that the cost of this self-insurance adds another 1 percent to the average per diem cost of detention.[34]

Capital Expenditures

The real cost of government-owned detention facilities should include some portion of the cost of building and outfitting them, but these capital and operating expenditures are not reflected in the public sector's operating budgets. Private firms, on the other hand, set their prices with the aim of recovering capital costs. The conventional way of doing so is to amortize these costs across several years and build them into the per diem rates charged the government for detention services. Were the government operating costs to include a portion of the amortized capital expenditures, the spread between the cost of public and the cost of private facilities would be even wider. Because we lack adequate information on the value of existing capital assets and past expenditures, it is hazardous to guess how much higher the actual cost of public detention in existing facilities is. If we compute the cost on the basis of new construction, however, the task is somewhat easier. Assume, for example, that the cost of construction averaged $20,000 per bed—which was about what the INS paid in 1986. Spreading that cost over the fifty-year life of the building would result in an additional cost per inmate of about $1.10 per day. This equals 3.6 percent of the reported average operating cost of the INS in 1986.[35] No estimates of capital costs were included in any of the calculations for the analyses in this essay, however.

Financing Costs

Were the cost of financing capital expenditures included in the reported costs of government-owned and -operated detention facilities, the per capita costs would be higher still and the gap between public and private costs wider. When private firms borrow money to pay for construction, they pay interest to those who provide the capital. The cost of borrowing is factored into the computation of per diem fees so that the hoped-for revenues will be sufficient to cover these financing costs as well. What is identified as an operating cost in the public sector rarely includes the cost of borrowing capital (although at the state and local government level, debt service is real and is easily denominated in dollars). The federal government has long been spending more than it takes in. One might argue that the government can borrow at no cost because it can merely increase its deficit; the cost of paying interest on bonds is shifted to other government accounts. Increasing the size of the deficit cannot be reasonably thought of as cost-free, however, because doing so has a number of undesirable results. Putting a dollar figure on such costs is difficult, but they are nonetheless real. Consequently, a more exacting comparison of public and private services would recognize that private contractors' prices typically reflect the costs of financing capital projects, whereas the federal government's reported operating costs do not.

The Privatization of Imprisonment: A Managerial Perspective

MICHAEL O'HARE,
ROBERT LEONE, and MARC ZEGANS

A first encounter with the debate about privatizing penal institutions reveals only two sides and two issues. Advocates contend that the private sector can produce better prisons and jails than the public sector. Unfortunately, privatization supporters seem to equate "better" with "cheaper, and no worse."[1] Because they focus almost exclusively on cost, even the most vocal advocates of privatization rarely show how privatization might improve the delivery of correctional services, not merely reduce correctional system cost.

Opponents see privatization as an ill-conceived attempt by market-oriented ideologues to reduce the size of government by eliminating the current government-run correctional system. They seem to equate "privatization" with "do it all in the private sector."[2] In this view of privatization, a self-contained prison— even a system of prisons—is "moved" from public to private ownership and administration. The government closes down the existing correctional system, and a small remaining staff contracts with private suppliers for services formerly provided by government employees. By viewing privatization as a dichotomous choice,[3] the opponents have failed to consider the numerous ways that privatizing parts of the prison or jail system might improve the quality of correctional services beyond merely reducing their costs.

Not surprisingly, both advocates and opponents invoke normative as well as analytic arguments to support their claims. These normative arguments typically rest on the idea that certain social functions are intrinsically governmental and others are not; government "should" provide the army, the private sector "should" provide automobiles. According to this normative conception of privatization, whether to privatize the operation of correctional facilities can be decided simply by determining whether they are intrinsically governmental or intrinsically private.[4]

The Idea of Privatization

We reject each of these characterizations of prison privatization. First, we observe that 1) no product or service can be produced wholly in the private sector or in the public sector;[5] and 2) no type of product or service is always attributed to only one sector.[6] As a result, "privatization" means something more incremental than the current talk of moving entire enterprises across the public-private divide would suggest.[7] Second, we observe that privatization works best when advocates seek quality improvement as well as cost reduction, and that privatization decisions are little informed by ideology.

Even in the most privatized industries, some activities inside government are essential to the enterprise,[8] and even the most nationalized forms of production depend on significant investment in private activity. The family farm in an industrial society will fail without government agronomic research, weather forecasts, and roads; at the other end of the spectrum, the army and navy procure weapons, uniforms, and research in the private sector. Similarly, the "public" correctional facilities presented as candidates for privatization routinely obtain such fundamental services as buildings, food, clothing, medical care, and rehabilitative services on contract from the private sector.[9]

As to the absence of private or public "monopolies," we note that even such typically "governmental" activities as legislation and taxation are common to private sector organizations. For example, private trade associations legislate standards for buildings and materials,[10] and electric utilities impose excise taxes on themselves to support research and development activities in that industry.[11] It is also true that few "private sector" activities are intrinsically private, although, by convention, many types of services are provided almost exclusively in the private sector.

As a practical matter, most productive activities can be carried out by government agencies, private organizations, or both. The typical case is "both," even when we choose to label the production process "public" or "private." This would seem to be as true of corrections as anything else. What are prisons, after all, but combinations of services such as housing, nourishment, confinement, punishment, and rehabilitation? Housing and nourishment are routinely provided in the private sector, but so, too, are confinement (as in private hospitals) and punishment (as when the commissioner of a professional sport levies a fine or suspension on a violator of league rules, or a private school teacher "makes" a child stay after school for violating a school rule).

We do not suggest a close analogy between a court's punishment of a criminal for assaulting a private citizen, and the National Hockey League commissioner's punishment of a player who assaults a member of another team with a hockey stick. But we do see much similarity between, say, the administration of the dormitory functions at the state prison and at the state university. Society is generally prepared to accept private housing at state universities without regarding public higher education as thus privatized. This is not because dormitory activities are incidental to the education function, but because a private housing market may provide options that are better suited to individual student needs than what a centrally administered housing office can provide.

The public has implicitly recognized that so long as we see our options as moving an educational enterprise—or even a prison—intact from the public sector to the private sector, we miss two important truths.

First, the borders dividing the public and private activities required for the performance of any social function, including prison services, are often fuzzy, representing a continuum of alternative, not discrete, choices. For example, state universities typically offer a mix of school-provided housing, private rental arrangements, and intermediate facilities such as co-ops and fraternities, which are privately managed, but open only to students. Similarly, some functions in correctional settings are performed by the private sector in one jurisdiction and by the public sector in others. Some prisons produce much of their own food, while others produce none. Few prison systems generate their own electricity or physically construct their own facilities without the help of private contractors. Some systems have extensive job-training programs in private firms; others teach skills in-house. We do not encumber public consideration of these policy decisions with the term "privatization," but these are surely privatization decisions.

Second, privatization, rather than being viewed as an outcome, might be viewed more usefully as a process. Parties who see privatization as an end in itself prefer contracting for prison support services to leaving them in the hands of the public sector, but tend to view such steps as no more than a partial victory. By contrast, those opposed to privatization tend to focus their attention on the prison functions that are intimately connected to society's formal relationship with the prisoner, such as prison management, guarding, and prisoner evaluation. They often dismiss the question of which prison support services should remain in-house and which should be contracted out as peripheral to the debate—an issue that can be resolved through classic cost-based, make or buy analysis.

Under the current terms of debate, privatization is an outcome either to be ardently defended or vigorously opposed. With this frame of reference, the debate tends to take on three forms: (1) ideological or philosophical arguments for and against the wholesale privatization of correctional services; (2) disputes about whether the public or the private sector is better able to manage jails and prisons; and (3) discussion relating to contract compliance and enforcement. By focusing on privatization as an outcome, however, those who take this view neglect perhaps the most important question facing the corrections field today: How do we do a better job of managing individual penal institutions and to what ends? As John DiIulio, Jr., has observed: "Based on our explanatory study of correctional institutions in three states, it appears that there is some relationship between administrative structure and prison conditions. The proper unit of analysis, however, is less the corrections agency as a whole and more the prison itself."[12] Therefore, we believe that rather than viewing "prison privatization" as an outcome, we should think of it as a process. The problem, then, is not to get the public-private line between the parts of the business of corrections in the "right place once and for all." Rather, the challenge is to define a specific set of benefits that correctional institutions are supposed to produce and continuously to seek new opportunities to relocate the boundary between public and private organizations in a manner that will provide the benefits being sought.

The important question we must address is: How are such movements likely to affect the work of corrections? Fortunately, when viewed as a process rather than as an all or nothing proposition, correctional privatization takes on the character of many other make or buy decisions. Managers regularly face such decisions, which can modify and clarify the boundaries between their organizations and the outside world. The basic text for such decisions is a 1942 Harvard Business School report that is still useful today.[13]

Sometimes these decisions are as routine and obvious as the decision by prison officials to contract out for prison construction. Often, however, they are neither routine nor obvious, but instead go to the heart of an agency's strategic purpose. Decisions by automakers to make or buy their own parts, for example, hardly seem to have the social significance of the decision about prison privatization, but from the perspective of managers and employees, such decisions are no less difficult or strategically important for the organizations involved.[14] It might seem to be a merely administrative or cost- minimizing matter for the U.S. Marines to decide whether recruits or outside contractors should provide food and maintenance services at Parris Island, but it is a choice that goes to the heart of our conception of what a marine is.[15]

One of the apparent obstacles to analyzing corrections privatization is the lack of experience against which to judge these important policy decisions. If we view such privatization as a special case of the more frequently encountered make or buy challenge, however, our base of relevant experience expands dramatically. Throughout the rest of this essay, we will use the make or buy experiences of others in considering how, and when, to privatize prisons and jails.

Boundaries as Managerial Instruments

Any productive enterprise that turns inputs into outputs combines and moves resources: goods, services, information, and money. Sometimes movement takes place within a formally delimited organization, as when the head of marketing presents the sales forecasts to the head of production, or the governor appoints a new commissioner of corrections. Sometimes this movement is between organizations, as when a supplier delivers parts to a manufacturer or the government collects revenue from a taxpayer. The public-private boundary and the formal division between organizations are only part of the complex set of boundaries and divisions that crisscross a productive enterprise. In this section, we will identify some of these boundaries and explore their importance. Our purposes are two. First, to examine the make-buy boundary in the context of the other boundaries managers must observe. Second, to demonstrate that the make-buy boundary is important, in part, because other kinds of boundaries often follow it, whether intentionally or accidentally.

If privatization is viewed as a boundary problem, perhaps the biggest single organizational difference between providing correctional services and buying them is that what moves across the boundaries of public and private organizations changes. When prison services are produced within government, many inputs—labor, capital, physical materials—must cross the boundaries between numerous private organizations and the public sector. Information flows from the public sector to the private sector to initiate and consummate these transactions. Information also flows within government to coordinate production once the inputs are assembled.

At first glance, privatizing prisons and jails would seem to reduce the number of public-private "border crossings"—because only the end product and not its inputs would have to cross the boundary from the private sector to the public sector. The resulting simplification of product and information flow alone would seem to argue for privatization. When we consider the information that must flow from the government to the private provider to secure appropriate prison services, the conclusion is far less obvious. It may be far easier to assemble relatively homogeneous inputs like bricks and mortar to produce prison services within government than to specify the complex and sophisticated "product" that a prison really is in enough detail to buy it "ready made," or to control the production process by contract.

Indeed, information flow, product specification, and control are the critical factors in the managerial analysis of privatization, and it is the boundaries within and among organizations that determine the various ways a manager can control and shape an enterprise. The study of these boundaries is almost equivalent to studying the reach of different kinds of managerial influence, or the manager's spans of control. To put the public-private boundary in context, we will briefly survey some examples of different kinds of control or influence and the boundaries they typically reach.

Spans of Control

Employment Authority

A durable managerial myth is the image of the manager "in control," barking out precise orders to a diligent and obedient staff that carries out these orders to the letter. An employee grants this kind of authority to management by general contract. In a first approximation, this sort of control appears tight because responses should closely match stimuli. Prison supervisors can order correctional officers below them to do specific things.

As every manager knows, however, an order whose authority is derived from contract obligations between employer and employee must be consistent with organizational and social norms, and explicit employment agreements. In a trivial case, a manager can send the office assistant (but not a secretary or the comptroller) out for coffee and donuts (but not for laundry). In a less trivial case, the warden has employment authority to tell the correctional officers to put prisoners in solitary confinement or to treat inmates with respect, but not to order them beaten.

Moreover, the relationship between order and response is stochastic, not rigid. The office assistant in our simple example might rush out for coffee and donuts, but return an hour later (having combined the errand with a trip to the post office), only to deliver cold coffee, no cream, and a croissant (because the store was out of donuts). Similarly, what the warden gets by giving a general order for decent treatment of inmates is likely to be highly variable and possibly quite far from what the warden had in mind. Public prisons do not ensure that they will deliver what the warden or the legislature wants, just because employment authority can be invoked.

Information Control

An entirely different kind of influence stems from the ability of an individual or agency to commit time to narrow segments of a productive process and consequently to develop command of detailed information. A subordinate's report to the corrections commissioner on prison food costs can enormously influence corrections policy simply because the subordinate can select alternatives and supporting data. Indeed, since the last thing the commissioner wants is to know every detail about food services, such selection and, therefore, control, is unavoidable. In this case, the control works up rather than down the hierarchy.

Control of information differs from formal employment authority in another significant way: It does not stop at the official borders of a firm or agency. This control, which can extend to legislatures, other organizations, clients, and suppliers, as well as to a manager's own employees, is often latent and delayed rather than explicit and immediate. Members of professional societies (doctors, lawyers, or corrections officers) are influenced by their training, disciplinary habits, jargons, professional associations, and formal and informal codes of ethics in ways that limit individual freedom of action.[16]

The specific limits of different kinds of information authority and control result from both expertise, or specialized knowledge, and the channels through which information can move. A police officer's span of control is communicated in part by a uniform. The uniform as a channel of communication enhances the officer's authority with respect to crowd control, but diminishes the officer's effectiveness in undercover work. In short, the formal channel of communication improves effectiveness in some dimensions but reduces it in others. This is why orders from the warden travel not only through formal organizational channels, but through informal ones such as those maintained by the guards' union and the inmates.

Our discussion of information control demonstrates that the value gained by clarifying organizational boundaries extends beyond the formal make or buy decision. Managers can clarify boundaries within organizations by giving one type of employee uniforms and another type street clothes; they can locate a particular staff function in a separate building or intersperse it with other activities;[17] they can multiply job titles or eliminate employee titles altogether.[18]

All of these choices, however, are constrained by the location of the make-buy boundary. Thus, correctional officers who are private employees are different from those who are public employees, even if the scope of their formal authority appears to be the same. Moreover, because of differences in information and employment authority, and public perceptions, a publicly employed prison guard working in a private prison will do a different job than would the same individual working in a public prison.

Control beyond Agency Boundaries

The limits of effective managerial control do not always match agency boundaries. In fact, some kinds of control are more effective beyond an agency boundary than within it. A political candidate with an important speech can affect the contents of a newspaper story more surely than the paper's own editor. A manager often hires a consultant precisely because the consultant's independent perspective buys the manager leverage that cannot be obtained from within.

That limits of control fail to match agency boundaries has special significance for the prison privatization issue. The power of prisoners to control their own environment is likely to vary greatly depending on whether security functions are performed by civil servants or contract employees. It is conceivable that the new patterns of information authority associated with prison management by private contractors will improve prison services in some dimensions and damage it in others. For example, complaints of inmate abuse may receive more attention if the offending officer is employed by a private contractor. Complaints about the food in the dining hall, however, may fall on deaf ears if the contractor is bound to extreme economy by contract.[19]

Market Control.   Purchasing outside an organization often results in more rigid conformance of response to stimulus than employment authority can. "Send a gross of no. 2 pencils, stock number 546-141" will more likely get the expected result than "go for coffee." Of course, the boss could say, "Go for a medium Maxwell House with one sugar, 10 ml of cream, and a chocolate-glazed donut." But he will not, or at least not for long. Employees will not tolerate being treated like automata. One reason for the more precise response in the pencil example is that purchasing is by necessity accompanied by detailed specifications (here, they are invoked by the words *gross* and *stock number*). The need for purchasers to provide precise procurement specifications is a consequence of the *difficulty* of communicating across organizational boundaries. Because the purposes and objectives of supplier and buyer diverge, clarity and specificity are essential to effective procurement. "Send some nice pencils" is a locution appropriate only to an interoffice transaction. The expense and awkwardness of contract enforcement across organizational boundaries also reinforce the need for detailed specification. The trick here is to use the apparent weakness of purchasing—the conflict of interest between buyer and seller—as an instrument to force specificity when it is desired.

The relevance of this observation to prison services is apparent. Unquestionably, one of the biggest challenges to effective corrections privatization is to write contracts that ensure the delivery of just what the public wants. This challenge, however, may prove to be one of the great hidden advantages of privatization. Hard as it is to do, such a contract must be written, and doing so can compel a clarification of purpose that is now so lacking in corrections. More generally, establishing boundaries where none previously existed—as in contracting out for prison services previously provided in-house—may increase prison managers' effective span of control in some dimensions.

Sometimes, however, the imprecision and ambiguity of general obligation employment contracts are preferable to the clarity and specificity needed in procurement agreements. The office assistant who brings back a croissant rather than a donut may well know something about the boss's preferences that is not specifically communicated in the order to "get coffee and donuts." Similarly, the subtlety of corrections issues, human rights matters, and justice may make a precise contractual arrangement of the type prison privatization requires quite unattractive. Analysis of a prison privatization decision, accordingly, focuses on where to draw the *various* boundaries of control and how each will contribute to the prison authority's strategic goals.

Life at the Edge

Viewing the privatization question as a problem of choosing where to draw, and how clearly to highlight, the important public-private boundary has two implications. First, if the pattern of information flow across the boundary is not well understood and consciously chosen, the decision will produce satisfactory results only by chance. Second, addressing privatization as a boundary-placing decision draws our attention to the importance of the personal and organizational dynamics at the "edge" of any organization.

What are the fundamental differences between the productive environments on the public and private sides of the boundary? Does placing this type of boundary between the two sectors make a difference?

Differences across the Boundary

Strategically important differences between the productive environments on the two sides of this public-private boundary fall in two categories: (1) differences attributable to operating conventions in the public and private sectors, and (2) differences that intrinsically distinguish public from private organizations.

Differences in Convention.   The operating conventions of the public and private sectors differ without reference to constitutional principle, and sometimes even in the absence of statutory regulation. For example, unions in the private sector can legally strike, whereas many public sector unions may not. Note that unions in both sectors can and do strike. The difference between the two sectors lies in the legality of the strike, the consequent willingness of individuals to strike, and the means managers can use in response to a strike, once begun.

We call this a difference in convention because there may be nothing intrinsic to public and private activities that necessitates application of this distinction to a particular activity. When school bus drivers in Boston went on strike in 1987, a proposed solution to the problem was to make these employees of a private bus company into public sector employees because public employees in Boston cannot legally strike.[20] It is hard to conceive of an intrinsic characteristic of public school bus driving that would make drivers less capable of striking, since the city proposed to use the same drivers to drive the same buses. The different operating conventions in the two sectors may affect the probability that a strike will occur, however, and they certainly alter the means for dealing with a strike if it does.

The no-strike convention in the public sector is no accident; some public activities are deemed sufficiently important to necessitate such a legal provision. The right to strike in the private sector is no accident either. In a competitive setting a customer can usually turn to more than one source of supply. Indeed, when public necessity argues against the right to strike in the private sector, the government intervenes, as in the Taft-Hartley injunctions against rail strikes.

What is relevant is not that there is a rationale for a particular convention, but that the applicability of a particular convention is unlikely to coincide perfectly with the formal boundaries of the public and private sectors. The lack of coincidence between convention and formal organizational boundaries creates opportunities to improve economic performance whenever a mismatch occurs.[21] Thus, if a no-strike rule is appropriate for most public activities, but not for all, it might be desirable to seek ways to privatize the exceptions and to allow the private sector convention to operate. Of course, the convention could be modified to allow for exceptions, but this might undermine the integrity of the underlying policy. For example, the army might be quite prepared to deal with a strike of civilian food service workers at a local base, but would object strenuously to giving military food service workers on that same base, who were performing the same tasks, the right to strike. Similarly, mismatches between organizational boundaries and operating conventions create opportunities for abuse. Making private bus drivers public employees to prevent them from striking could undermine the integrity of the no-strike law. If labor organizations come to see the no-strike rule as merely a convenience to stop legitimate employee actions, their willingness to support no-strike rules necessary for public health and safety may be jeopardized.

We choose the strike issue as an example of a difference in the conventions of the public and private sectors not only because it is familiar, but because it will require direct attention in any correctional privatization. At a minimum, a private contractor will have to make different arrangements to protect the enterprise against work stoppage than would the Department of Corrections. The strike example points to the larger question: If prisons are to be privatized, can adequate safeguards of the public interest be achieved through contractual arrangements?

Since the likelihood (as opposed to the legality) of a strike by public sector employees is influenced by convention rather than intrinsic sectoral differences, the contractor who takes over a going state enterprise, employees and all, will find the strike problem very different from that encountered by the contractor who supplants state employees with new ones recruited from the private sector. The willingness or lack of willingness of public employees to strike is only loosely correlated with the legality of the action; culture plays an important role in determining employee behavior. The time it takes to cultivate and establish a new working culture will determine whether this convention will be a factor for or against privatization in any given case.

Indeed, the rigidity of long-established cultures may well be an argument *for* privatization. Just as constructive work cultures are difficult to establish, unconstructive ones are difficult to correct. It is sometimes easier to create an entirely new culture than to fix the one at hand. These opportunities, whatever their implications for a specific privatization decision, are unlikely to emerge in the cost-oriented analyses that typically accompany public policy deliberations—although the political process is often quite responsive to such opportunities.

A case in point is the reform of the Massachusetts Department of Youth Services initiated by Commissioner Jerome Miller in 1971–1972.[22] When Miller took over the management of the department in 1969 there was a pressing need for innovation in the delivery of youth services, but the existing culture was an overwhelming obstacle to change. As long as youth services were provided in state schools, a network of conventions, habits, and expectations made it almost impossible to make innovations in care delivery. The buildings themselves seemed to impose an obligation not to waste resources by housing offenders outside them. The communications links between school supervisors and legislators did not carry information about care delivery, and did not carry authorization to experiment. The civil service system gave implicit instructions, backed by law, to perform tasks according to written job descriptions that embodied the traditional way of delivering youth care.

Moreover, Miller was not able to specify the particular innovations needed to improve youth services. He was able to articulate things that should stop—mainly, the abuse of youth—but he was not able to articulate things that should start. Thus, even if given a free hand, he would not know what to make or buy.

After disappointing attempts to fix the existing system, Miller sought to create an entirely new one through the privatization of youth care services. The decision to privatize produced three critical results.

First, it became obligatory for care providers to find different ways to do their jobs. Only by distinguishing themselves from other providers competing for state contracts could they stay in business, and the department made clear that it was looking for new kinds of care, not just marginal cost reductions. The environment of care providers and potential providers changed from one that rewarded innovation with indifference or punishment to one that gave an inventor resources with which to demonstrate and refine innovation.

Second, privatization created different patterns of information flow concerning youth care. When the schools were state agencies, every administrative problem in community relations, food service, physical plant, and so on had an easy route to the commissioner's office, both directly and through the legislature. Each of these areas was important to care delivery, but all of them together prevented a focus on new kinds of care because they absorbed the attention of the commissioner and the staff. Contracting, in contrast, filtered these "micromanagerial" issues out of the commissioner's in-box. In addition, information began to flow between providers and the larger world of psychologists, educators, and social workers through the less focused network of professional associations and relationships. By removing the formal division between providers and the rest of the world, privatization opened up opportunities for new ideas to circulate informally and at relatively low risk.

Third, written contracts helped clarify the department's aims and the means to achieve them. With privatization, schools were required to describe the care being provided beyond the most rudimentary elements of nutrition, beds, and escape prevention. Under the old system, schools could be in the youth care business for years without having to explain exactly what was being done for youths in the important areas of training, socialization, and affection. Providers and administrators alike now had to confront a written contract, a promise of actions and responsibilities that forced them to think about what the youths really needed and what services might provide it.

As the Massachusetts experience with privatization at the Department of Youth Services indicates, the many differences in operating conventions between the public and private sectors make the boundary important. In addition to differences in personnel policy, there are differences in procurement systems and contracting arrangements and even differences in accounting practices. All are likely to be quite significant in any individual privatization decision. Because they are conventions, these differences can often be replicated or resolved by organizational reforms other than moving the public-private boundary. Thus, if public sector procurement methods do not provide prison food services in a cost-effective and responsible manner, the prison might be privatized so it can buy meals as a business does—but public procurement methods could also be changed.

The wise manager, however, might seek out opportunities to use differences in convention rather than fighting or undoing them. Other things being equal, we think the opportunities afforded by privatization to free corrections from some of the most troubling rigidities and irrationalities of public managerial conventions constitute one of the strongest arguments for experimentation in this area.

Intrinsic Differences. To this point we have considered implications of privatization that had little to do with the intrinsically public or private character of the service provider. Indeed, we noted that differences in operating conventions in the public and private sectors may tell us little about "publicness" or "privateness" per se. Some characteristics of public and private production, however, are not merely conventions, but are intrinsic to our conception of public and private institutions.

For the most part, these intrinsic differences exist in the heads of consumers and participants in the productive enterprise and not in the external manifestations of productive activity. What is intrinsically public about the actions of government has most to do with how people feel about it. These differences, it should be emphasized, are not illusions or "merely" symbolic. Portions of fried potatoes that cannot be distinguished by any physical means are different products when they come from McDonald's, a soup kitchen, ARA Services, Inc., or your mother.

Public and private production differ in two primary ways. The first is that public actions have the authority, mandate, and consent of society as the consequence of collective choice; they are the concrete manifestation of what we *want to do* as a group. The second is that public actions serve a symbolic purpose; they are what we want to *see ourselves choosing to do* as a group. They are a significant part of what it means to be a political collectivity rather than an atomistic plurality.

These intrinsic differences are the principal argument for our proposition that privatization is not an all-or-nothing choice. No matter how much of the daily activity of imprisoning is performed by people drawing paychecks from private firms, incarceration that begins with a judge's sentence will be a public act in the perception of the people it affects. It is, therefore, essential to look closely at the different parts of the corrections business to determine which activities most essentially symbolize the special relationship between the convict and the state, and which are peripheral. For example, some critics see the use of deadly force or superincarceration (solitary confinement or reassignment to a "tougher" institution) as being in this sense the kernel of publicness in the corrections business. If this view holds, corrections departments would look for ways to keep security and internal discipline in the public domain even if they had chosen to privatize a great deal of corrections production.

It may be impossible or unwise to distinguish particular activities in this way. Perhaps publicness is a diffuse integral property of corrections, and prison food is just as important a manifestation of the public's concern with the convict's future as riot control. In this case, the government would seek ways to imprint literally private acts with semantically public significance, as it has learned to do with private education (by accreditation, curriculum supervision, and the pledge of allegiance) and the private services of defense lawyers (by making them officers of the court).

Intrinsic differences between the public and private sectors not only impose obligations for policy design, but also help predict the effect of privatization experiments. These differences lead to different expectations among workers and consumers, and ultimately to tolerance for different forms of inefficiency. For example, in many states, the public has a high level of expectation for service from local fire departments, but (often) a low level of expectation for service from the Department of Motor Vehicles. To privatize a fire department will create the expectation that the profit motive will mean lower-quality service; privatizing the licensing bureau may well yield the opposite expectation. Because expectations play an important role in service production—and are often self-fulfilling—these realities ought to enter the calculus of any analyst contemplating a make or buy decision.

We would counsel taking advantage of this reality by aligning the physical and institutional organization of production with our ideological conceptions of production. When individuals enter a shelter for the homeless, it is typically necessary to frisk them for drugs and weapons. This inherently demeaning experience can sometimes be made more acceptable if the search is conducted by a volunteer wearing street clothes and working in the basement of a church. The same act performed by a uniformed police officer in a state-owned institution is an intrinsically different activity, just as it would be different if the person doing the frisking were an employee of a for-profit firm under incentive contract with a municipality.[23] In this instance, the same physical act of frisking is fundamentally altered by the redrawing of organizational boundaries between the public and private sectors.

The opportunity to align the organization of production with ideological conceptions carries a corresponding risk—that decision makers will use ideology as an excuse to perpetuate existing organizational arrangements. Thus, we might admit that we would not invent the current postal service if it did not exist, but argue against its privatization on the grounds that the postal service played an important historical role in shaping the nation. There is some merit to this argument, but we also may have some difficulty in deciding just how far to go with such reasoning. Trying to determine whether the public essence of the mails is found in a kernel activity or is diffused throughout the system can help.

A second risk is that privatization decisions will not be made on the basis of positive attempts to use the ideological characteristics of organizations for social advantage, but instead that stereotypes will be exploited to satisfy short-run ideological self-interest. The fervor with which advocates of privatization make their case often seems motivated less by the desire to better align the boundaries between the public and private sectors than by the desire to wipe out the public sector.

Consequences of the Boundary Itself

If public officials contemplating correctional privatization must consider operating conventions on both sides of the public-private boundary, they also must consider the organizational consequences of the boundary itself. These consequences derive from the ability of an organizational boundary to act simultaneously, and selectively, as a barrier, as a conduit, and as a processing step in itself.

The public-private boundary separates an organization into two legal persons. The fundamental importance of this separation is the access it provides to the courts and to the law of contracts, which in turn makes the process of dispute resolution predictable and formal. When the Department of Corrections engages the Labor Department to provide job training, through a memorandum of understanding, surprises and disappointments must be ironed out through negotiation or at the governor's desk. These are informal and relatively unpredictable processes, and both parties' knowledge of this uncertainty affects their behavior in a variety of ways. In contrast, purchasing job training from a school or factory involves a contract that will be interpreted as conditions change according to rules and precedents that both sides' counsels can predict with relative certainty.

As barriers, organizational boundaries filter certain kinds of information—especially information normally transmitted informally and qualitatively. One of the most important managerial uses of a make-buy boundary is to protect an organization's ability to focus on what it needs to see clearly and ignore what it does not. In particular, most of the daily operational crises in a supplier's organization will be kept off the purchasing agency's director's desk. Of course, subtle alternatives in the application of production methodology will be precluded as well.

Organizational boundaries are, however, highly permeable to information that is fixed in goods and services or that can be described numerically, especially accounting information. A make-buy boundary forces an inventor to reduce a vague idea or proposal to a specific testable example, or to find a way to measure its improved performance in dollars (often as a reduced sale price) or in measurable efficiency improvements.

Finally, as a processing step, a boundary of this kind transforms products into inputs and vice versa. Whatever the suppliers deliver across a make-buy boundary looks to them like a finished product, and this perspective is another opportunity for focus. It is also an opportunity for process innovation stimulated by competition between suppliers of inputs. In general, private sector organizations are taught to do their work better or faster by the person selling the product or service that makes the improvement possible.

Placing the make-buy boundary in the right place means locating the boundary where it is most useful to make inputs look like final products. This notion brings us to what we consider the most important issue bearing on prison privatization in the existing corrections context: How can privatization promote innovation in this industry?

Dynamics of Privatization: Procurement and Innovation

It is widely recognized as one of the most important qualities of a make-buy boundary that the selling side can be divided into many organizations. Creating the potential for supply by multiple vendors, in turn, makes competition possible. The primary benefit of this competition is product differentiation: The corrections commissioner can choose among several ways to perform particular prison activities, each presented by someone who must make a distinctive offer in order to survive. But will the commissioner, instead, simply see four proposals for the same thing that differ only in price? Or, by demanding that the private sector behave "just like government," will the commissioner waste the opportunity entirely? When the state of Tennessee issued a Request for Proposals that specified its demands in such detail that the document ran to 415 pages (because it incorporated all policies and procedures that had been developed by the state Department of Correction), none of the major private firms had any incentive to respond.[24]

To answer these questions we need to consider two different kinds of innovation that private sector experience indicates are difficult to generate in the same organization: cost reduction and product improvement.

It would be a tragedy if the experiments in prison privatization that now seem imminent resulted in provision of the same (often inadequate) service that exists now, for a few dollars less or even for many dollars less. We are disheartened by the willingness of some to consider wholesale privatization of prison systems, especially using a single contractor, and by the relentless effort to focus on cost rather than product quality as a motivation to privatize. One of our hopes is that privatization will fractionate the production of incarceration, making it possible to provide many different kinds of jails and prisons within a single administrative unit such as a state.

Indeed, one of the outstanding successes of the privatization of youth services in Massachusetts was the establishment of this polyvalent mode of operation. Like every important managerial decision, Miller's actions illustrate the necessity to recognize the existence of, and choose among, vulnerabilities and advantages. As a procurement decision, the Department of Youth Services story serves as an illustration of the dimensions of privatization, here in the context of dynamics, that we consider most important.

Recall that Miller was unable to specify what kind of youth services he wanted, though he expected to be able to recognize improvement when he saw it. In inviting proposals from contractors, he deliberately took advantage of the variety of alternatives competition could provide. In selecting suppliers and signing contracts, the department was forced by the clarity and specificity that buying demands to think specifically and consequentially about exactly what was being done for the youths under its care; both of these effects were to its advantage.

As soon as contracts were in place, however, this same clarity and specificity posed a challenge that confronts every manager who obtains services by purchase: how to avoid constraining suppliers' innovative energies to focus only on cost. While operating under contract, a supplier is constrained not to innovate in product quality; anything very different from what was originally contemplated will violate the contract. On the other hand, innovations that reduce the cost of the contracted service will pay off at once.

This tendency is reinforced if the contractor has the reasonable expectation that the next contract will be let in response to a Request for Proposals that describes the existing product. This expectation is consistent with a sequential, two-step procurement process: First, the product is specified; second, it is procured from the competitive bidder offering the lowest cost. Of course, bids are not always let strictly on a cost basis, but the sequential process of specifying the product—even if it includes the specification of nonprice factors—tends to sacrifice opportunities for individual competitors to differentiate themselves from their competition on their own terms; rather, they are constrained to compete on terms specified by the procurement agency.

Consider the actual experience of two real companies competing for the recently privatized service of cleaning government buildings. Company A provides cleaning services on demand; that is, it washes walls when they are dirty and waxes floors when they require it. Company B, in contrast, provides cleaning services on schedule; that is, it washes walls and waxes floors on some specified periodic basis, say, monthly. To make its strategy work, Company A uses sophisticated management information systems and relatively high-priced, skilled labor. Its total costs for keeping any building clean for a year are low, though its unit costs (for mopping a hundred square feet of floor, for example) are high. Company B needs less sophisticated information and uses lower-priced, less skilled labor. Its unit costs are low, but because it must do more mopping and waxing for a given level of overall cleanliness than Company A, its total costs are about the same—as might be expected in a competitive industry. Company A, however, is widely acclaimed for superior quality, consistency, and good employee relations.

Now let us impose the governmental procurement process on these two competitors. If the procurement officer specifies cleaning on demand, Company A will likely win the bid and Company B will cry foul, arguing that it was effectively precluded from bidding. Of course, if the procurement officer specifies cleaning on schedule, Company B will likely win the bid and Company A will do the complaining.

In this example, there would likely be only one bidder for either alternative. To get more bidders—a goal of many procurement operations—would require one of two things: either more competitors must pursue similar production strategies, or the Request for Proposals must be carefully crafted to allow various definitions of the service being sought. With the former strategy, differentiation will presumably be oriented to cost reduction. The second strategy, deliberately inviting product innovation through the procurement process, requires strong managerial commitment in the face of many countervailing forces. A "loose" Request for Proposals can appear to allow unaccountable or incommensurable proposals, and may be hard to defend to a hostile legislative committee or a suspicious journalist. Competitors may cry foul, and the contract administrator will probably have to work harder to supervise the successful bidder. Managers of procurement processes that generate innovation and experimentation will have trouble giving the impression that they run a tight ship and may even appear not to know what they are doing.

Our key point is that the information flows necessary to manage *across* the public-private divide may increase the attention paid to cost at the expense of innovation and quality over time unless these pressures are actively resisted. Although cost focus may be appropriate for many governmental procurement situations, it may not be appropriate for procuring prison services. If policymakers believe that prison services can benefit from an innovation and quality stimulus, and expect privatization to provide that stimulus, they must take care that the procurement process does not undermine this strategic objective.

Whether redrawing the organizational boundaries of industry increases or decreases the pace of technological innovation, it almost surely changes it. Unless the analyst considering prison privatization has carefully considered the implications of privatization for innovation, the analysis is incomplete.

Conclusion

We have attempted to view prison privatization from a managerial perspective. In doing so, we conclude that there is no general prescription to privatize correctional services or not. Instead of a general rule about the direction of movement of the private-public boundary, we offer something potentially more useful: a way of thinking about such opportunities as they arise. Our analytical approach to privatization has three key elements.

First, it is important to think of privatization as an incremental process rather than as an all-or-nothing policy alternative.

Second, "privatization" is a state of affairs that cannot be avoided; some part of corrections will of necessity be carried on in the private sector. Nor, for that matter, can prison privatization ever be achieved completely. The incapacitation, punishment, and rehabilitation of criminals is a governmental act no matter who signs the practitioners' paychecks. Appreciation of this reality greatly enriches the menu of choices available to the public because it makes it much more difficult for ideologues and special interests on either side of this debate to eliminate otherwise viable policy options by a simple wave of the hand.

Third, privatization is principally an issue of fit between the strategic purposes that society seeks to achieve through imprisonment and the currently available means to do so. Deliberations should start with a list of objectives, not with a presumption for or against privatization. Society can then ask where the public-private boundary ought best be positioned to achieve these ends—not just in the abstract, but taking into account the practical realities of the particular set of circumstances in which the question is posed.

An appreciation of the extent to which the issue is one of fit leads to an understanding that the opportunities to shape the *various* boundaries that are moved when prison privatization occurs are, in fact, much greater than those captured in the current privatization debate. Once again, this is an argument for innovation through experimentation and testing, not through wholesale commitment to any one way of doing the business of corrections. Such experimentation and testing should never end, for there will always be possibilities for improvement. There should be a constant search for ways to realign the boundaries between the public and private sector.

We cannot guarantee that experimentation will ensure that boundaries are properly chosen and correctly placed. We can guarantee, however, that the failure to experiment ensures that they will be wrong.

A final observation. As we noted at the beginning of this essay, practice and the average citizen may well be ahead of theory when it comes to understanding the realities of privatization. In their efforts to construct simple models and keep research tractable, analysts may miss the richness of public and private organizational forms already available in the real world. If they focus on prison privatization as a dichotomous decision between public and private provision of a specified set of services the corrections system already provides, they will miss the essence of both the opportunities and pitfalls of privatization.

The choices are not dichotomous and the goods and services are not specified. The service now called imprisonment is itself conditioned by the means of its production. Many analysts are undoubtedly prepared to describe how society can use privatization to lower the cost of the prison services now being provided. We certainly do not object to cost reduction. We prefer, however, to view privatization as a means to improve the delivery of prison services. If the full range of possible public and private collaborations is used to do a better job than is now being done in operating this nation's penal institutions, cost reduction will merely be a pleasant dividend.

The many untested available alternatives make a strong case for privatization as a way to proliferate new means for delivering prison and jail services. Today's policy debate over prison privatization affords an excellent opportunity for society to embark on a path of innovation in the delivery of correctional services by making better use of its private as well as its public resources.

Public over Private: Monitoring the Performance of Privately Operated Prisons and Jails
MICHAEL KEATING, JR.

History suggests that the delegation of correctional functions to contractors has often resulted in abuse and exploitation. Common sense confirms the lesson of history; most people are naturally suspicious of a proposal that links punishment to profit. In the past two decades, however, repeated judicial revelations of shocking conditions in prisons and jails throughout the country raise fundamental questions about our ability to provide decent, effective incarceration even in public (never mind private) correctional facilities. For all of these reasons, virtually every commentator on the privatization of corrections, critic and proponent alike, agrees on the need for strict accountability.

There is, alas, much less agreement on exactly what constitutes accountability and the extent to which it should establish the levels of performance providers must attain; the mechanisms for ensuring compliance with fiscal, operational, and ethical standards; or devices to obtain the proper interplay of public and private oversight responsibilities.

What follows is an analysis of this issue of accountability as it relates to the private management of correctional institutions. The inevitability of expanding experimentation with the purchase of correctional management services is accepted as a given; the focus here is on the need to effectively hold private providers of correctional management services accountable for the services they provide.

The Reluctant Appeal of Privatization

The seductiveness of correctional privatization is apparent. The ability of the private sector, unburdened by mechanisms for obtaining public approval, to respond quickly and flexibly to mounting overcrowding pressures alone is powerfully alluring to local officials who are subject simultaneously to intense criticism for their failure to protect the public and to judicial censure for operating inhumane facilities. In the 1980s, a decade marked by revived respect for business and the remorseless denigration of government, it was probably inevitable that private enterprise would eventually be seen as the deus ex machina for those most perplexing of public institutions, prisons and jails.

Considering the appeal of the concept, it is surprising that there has been such substantial opposition to the private management of prisons and jails. Some of it, no doubt, has come from disgruntled vested interests (e.g., public employees' unions); some springs from liberal sensitivity to the injection of market system principles into an area that has traditionally been a governmental responsibility; and some represents nothing more than local resistance to potential sitings of unwanted new facilities, public or private. These reactions were all predictable, but there appears to be more at stake here. Perhaps it is the symbolism involved, as touched upon elsewhere in this text, or a hesitation to delegate to private citizens so critical an element of the state's police power, or just antipathy toward the notion of profiting from imprisonment.[1] Whatever the cause, the country's approach to correctional privatization has progressed at a snail's pace. Numerous institutions for juveniles, halfway houses, and prerelease centers, all involving many of the same legal and policy issues as their more secure correctional counterparts, are in the hands of private entrepreneurs; yet there seems to be a strong reluctance to turn over secure institutions to the private sector.

The reluctance also reflects, in part, concern over issues of control and accountability. Left to their own devices and confronted with the exigencies of the marketplace, it is feared, entrepreneurs may reduce staff, staff training, programming, and other services to squeeze operating costs, all at the expense of prisoners. Likewise, entrepreneurs may be unable to resist pressure to maintain a full house even if it means delaying or preventing releases. It is this tension between the maximization of profits and the duty to provide decent, humane, and fair incarceration that arouses the concern of many over proposals for privately operated prisons and jails.

Past efforts to handle this tension constitute an ugly chronicle of exploitation.[2] How likely is a repetition of this sordid history? Have correctional systems and management techniques improved sufficiently to prevent the recurrence of such abuses? Do we now know enough to impose an accountability requirement on private correctional managers? There is a need to find answers to these questions.

Hard-Won Accountability

Before delving into the mechanics of accountability appropriate to privatized corrections, it may be useful first to analyze what we mean by the term. Accountable for what? Accountable to whom?

The latter question is easier to answer than the former. One of the clichés in prison reform literature is that until recently most prisons and jails were closed fiefdoms. Implicit in the metaphor is the acknowledgment that reigning wardens and sheriffs were long accountable to no one for the manner in which they ruled their institutions. Until the 1960s, the courts virtually ignored prisoner petitions.

All of that is now vastly changed. Courts, the media, politicians, and the general public have all cooperated over the past twenty years to undermine the isolation of correctional facilities, to increase substantially public access to them, and to hold their operators accountable for their actions. Although the need for security in corrections ensures that public access will never be absolutely free, prison and jail officials these days are not much less accountable for their performance than their hospital or school counterparts. They are answerable, in varying ways and to different degrees, to prisoners and their families, attorneys, judges, elected executives, legislators, media representatives, and the public. The enormous public resources increasingly being devoted to corrections inevitably entails closer political scrutiny, and in no other public institution are clients quite so ready to file suit against the administrators and staff.

None of this new accountability came easily. It required the disasters of Attica and New Mexico, the civil rights movement and the mandates of activist federal judges like Frank Johnson, Robert Merhige, Raymond Pettine, and Wayne Justice to breach the fiefdoms and to bring correctional facilities into the mainstream of public institutional accountability.[3] Nor are these gains easy to maintain. Pressures to restrict judicial oversight continue, and there are some signs that the appellate courts are ready to impose more restrictive limits on judges in the corrections arena.

What privatization adds to this mix is an additional administrative or bureaucratic layer that inevitably makes accountability more difficult and costly. Indeed, some worry that it will make accountability impossible. The trick is to make sure that the processes and mechanisms developed in ad hoc fashion over the past twenty years for holding public correctional facilities more accountable are applied in all of their vigor to the private sector.

Because there has been significant experience with contracting in human services, though not in the management of secure correctional facilities, the notion of what constitutes accountability is understood reasonably well.[4] Accountability has three important elements. The first addresses finances and asks whether the private entity has expended public funds only for authorized purposes and in accordance with its approved budget. The second element, which covers all other aspects of a private operator's contract with the public agency, monitors and assesses the contractor's performance of services required by the contract. A third component more properly constitutes evaluation; on the basis of the data generated by the other two elements, it seeks to determine whether contracting with this or any other private entity to operate a correctional institution makes sense for the governmental agency.

This essay focuses almost exclusively on the second of these three elements; a word about the others is in order, however. The auditing mechanisms developed by public agencies to oversee the fiscal performance of contractors in a variety of social service contexts are fully applicable to privately operated prisons and jails. There is a rich literature on, and ample practice in, fiscal auditing available to provide guidance to correctional agencies on how best to assess the financial aspects of a contract. One notable, recurring difficulty in this area has been the persistent failure to meld financial and program monitoring effectively. For bureaucratic reasons, auditing and program monitoring functions and personnel seem inevitably to be compartmentalized, and there is rarely an adequate exchange of information between the two. As a result, valuable insights about a contractor's incipient difficulties, whether fiscal or programmatic, are not communicated, and opportunities to anticipate and resolve problems are routinely lost. A much closer working relationship is needed between financial and program monitors, with a frequent and free interchange of information, observations, and intuitions.

Evaluation, as opposed to monitoring, focuses on the success of a particular strategy in meeting overall agency needs. The pro-privatization literature is full of claims about the potential efficiency of privately operated facilities compared with that of publicly operated ones. The rhetoric here is usually no more specific than the generic boasting characteristic of the Republican ascendancy in the 1980s. Putting aside the theoretical difficulties involved in comparing costs and competence in the delivery of public and private human services, there is simply insufficient baseline data available for accurate, comparative cost-efficiency and cost-benefit calculations in corrections. Jurisdictions exploring privatization ought to begin with a careful analysis of their current institutional costs and their goals for prisoners so they will be in a position eventually to assess realistically the comparative value of their contractors' performance. Without basic data on the current costs and goals of public facilities, it will be impossible later to assess in any meaningful way the reliability of private operators' claims of enhanced efficiency.

Privatization provides correctional managers with an opportunity not only to identify and clarify goals, but also to create incentive structures designed to promote the attainment of these goals. The traditional client-centered measurement in corrections has been the elusive and chameleonlike notion of recidivism. Managers can use privatization to develop and test the efficacy of programming aimed at accomplishing other goals for prisoners, including the increase in educational levels and the acquisition of job skills and subsequent employment. By requiring contractors to pre- and post-test prisoners in educational and vocational attainments and by linking positive results to financial rewards for the contractor, thoughtful public correctional managers can shape private prisons and jails in hitherto unavailable ways. If contracts focus solely on escape prevention and safety enhancement (both essential concerns, to be sure) but exclude rehabilitative goals, then privatization can be expected to continue, or even accelerate, the present trend in corrections toward simple warehousing.

Although fiscal integrity and evaluation are important, by far the most complex and challenging aspect of accountability is the effective monitoring of a contractor's performance. This function embraces both a precontractual assessment of the private operator's capacity to deliver promised services and a subsequent determination of whether the services actually provided meet contractual requirements. The precontractual phase weighs the adequacy of a contractor's facility and the size, qualifications, training, and experience of its management and staff. Also included is a review of the contractor's policies and procedures, staffing patterns, job descriptions, and ability to provide such critical services as medical and mental health care, food services, and programming. All of these factors must be assessed while the correctional agency is reviewing bids and selecting a contractor, but they must also be confirmed periodically throughout the life of the contract. The subsequent assessment of a contractor's performance focuses on whether the private provider has operated its facility in accordance with the terms of the contract, which spells out applicable standards or includes by reference other relevant standards, rules, regulations, or statutes. This postperformance measurement looks at results; the precontractual review assesses capability. For example, a correctional agency will want to review a private operator's disciplinary and classification procedures during the bidding process to determine its ability to deal with these issues in a way that meets legal and professional standards. Later, to gauge the competence of the contractor's performance, the agency will review and analyze the records of these procedures and observe hearings to ensure that the contractor's practices actually conform with policy and thus with the contract.

Contract reviews measure the competence with which a contractor delivers correctional services, while at the same time respecting the rights of clients, whether detainees or convicted offenders. Order, amenity, and service are the subjects of a public agency's monitoring.[5] Order includes inmate safety and escapes; amenity addresses those aspects of institutional life designed to meet the basic needs of inmates, like medical care, food, and recreation; and service refers to efforts to reintegrate prisoners into the general community, like education and vocational training and counseling. All three must be accomplished or provided in ways that comport with the individual dignity and worth of prisoners.

This kind of accountability, which seeks to answer the question of whether the contractor is performing well, has two basic stages. First, clear operational standards by which the contractor will be judged must be identified and articulated. Second, the correctional agency must develop effective monitoring mechanisms to determine whether the contractor consistently meets these standards. Fortunately, sufficient work has been done in both areas in the past two decades to justify some optimism that the development of an acceptable accountability process is possible.

Standards

Standards cannot be discussed sensibly in the abstract, without reference to the goals they reflect. Unfortunately for the development of standards, correctional institutions have long been buffeted by disunity over ultimate ends. Rehabilitation as a desired outcome of corrections mixes poorly with other classic aims of the correctional process—incapacitation, retribution, and deterrence. Custodial and rehabilitative functions in corrections have long competed for funding, staff, and priority. Custody has remained clearly dominant; nonetheless, most institutions have developed and maintained, sometimes grudgingly, a variety of rehabilitative services.

In recent years, the confusion regarding correctional mission has become even more pronounced because the goals of the broader sentencing structure and the overall criminal justice system are being increasingly skewed in the direction of incapacitation, retribution, and deterrence. In response to an angry and frustrated public, police, prosecutors, and courts are committed to the conviction and incarceration of ever-growing numbers of offenders. This has occurred without a concomitant increase in available jail and prison beds. The resulting overcrowding seriously undermines the rehabilitative objectives of the correctional process.

One of the ironies of the privatization movement in corrections is that privately operated prisons will probably escape the worst ravages of overcrowding. Private operators will be able to write into their contracts a cap on the populations to be assigned to their care, whereas their public counterparts must accept whoever the courts send. There may, of course, be strong internal pressure on private operators to welcome overcrowding, which will drive per capita costs down and earnings up, but correctional agencies are in a strong position to control any such proclivities contractually. By keeping private facilities relatively immune from overcrowding, public correctional systems may resume the effort to reconcile competing correctional goals. Not all public systems, however, will be able to resist the temptation to farm out their overcrowding problems to private operators, in which case the potential for exploitation of prisoners by private contractors will be greatly enhanced.

Developing Standards for Care and Keep

Any discussion of the standards currently applicable in corrections must begin with the United States Constitution. When federal courts in the mid-1960s first intervened to stop the isolation of state-operated prisons and local jails, the standards applied were derived from the Bill of Rights. Earlier decisions had extended to state agencies and operations the protections incorporated in the first ten amendments, and once judges abandoned the "hands-off" doctrine (which required courts to defer to the administrative expertise of correctional managers in considering allegations of abuse), the floodgates of judicial intervention in corrections were opened.[6] Probably no other event of the present generation has had so dramatic an impact on accountability in corrections. Beginning with decisions on disciplinary procedures in California prisons, federal courts across the nation applied the Bill of Rights to conditions, policies, procedures, operations, and services in all sorts of correctional institutions. The underlying premise in all of these decisions was that it was the role of federal courts to intervene when state and local authorities failed to control the abuses of correctional managers and to hold them accountable for operating inhumane facilities in violation of prisoners' basic constitutional rights.

The federal judicial wave is currently ebbing from the correctional shore, but the reemerging terrain is nonetheless greatly altered. Left behind are constitutional standards that will endure in areas like medical care and discipline. More important still, procedural vehicles whereby prisoners can subject the actions of correctional administrators to judicial second-guessing have been fashioned and are relatively readily available. This means that allegations of abuse and neglect are much more likely to be heard and evaluated today than they were in the past.

In their efforts to redress flagrant abuses, the courts initially identified broad constitutional norms, with which all correctional facilities must conform. Numerous subsequent judicial decisions on prisoners' rights clarified the meaning, interpretation, and application of these broad constitutional standards. The result is a body of law affecting conditions, procedures, and services that forms a core of constitutional standards by which the administrators of all prisons and jails will be judged.

Legal commentators who have considered the relevance of these constitutional standards to privately operated facilities concede unanimously that the Constitution will be applied no less vigorously to private facilities than to public ones.[7] Section 1983 of the Civil Rights Act, the procedural vehicle for initiating suit on constitutional grounds against correctional administrators, institutions, and systems, will be equally available in institutions operated by private entities under contract to state government, meaning that the same constitutional standards applied routinely to state-operated correctional facilities will apply in privately operated ones.

It is not just the Constitution that establishes operating legal standards that correctional facilities, both public and private, must meet. Every state has adopted statutes to regulate correctional operations. Some states have legislated little more than a simple structural outline, broadly identifying the goals of public correctional entities, while others have enacted voluminous, specific statutes incorporating extensive and detailed operational standards.[8] States with sparse legislation tend to supplement their statutes with detailed regulations governing the operations of state-run facilities. Recently, a number of states have developed statutes, regulations, or standards for all county and municipal jails within the state. Whatever the form of the local statute, private facilities can expect to be held accountable for meeting all of the legal standards applicable in their jurisdiction.

Privatization in any state, moreover, will require specific statutory authorization, which may contain detailed operational criteria, or may adopt by reference already existing statutory or regulatory criteria. The tendency is for jurisdictions with extensive criteria for public institutions simply to authorize the establishment of private facilities, whereas jurisdictions with few existing legislative standards tend to enumerate at least some operational requirements in their authorization of private institutions.

These legal standards, whether derived from constitutional, statutory, or regulatory sources, as well as the extensive case law interpreting and applying them, all represent the state's active effort to control public correctional facilities and hold their administrators accountable for implementing some fundamental measures of decency and humanity. Simultaneously with this development and, in part, in reaction to the state's intrusion, correctional officials themselves have undertaken not only to articulate standards and develop accountability mechanisms that transcend the bare legal minimum defined and imposed by the state, but also to incorporate the best professional correctional expertise.

Beginning with the work of the National Advisory Commission on Criminal Justice Standards and Goals in the early 1970s and culminating in both the promulgation of standards by the American Correctional Association (ACA), and the adoption of a mechanism for the accreditation of institutions comporting with ACA standards, correctional professionals have engaged in an unprecedented effort to identify standards of acceptable correctional practice. Nor has interest in defining standards been confined to correctional personnel. The American Medical Association issued standards for correctional health care; the American Bar Association developed guidelines for prisoners' rights; the National Sheriffs' Association addressed conditions in jails; the American Public Health Association looked at medical care and sanitation; the National Fire Prevention Association published fire safety standards for correctional facilities. At the beginning of the 1970s one could only guess what an effective jail or prison might look like; by the mid-1980s there were standards everywhere defining acceptable policies, procedures, and practices for virtually every facet of institutional life.

The importance of this development for the purpose of accountability cannot be overemphasized. The subjectivity of terms like "humane," "effective," and "well managed" dilutes accountability and makes it virtually impossible to evaluate institutions and systems objectively. In the earlier legal context, the constitutional concept of "cruel and unusual punishment" was vague and, as a result, only marginally useful as a yardstick for assessing conduct. The abstract concept needed to be applied and analyzed in specific cases to generate an objective and functional meaning. Correctional administrators, likewise, needed to dissect "good management" and define the specific practices and policies that underlay the concept.

The logic of the resulting professional standards is straightforward. By spelling out in detail the requirements seen as critical by correctional administrators and others involved in corrections, the standards seek to create measurable, objective management norms for the operation of prisons and jails. The development of each set of standards involved a host of officials and experts working together over long periods. The standards thus represent a distillation of the very best theories and practices available in correctional management.

Reviewing the full array of legal and professional canons, one perceives vast differences in their scope and detail. Take, for example, medical care. The Constitution, via the Eighth

Amendment's ban on cruel and unusual punishment, prohibits deliberate indifference to the medical needs of prisoners; state statutes or regulations generally require correctional agencies to provide "adequate" health care; the American Correctional Association outlines service and structural requirements in about four pages of standards and commentary; and the American Public Health Association provides a whole volume of standards covering every conceivable aspect of correctional health care. The standards, moreover, are generic; they are intended for institutions of all shapes, sizes, and varieties. Specific application in a particular facility requires that the standards be refined and tailored to local needs.

The development of standards has altered dramatically the face of corrections. Historically, government exercised little control over prisons and jails. Legislatures and elected executives were content to allocate funds and delegate control of correctional facilities to their principal keepers. Standards for measuring performance were minimal: Let there be no riots, escapes, or other events that were risky to the political establishment. Now, however, governments, courts, and the correctional profession itself have all generated a web of standards that provide both general and specific measures for assessing the quality of institutional life. It is critically important that this development not be lost in any future transition to privatized corrections.

The traditional vehicle for the application of standards in the privatization context is the contract between the purchasing governmental entity and the private correctional operator. The contract incorporates the norms of conduct to which a private contractor will be held. The development of a contract thus provides contracting correctional agencies an opportunity to encourage the expanding use of standards. No one can obligate public institutions to meet other than constitutional or legal standards; public agencies, however, can compel private providers to meet professional or other more exacting standards as a condition of obtaining and holding a contract.

Like most opportunities, this one has risks. Contracting in human services, as we have seen, is not new, and the process for announcing available governmental work, specifying the conditions under which it must be undertaken, supervising the submission of bids, and assessing the relative merits of competing proposals has become a fixed ritual of our time. On the correctional scene, the process has been used successfully to elicit and award contracts for food services, medical care, and the management of community-based halfway houses, prerelease centers, and secure juvenile facilities. The same process will inevitably be used to manage contracting for secure, adult correctional facilities.

One of the attractions of privatized corrections, presumably, is the opportunity it provides to do things the public sector cannot do or cannot do well, to experiment and identify things that might be done better or differently in the private sector. The Request for Proposals, a key document in the contract bidding process, spells out an agency's requirements in offering any specific work for bid. To realize the opportunity for change offered by privatization, the request must incorporate useful standards without stifling all possibility of doing things differently. A request that incorporates every potentially applicable standard may well scare off all prospective bidders.

The contracting agency must winnow from all available norms fundamental standards directly related to the state's control function. The public sector's basic obligation here is to preclude any potential for the exploitation or abuse of prisoners while encouraging the prevention of escapes, ensuring safety, and providing basic services. Although constitutional and legal standards address these fundamental concerns in part, contracting agencies need to go beyond the legal minimum since they are turning over to private entrepreneurs their inherent power to incarcerate detainees and offenders. Thus, the detailed and specific standards incorporated in the Request for Proposals (and, subsequently, in the contract) ought to focus on these basic issues of control.

The inclusion of additional standards in the request is a matter of management art rather than necessity. A requirement simply to provide "adequate" recreational facilities and programs, for example, is probably preferable to a demand for facilities of specific dimensions and personnel with enumerated recreational experience. Although the aim is to ensure that recreation will be provided, it is not directly related to basic control functions, and in addition, the private operator should be given the freedom to meet the need in creative and innovative ways.

In fashioning a Request for Proposals that ensures adequate control and encourages creativity, a contracting agency might adopt the following strategy:

1. Include specific, detailed requirements for inmate safety, security, and the provision of essential services.

2. Identify any operational standards the agency endorses and offer financial incentives for complying with them. For example, in the area of medical care, a contractor might award a provider a modest bonus for meeting American Medical Association standards and a more substantial one for meeting those of the American Public Health Association.
3. Identify specific goals for prisoners and include a structure of incentives for the accomplishment of these goals.

The proffered strategy, obviously, is rooted firmly in free market principles, which seems appropriate in this context. The incentive structure is designed to arm the contracting agency with indirect and economic controls over the private jail or prison operator. Public agencies would do well to remember that this kind of contract entails a shift over time in the economic power of the contracting parties. During the initial bidding process, the public entity holds all of the cards and can dictate terms, but once work under the contract commences, the balance of power changes in favor of the provider, especially if the private entity is entrusted with a significant part of the public agency's incarcerated population. The public agency can swiftly become hostage to the imperative of maintaining space for its prisoners.

Because the health of both public and private entities here is critical, neither should be permitted to exploit its temporary advantage. Bidding and budgeting procedures must be constructed carefully; they must be flexible enough to allow subsequent change orders but definitive enough to constrain "bait and switch" tactics by providers willing to bid low before racheting prices through the roof in renewal negotiations once a dependency is created. Public entities must understand that, unless they are a federal or large state agency, the ability to terminate a private provider's contract promptly and painlessly is largely mythical. Even the opening up to rebidding of an existing contract can prove traumatic if the contract involves heavy capital commitments, considerable staff, and a significant number of prisoners. The inclusion in a contract of a structure for incentive payments, as recommended here, provides the contracting agency with some economic leverage for the duration of the contract and enhances continuing public control over the private entity. Contracts may also include negative incentives, or monetary penalties, for failure to meet basic control standards or provide essential services. The parties to a contract need to be flexible in determining costs because of the many variables that complicate accurate budgetary estimates in corrections, but it is equally important that the public agency retain some measure of financial control.

One last word about contracts. Few models are available of this type of working agreement. Public agencies and their attorneys are free to create imaginative and effective instruments intended to make the supervision and regulation of private providers less painful and mysterious for both the public and the private parties. History suggests, however, that state agencies are unlikely to take advantage of this opportunity. The chief reason is that the legal and purchasing or contracting functions in most state and local governments are divorced from the operational components. Operational managers typically draw up operational specifications, which are then turned over to legal or contracting people for inclusion in a Request for Proposals. Operational personnel may or may not know about available standards; legal and contracting personnel almost surely will not. The result, not infrequently, will be an overlybroad and vague set of specifications that eventually will be incorporated into an equally murky contract. If the criteria in a contract are difficult to interpret and apply, accountability may not be effective. The way to avoid this is to encourage close collaboration between operational, legal and contracting personnel in developing specifications for the Request for Proposals, as well as the final contract, and to provide all of them with model contracts and an orientation to this new substantive area of correctional contracting.

Effective monitoring and accountability, then, begin with standards; no one can judge whether a private operator's jail or prison is "adequate" or comports with contractual requirements in the absence of clear contractual mandates. Contracting agencies must think through what they want of their private operators and adopt specific requirements that define goals and guide contractors without precluding flexibility and innovation. We do know how to run a safe and humane prison or jail. The challenge is to translate that knowledge into contractual standards that protect prisoners and encourage the improvement of institutional quality.

Monitoring Mechanisms

In the past two decades, the turbulence in the field of corrections has spawned a much richer understanding of the dynamics of effective correctional management. The same events
have also spurred the development of a variety of mechanisms
for monitoring the performance of correctional facilities. Indeed,
these mechanisms have sometimes served as the key catalyst in
the reform of correctional institutions and systems. They also
provide useful monitoring possibilities for correctional agencies
about to contract with private jail and prison operators. What
follows is a brief catalog of the devices and processes available
for monitoring, together with some guidelines for their implementation or use.

Contract Monitoring

Although contracting for the management of secure adult correctional institutions is a recent development, correctional
agencies have long hired private entrepreneurs to provide a variety of services, as previously noted. In addition, deinstitutionalization in juvenile corrections and mental health has
encouraged widespread contracting in these two related fields.
The result is a relatively extensive body of experience with the
contracting process, including the difficult task of monitoring
private providers' performance.

We have already examined the initiation of the contractual
process though the issuance of a Request for Proposals and the
solicitation of bids. Once submitted proposals have been reviewed and evaluated, the agency negotiates a final contract
with the prevailing bidder. Over the years, agencies have developed processes for the assessment of proposals that are sufficiently sophisticated to circumvent the necessity always to
award contracts to the lowest bidder, no matter how dubious the
bidder's credentials, capabilities, or overall proposal. These processes will be needed as never before in the review and award of
prison and jail management contracts.

Contract review traditionally includes the collection and review of documents, personal observations or site visits, and a
financial audit. Human services agencies that let contracts for
residential programs often supplement their effort to monitor
contracts with program reviews focusing on the services pro-

vided by the contractor. In these agencies, contract reviews are usually perfunctory, infrequent, and focused primarily on finances. Whether reviews are unified or separated into operational and financial functions, someone at the agency level collects documents, visits facilities, and checks finances. Each of these elements is vital to effective oversight.

Document Review

This aspect of monitoring requires the private contractor to supply the public agency's oversight personnel with a steady stream of paperwork documenting the contractor's operations. In the correctional context, this might include statistical data and specific periodic reports on population, classification, discipline, grievances, serious incidents (e.g., physical assaults on staff or inmates, sexual assaults, arson, suicides and attempted suicides, escapes, and disturbances), and programming. Although an assessment of a contractor's policies and procedures in these and other areas precedes the grant of a contract, the public agency will also want to review them at regular intervals.

Observation

Typically, contract personnel visit a private operator's facility at least annually to conduct an in-depth inspection and analysis of facilities, operations, and staff. When well planned and executed, these reviews can be thorough and exacting.[9] They often include structured interviews with administrators, staff, and clients; physical inspections of facilities; direct observation of services and programs; and attendance at hearings and meetings. Normally an extensive report of the inspection team's findings and recommendations follows, which serves to uncover or anticipate problems, initiate technical assistance, or promote the modification or termination of the contract.

Annual or semiannual inspections of privately operated secure correctional facilities are simply not enough. Mental health and juvenile correctional agencies that contract for residential programs typically assign full-time personnel to visit contract residences on a regular and frequent basis. In its statute authorizing the state's Department of Corrections to contract for correctional services, Florida requires the department to appoint a contract monitor to document adherence to the contract, although the statute requires only an annual audit.[10]

There is no magic in the use of a full-time monitor, who may be seduced by the contractor's overt corruption or subtle cooptation. The effectiveness of any monitor in this demanding and complex role will be determined by the individual's background, competence, tact, shrewdness, and authority. Whistle blowing can be a lonely and onerous profession.

Financial Audit

No contacting agency has to be persuaded of the importance of financial monitoring. Again, perhaps the greatest weakness in this area is the failure to utilize effectively the information generated in fiscal audits to anticipate and head off operational problems. More and better coordination of financial and operational monitoring are needed.

Contracting governmental agencies differ widely in both the frequency and depth of their performance monitoring of contracts. Even agencies with substantial contracting and monitoring tend to be understaffed, and oversight responsibilities are assigned as an additional, and often peripheral, duty to otherwise busy central office staff. The result, not infrequently, has been that inspections are performed only annually or once every three years; documentation is accumulated but not reviewed; and financial audits become by default the basic monitoring tool. When this occurs, effective monitoring ceases. Such erosion in the monitoring of contracts for secure correctional facilities will help to re-create those fiefdoms it took so long to dismantle.

Accreditation

Following the lead of other public institutions like hospitals and schools, correctional administrators in the 1970s developed a process for certifying institutional compliance with emerging standards of effective management. The accreditation process, developed by the American Correctional Association (which now dominates the field), has undergone organizational changes. After enjoying independence for a decade, the Commission on Accreditation, the initial reviewing body, returned to the ACA fold in the mid-1980s.

Accreditation requires an institutional or departmental applicant to undergo an extensive examination of conditions, operations, security, programs, staffing, training, services, management, and so on. The ACA's review has many of the same components discussed in the section on contract monitoring. There is an initial review of paperwork; facility inspections follow, and a report is then prepared, which allows an applicant a designated period within which to rectify identified deficiencies and thereby qualify for certification as a facility operated in compliance with the ACA's standards.

The accreditation process differs from contract monitoring in two important respects. In the former, inspections of facilities are conducted by a team of senior, experienced correctional administrators from other jurisdictions, who generally are far more qualified to assess institutional performance than state or local central office bureaucrats. An accreditation review does not include a financial audit, however. An accreditation team may examine a facility's ability to conduct financial planning and maintain fiscal controls, but it does not audit income and expenditures.

Accreditation is not cheap. The fee depends on the size of the applying institution or system and must cover all administrative and personnel expenses incurred in the review, evaluation, and preparation of reports. Subsequent reviews for continuing accreditation normally occur in a three-year cycle, with additional charges for each reevaluation.

The ACA does not have a monopoly on accreditation. Just as other groups of professionals with an interest in corrections have developed their own standards, so too, have accreditation groups put together accreditation vehicles. For example, a National Commission on Correctional Health Care evolved out of the American Medical Association's work on institutional health care standards; it currently manages a nationwide program for reviewing and certifying health care services in correctional institutions.

When a national body conducts the inspection and certifies compliance with standards, the strength of the accreditation process is a function of the skill, experience, and independence of the reviewing teams. A major disadvantage of the accreditation process is that reviews occur infrequently, and certification documents compliance with standards for only a brief period. In addition, the high cost of accreditation may often be prohibitive.

Court Models

Courts created institutional masters, the quintessential judicial monitoring mechanism, because defendant correctional bureaucrats were unwilling or unable to implement remedial orders after their institutions or systems were found to be unconstitutional or otherwise unlawful. Most institutional masters have been appointed in cases involving adult correctional facilities; they have also been used in other contexts such as juvenile corrections, facilities for the mentally handicapped, public housing, and special education. In the normal course of judicial events, the parties themselves are expected to police the enforcement of remedial decrees. Generally, only in cases where the parties have been unable effectively to bring about compliance through their own efforts, or in particularly complex cases where the plaintiffs cannot be expected to police the court's decree (as, for example, when a whole state's correctional system is declared unconstitutional), will the court appoint a master. Occasionally, courts have appointed an independent committee to oversee compliance with a court order, but this has not been a favored or an effective alternative.[11]

The responsibilities of a court-appointed master in a correctional case correspond with those of monitors designated to assess the performance of private contractors. Whereas the master holds the defendant institution or department to the standards contained in the remedial order, the monitor upholds the applicable standards as set out in the terms of the contract. The designation used by several judges to describe the master's role is the "eyes and ears of the court." The institutional master has free run of the subject facility and may meet alone with prisoners, staff, or administrators. Typically a master will make periodic reports to the court detailing the defendant institution's compliance (or noncompliance) with the terms of the remedial order and, where appropriate, making recommendations to ensure future compliance.

The subject matter of a mastership may vary from a single, specific issue like medical care or discipline to the widest possible range of issues.[12] A so-called omnibus suit may deal with physical conditions, staffing, medical care, sanitation, food services, mental health, programming, recreation, classification, and discipline.[13] In these cases, the master's substantive reach is no less broad than a public agency's in monitoring the operations of a private facility with one exception. A master does not typically audit financial records.

In many respects, the mastership provides a useful paradigm for monitoring the operations of a private prison or jail. Masters throughout the country have proven to be exceptionally effective monitors. Putting together a successful mastership, however, is expensive. The annual operating budget of the mastership established in a Texas prison case, which admittedly covered all of the adult facilities in that state, was about $700,000.[14] Yet, although the absolute cost was high, the annual cost per prisoner in that case was only about $30. The mastership in Rhode Island, with a population of only 1,400, involved an annual cost per prisoner of approximately $35. If this latter figure were used to calculate a monitoring rate for a privately operated facility for 400 offenders, the daily rate per prisoner would be about ten cents.

Interestingly, the Corrections Corporations of America, the acknowledged leader among private correctional enterprises, has put on record its intention to utilize monitors "at least to the same ratio as the court has provided monitors in Texas."[15] Private entrepreneurs seem to know that they cannot scrimp on monitoring.

Administrative Mechanisms

In the early 1970s some correctional systems began to develop innovative mechanisms designed to encourage prisoners to express and seek redress of their grievances. As alternatives to judicial intervention and as useful management tools, the resulting mechanisms have had a history of mixed success. At least three kinds of mechanisms emerged and have endured.

Ombudsmen.   Several jurisdictions have adopted a modified version of the Scandinavian ombudsman, a public official authorized to investigate and resolve complaints against governmental agencies. In the original version, the ombudsman was a respected public figure, appointed by the legislature and independent of the bureaucratic structure to be reviewed. The ombudsman could not impose decisions, but relied instead on persuasion and the authority to publish findings and recommendations to get parties in a dispute to settle.

The major difference between the Scandinavian model and its correctional application in the United States has been the deletion of the model's traditional and vital independence. Correctional ombudsmen are usually hired and supervised by the managers of the institutions or agencies they monitor. They also tend to be middle-level correctional bureaucrats, rather than prestigious members of the community with impeccable reputations. Finally, the original notion of an ombudsman presupposed the existence of an administrative grievance process to winnow out and resolve most complaints, leaving only more serious, systemic problems to the ombudsman. Typically in this country, a correctional ombudsman also serves as a substitute for an administrative grievance process and is usually swamped by a flood of complaints.

The prime advantage of an ombudsman mechanism is the assurance it provides that someone in the system receives, responds to, and attempts to resolve complaints. Typically, ombudsmen have direct access to top institutional or departmental administrators and, when effective, they can have a significant impact on policy and its implementation. A 1980 study found some form of correctional ombudsman in seventeen prison systems and thirteen jails, so the device is clearly popular.[16]

Grievance Procedures.   Formal grievance procedures generally involve the submission of complaints to a designated individual in a facility. A grievant who is dissatisfied with the resolution of the complaint can appeal to higher supervisory levels in the institution and the department and, in some instances, to an individual or body outside the correctional entity. Any external review in such a process is advisory, not binding.

In most grievance procedures, appeals are taken through the different levels of supervisory staff and administration. Some procedures, however, directly involve prisoners, line staff, and outsiders in making or reviewing decisions. In the most sophisticated and successful of this type of procedure, inmates and staff collaborate to mediate disputes within facilities, and final appeals may go to an outside arbitrator appointed by the American Arbitration Association for review and for an advisory opinion. Such a procedure has been utilized in the California Youth Authority since 1974. Every year an independent audit of the process is conducted by an agency without ties to the Youth Authority, and the audit results are reported to the California legislature.[17]

When structured and implemented with care, grievance procedures provide a mechanism through which prisoners' allegations of abuse and mismanagement can be heard, evaluated, and responded to swiftly and efficiently. Such procedures can also provide an invaluable management tool for correctional administrators genuinely interested in closely monitoring their facilities. Grievance procedures are the creation of management, however, and sometimes uncannily reflect an administrator's willingness to control staff. Only when a correctional manager is committed to making grievance procedures work will they be useful monitoring mechanisms.

Grievance Commissions. A few states have developed mechanisms that have features of both the ombudsman and the multilevel grievance procedures. In these systems, a commission consisting of people from outside the correctional establishment is assigned an investigative staff and receives and investigates complaints. Staff investigations are submitted to the commission for hearings and decisions, which are, in turn, communicated to the correctional administrators in the form of recommendations. Before complainants may submit their grievances to the commission, they are normally required to exhaust existing institutional grievance procedures. Maryland, North Carolina, and New York have instituted grievance commissions that receive complaints from all facilities within their respective states.[18]

The value of all of these mechanisms for the monitoring of private prisons and jails is the guidance they provide for the development of processes to ensure that aggrieved prisoners in privately operated facilities have access to public officials. One danger of privatization is that the addition of an extra layer of bureaucracy will hinder prisoners' ability to complain about treatment and services. Agency personnel involved in contract monitoring tend to look at documents and programs and talk to administrators and staff. When, and if, interviews with prisoners are scheduled (they rarely are), they are few and tend to be brief. Prisoners need a readily available channel through which they can communicate allegations of abuse or ill treatment to extrainstitutional, corporate administrators of the private operator and administrators of the contracting public agency. This is a critical component of any effective process for ensuring accountability.

Public Scrutiny

One of the most useful means for the prevention of prisoner abuse in correctional institutions is a frequent, continuous, and significant public presence. Once unthinkable in corrections, such public presence is today commonplace. It assumes many forms, ranging from attorneys who visit regularly and provide structured legal services for prisoners to volunteer groups of every description.

In a number of jurisdictions throughout the country, external groups of volunteers with an interest in corrections have provided invaluable services to facilities and their managers. The Pennsylvania Prison Society and the Alston Wilkes Society in South Carolina are two of the better known groups. Such organizations can provide an outlet for prisoners ignored or frustrated by the system. They can also both marshal support for the correctional establishment on key public issues and supplement meager program resources.

In the normal course of events, the emergence of such groups is largely a matter of serendipity, but contracting public agencies can require private managers of prisons and jails contractually to develop and utilize volunteers or volunteer organizations. For example, a private operator might be required to put together an advisory or visiting board that periodically reviews and evaluates conditions and programs in the facility. Civilian review boards in law enforcement provide a paradigm for this kind of external, voluntary oversight body. The board could be required to include professionals, media representatives, and minority advocates from the local community. It would not be difficult to structure and fill positions on such a board. Because of the amateur standing of its members in correctional matters, the board would not be a substitute for external professional monitoring, but as a sounding board for general conditions and a prophylactic measure against the abuse of prisoners, it could be invaluable.

There are, of course, limits to the usefulness of public scrutiny. Community representatives can easily be persuaded by correctional officials that harsh measures are necessary for security. Volunteers, moreover, tend to burn out quickly and often lack the endurance necessary for sustained, long-term involvement. Despite these shortcomings, contracting public agencies ought to consider a requirement that private providers develop plans to promote public scrutiny within their facilities.

No single one of these various monitoring mechanisms will suffice to hold privately operated jails and prisons sufficiently accountable or ensure the required level of control over their operations. A rich mixture of all of these approaches is needed, including traditional contract or performance monitoring; some form of regular external review, whether through accreditation or the equivalent of a court-appointed master; a mechanism for encouraging presentation of and responding to prisoners' grievances that allows appeal to the public agency; and some structural form of public involvement in the operation of the private facility.

To some observers these multiple requirements may seem redundant and excessive, but prisons and jails are artificial and unnatural institutions that generate powerful barriers to the collection of data for those obligated to observe and evaluate such institutions. Among prisoners, the fear of reprisals from staff and administration, powerfully impeding the flow of information about conditions and events, is reinforced by the inmates' taboo against "snitching," which leads them to view with suspicion any private conversation between a prisoner and the minions of the system. The staff has its own caste system, firmly rooted in solidarity, and typically confronts complaints with closed ranks. Administrators are hesitant to appear lukewarm in their support of staff, even when serious errors in judgment have occurred, for fear of eroding staff authority and control over the inmate population. A factual assessment of alleged abuses in such an environment requires multiple and redundant means for generating accurate information.

For all of these reasons, it is essential to structure accountability in diverse and imaginative ways. Indeed, even the plethora of approaches to monitoring suggested here is probably insufficient. Other measures, like exit or postrelease interviews with a randomly selected cross section of prisoners incarcerated in privately operated facilities, need to be considered and implemented. Contracting public agencies must be innovative in developing control mechanisms commensurate with the awesome public responsibility being handed over to the private sector.

Once a public agency has decided on a mixed structure of monitoring devices, they must all be included in the contract with the private prison or jail operator. Early correctional privatization contracts have neglected to detail monitoring provisions and, in practice, the monitoring of these contracts, not surprisingly, was weak.[19] The contract itself must commit the parties to effective monitoring.

Perhaps the ultimate answer to accountability in this context is for the handful of functioning court-appointed correctional masters throughout the country to take a page from the

privatizers' ledger and form an independent, private corporation, called, let us say, Accountability, Inc., to monitor private
prison and jail operators. The possibility, though offered face-
tiously, suggests that sufficient experience and expertise exist
to develop effective monitoring and control mechanisms in privatized jails and prisons, and that is encouraging news.

The Duty to Govern: A Critical Perspective on the Private Management of Prisons and Jails   JOHN J. DIIULIO, JR.

> Some twenty years ago several pious individuals undertook to ame-
> liorate the condition of the prisons. . . . While new penitentiaries
> were being erected . . . the old prisons . . . became more unwholesome
> and corrupt . . . so that in the immediate neighborhood of a prison
> that bore witness to the mild and enlightened split of our times,
> dungeons existed that reminded one of the barbarism of the Middle
> Ages.
>
> —Alexis de Tocqueville, *Democracy in America*

Introduction

The privatization of corrections is the latest, albeit unfinished,
chapter in the history of penal reform in the United States. Like
most previous penal reform movements, the privatization movement can be understood as a response to escalating costs, rising
inmate populations, and a broadening consensus that the government has failed to handle adjudicated offenders in ways that
achieve one or more of the following goals: public protection (or
incapacitation); deterrence (specific and general); punishment
(or retribution); and the rehabilitation (or reformation) of convicted criminals.[1]

Like previous generations of penal reformers, the privatizers
are motivated by a mixture of self-interest and high ideals. On
the one hand, they are out to make money for themselves and
their investors; on the other hand, they seem convinced that they
can help to improve this country's ailing corrections complex.
They pledge to operate in an abuse- and corruption-free manner,

and they claim that their ultimate mission is to make prisons and jails safer, cleaner, more productive, more lawful, and less expensive to build, finance, and administer. In public, the privatizers are reluctant to predict that they can also reduce rates of recidivism; in private, however, they are bolder.[2]

This essay focuses on one major facet of the privatization movement: the private management of prisons and jails. The central questions posed by such management are normative. Should the authority to administer criminal justice in prisons and jails, to deprive citizens of their liberty, and to coerce (even kill) them, be delegated to contractually deputized private individuals, or ought it remain in the hands of duly authorized public officials? Should the care and custody of citizens detained or incarcerated for the commission (or suspected commission) of crimes be placed in the hands of nonpublic, profit-making organizations? Who should manage our penal institutions and by what authority?

My analysis of the normative questions posed by private prison and jail management is based on four sets of assumptions. First, at this stage, it is simply impossible to answer most of the important empirical questions raised by the privatization movement.[3] Despite a variety of claims to the contrary, there is absolutely nothing in either the scholarly or the nonscholarly literature on the subject—no journal article, no government report, no newspaper story, no conference proceedings, no book— that would enable one to speak confidently about how private corrections firms compare with public corrections agencies in terms of costs, protection of inmates' civil rights, reliance on particular management technologies, or any other significant dimension. The necessary comparative research simply has not been done, and reliable empirical data are still scarce. Sophisticated theoretical speculations, colorful anecdotes, impressionistic "before and after" surveys, and raw statistics are in ample supply, but there is as yet little dependable information to tell us how, whether, or at what human and financial cost privatization will succeed or fail. None of the essays in this volume, including this one, bring us any closer to definitive answers, though they may bring us nearer to definitive questions.

Second, however one answers the normative questions surrounding private prison and jail management, it is a mistake to conceptualize privatization as an "either or" issue. The privatization of corrections involves multiple policy alternatives, only some of which provoke substantial normative controversy.[4] For instance, if we think in terms of administration, construction, and finance, then privatization presents us with at least eight distinct bundles of policy alternatives (ranging from all-public to all-private) for each of at least seven discrete correctional activities (higher-custody prisons, lower-custody prisons, jails, other secure facilities such as juvenile centers, probation, parole, and nonincarcerational programs such as restitution).[5] It is crucial that correctional decision makers recognize the various possibilities, study them in light of their own agency's immediate and long-run needs and resources, and carefully scrutinize all empirical and normative generalizations about "privatization."

Third, the normative questions raised by private prison and jail management are extremely thorny. To even begin to address them adequately requires broad-gauged moral reasoning grounded in the history of the subject, in a detailed knowledge of how correctional facilities actually operate, and in some understanding of the politics of corrections. With few exceptions, existing commentaries on the normative dimension of private corrections fail in every department—the moral reasoning is narrow; the grasp of correctional history is shallow; the understanding of correctional politics and administration is negligible or nonexistent.[6] In addition, two mistakes are often made in handling the normative questions related to private prison and jail management:

1. The substitution of empirical for normative criteria, and assertion of the concomitant notion that if it could be shown beyond any reasonable doubt that private management improves (or worsens) correctional services, lowers (or increases) costs, and exceeds (or falls below) constitutional requirements, the normative questions would be resolved.[7]

2. The focus on the profit motive of the privatizers, and assertion of the concomitant notion that the central moral conundrum posed by private management is not whether the authority to administer justice behind bars ought to be delegated by contract to private, nongovernmental entities, but whether the private contractors ought to be paid for or to profit financially from their services.[8]

Fourth and finally, the private management of prisons and jails poses first-order questions of constitutional governance. Who shall be punished under law, for what, how, and by what authority? Where does the government's responsibility to govern begin, where does it end, and how (or how far, if at all) may it be delegated?[9] To a remarkable degree, twentieth-century political scientists have ignored both the practical and the philosophical challenges of administering criminal justice in a constitutional polity.[10] Their lack of guidance, however, need not leave us intellectually flat-footed, for there is an earlier and wiser tradition in political science, embodied superbly in the writings of James Madison and Alexander Hamilton, to instruct us on how to approach such challenges. History, the Founding Fathers counseled, "is the oracle of truth,"[11] and experience "the least fallible guide of human opinions."[12] To them, history was moral philosophy teaching by example.[13] Let us begin, therefore, with the lessons of the past.

Lessons of the Past: Guides for the Future?

In 1833, Alexis de Tocqueville and Gustave de Beaumont expressed grave reservations about the role of private contractors in the administration of penal facilities. With regard to the contracting system in their native France they wrote:

> With us the same person contracts for the food, clothing, labour, and sanitary department of the convicts—a system equally injurious to the convict and the discipline of the prison; to the convict because the contractor, who sees nothing but a money affair in such a bargain, speculates on the victuals as he does upon the labour . . . and if the labour is less productive than he calculated upon, he tries to balance his loss by spending less for the support of the convicts, with which he is equally charged. . . . The contractor, regarding the convict as a labouring machine, thinks only how he can use him to the greatest advantage for himself . . . and he cares little if the expenses of the convict are made to the injury of good order.[14]

Beaumont and Tocqueville believed that prison authorities in the United States had avoided such problems by the use of "a different contractor for each branch of industry; the contracts being thus multiplied, the contractor cannot obtain in the prison more than a limited and passing influence."[15] But even in the United States, they observed, "the presence of the contractor or his agents in the prisons has been found to be not without its inconvenience."[16]

For much of the nineteenth century and as late as the 1960s, prisons and jails in many parts of the United States were privately owned and operated. In the current debate over private sector involvement in corrections, these precedents have not been duly acknowledged. In Texas, California, Michigan, Louisiana, Oklahoma, and many other states, all or part of the penal system has at one time or another been administered privately. As a few examples should suffice to show, the premonitions of Tocqueville and Beaumont were if anything too mild. The pre-1980s record of private sector involvement in corrections is unvaryingly bleak.

In the nineteenth century, Texas leased its penitentiary (which survives today as the Huntsville "Walls" unit) to private contractors.[17] For a few dollars per month per convict, the contractors were allowed to sublease their charges to farmers, tanners, and other businessmen. It was not long before the inmates began to appear in poor clothing and without shoes. Worked mercilessly, most convicts died within seven years of their incarceration. Escapes and escape attempts were frequent. Conditions were so horrid that some inmates were driven to suicide while others maimed themselves to get out of work or as a pathetic form of protest.[18]

The Civil War decimated several penal systems in the South. Louisiana, Arkansas, Florida, Virginia, and Georgia were among the states that responded by leasing out their entire convict populations to private contractors, or by granting contracts for work to be performed behind the walls, or both.[19]

Even in the antebellum South, however, contracting was not unknown. Louisiana, for example, began contracting in the 1840s. In the Reconstruction Era, the state's prisoners were under the private control of one Major Samuel Lawrence Jones. For a quarter century, Jones ran the most corrupt and brutal regime in Louisiana's sordid penal history.[20] As in other states where contractors ran amok, Louisiana's State Legislature launched investigations and issued damning reports. But nothing happened; indeed, over a decade elapsed between the introduction of the state's first antilease bill and the lessee's exit from Baton Rouge. Well into the 1940s, the Louisiana penal system was a business administered by leaseholders out to make profits from the labor of unskilled and semiskilled convicts. Public officials used the system as a patronage mill, awarding contracts to friends, relatives, and political loyalists.[21] As in other Southern states where contractors assumed a large measure of control over prison and jails, Louisiana's inmates— most of them blacks and dirt-poor whites—were treated as "slaves of the state" though it was not the state that had them in hand.

In Arkansas, where the contract system had rapidly degenerated into a system of legalized inmate abuse, profiteering, and graft, a Progressive Era governor made the deplorable condition of the state's penal facilities a key political issue. He published an essay on the subject in March 1913.[22] In Virginia, the contract system was operated without regard for either prison discipline or the inmates' health and safety; escapees were not recaptured; prisoner mortality rates soared.[23] "Yet the profits from the contracts and the desperately needed relief from overcrowding . . . kept the contract system in operation."[24]

The same basic story can be told concerning other jurisdictions.[25] The era of for-profit corrections, stretching roughly from 1840 to 1960, came to an end in most places largely as a result of three factors. First, public scandals and journalistic exposés revealed the contract system's weaknesses. Second, there was a decline in the demand for the kinds of products that unskilled, uneducated convicts could produce, and a concomitant increase in the mobilization of political (mainly labor union) pressures against the production and sale of prison-made goods. Third, politicians and prison officials, often at great risk to their careers, spoke out against the system and argued in favor of the public administration of prisons and jails.

Clearly, the pre-1980s record of private sector involvement in corrections is damning. But what, if anything, does this history teach us? Are these lessons of the past proper guides for the present and the future? Could such gross abuses occur today before a watchful court (taking a stance well beyond the "hands-off" doctrine) and the scrutinizing media? The best answer is, Probably not, but be very careful.

Increased external monitoring aside, in the last few decades the corrections profession has made enormous progress.[26] There are now some twenty-five private corrections firms.[27] Many of them, no doubt, are fly-by-night enterprises. Several, however, such as the Corrections Corporation of America (CCA), are led by some of the most seasoned and respected corrections professionals in the country. As of this writing, no private institutions or programs have been plagued by serious, systemic cases of inmate abuse or political corruption. Indeed, the CCA and its competitors have kept an enviably clean slate.

History nevertheless teaches us to be extremely wary of the claim that the slate will remain clean so long as contracts are detailed in accordance with the highest current correctional standards. The previous era of private corrections was influenced by contracts every bit as "tight" as those being drafted today. Consider, for instance, the following passages from a typical 1906–1907 "share system" contract between the state of Texas and a private party (a "widow woman").[28] Texas agreed to supply "a class of convicts, who, because of youth, old age, or some physical infirmity, are not suited for contract farms or railroad work, but who are, nevertheless, capacitated to perform labor on a share farm." Texas agreed to "clothe and feed said convicts in accordance with the rules and regulations of the Penitentiaries," and to "furnish anything necessary and incidental to the management and keeping of said convicts not specially contracted to be performed by" the private party. Among other things, the latter was to provide "the necessary shelter for (the convicts') protection" during "rain or bad weather"; "transportation . . . to and from the Railroad depot"; and "a good Prison House, Hospital, Dining Room and Kitchen for the convicts, as is prescribed by the rules."

The record in Texas and other jurisdictions shows that such contracts were violated routinely by both parties. In the language of Madison, these finely worded contracts were mere "parchment barriers."[29] There is no reason to suppose that words on paper embossed by public officials will do anything to check abuse and corruption if the political will and regulatory force of the government are absent.

Today, the Immigration and Naturalization Service (INS) has what might be considered a model contracting and monitoring process. Prospective contractors respond to detailed INS publications calling for specific correctional services. Normally, for each request the INS receives several dozen proposals. A panel of three or four INS officials screens the proposals, usually eliminating most of them as "nonresponsive" either because they carry price tags higher than what the government has budgeted, or because they address only a part of the government's request, or for other such reasons. The "responsive" bids are then graded on a 100-point scale according to a 70–30 point system. A maximum of 70 points is given to the proposal that best meets or exceeds the minimum standards specified in the government's request. A maximum of 30 points is given to the lowest bidder, and a fraction of 30 points is given to the other bidders in proportion to the lowest bidder (e.g., lowest bidder's price is $1 million, next lowest bidder's price is $2 million; the former gets 30 points, the latter gets 15). Because of the 70–30 point system, contracts do not always go to the lowest bidder. Almost without exception, the proposal that wins 70 points is one that goes beyond what the government requested and that, in the words of one INS official, "counts nails" and offers an "enhanced program." On major INS requests (e.g., to build and operate whole facilities), winning proposals are about the size of a Sears, Roebuck Christmas catalog. They contain little vague language. For example, they do not state that the contractor shall "provide adequate recreational services"; instead, they specify such things as the number, size, and location of recreation rooms and the exact kind of Ping-Pong tables to be used (even down to their height and weight!). Together, the government's request and the winning proposal become the official contract. The INS supervisors literally walk around their private facilities with the bulky documents in tow. Monitoring contractor compliance and measuring contractor performance would thus seem to be a fairly simple and routine task.

Even with the INS contracting and monitoring system, however, there are at least three causes for concern. First, the CCA and its corporate competitors are entitled by law to restrict access to their proposals. Because the proposals contain "trade secrets," they are not open to public or media scrutiny (not even via the Freedom of Information Act). Since the winning proposal (together with the government's request) is the official contract, and since the proposal selection process is also secretive (in order to protect each firm's trade secrets), everything depends on the good sense and integrity of a few INS officials. There is every reason to have such unqualified confidence in the present INS staff, but what about future staffs? And what about the equivalent officials at the state and county levels?[30]

Second, although the contract's specificity may help to guarantee accountability, it does so at the expense of administrative flexibility. A major selling point of the privatizers is that they can be more innovative (and ultimately more efficient) than public providers of correctional services. A contract that "counts nails," however, makes it difficult for the contractor to allocate resources freely, to make staffing changes, and so forth. Of course, on-site monitors could be empowered to grant variances that would enable the contractor to operate outside the terms of the contract. Obviously, however, there could be problems with such a grant of regulatory discretion, whether exercised on a loose, ad hoc basis ("initial a variance slip") or on a more formal basis ("clear everything through Washington").

Third, there is a danger that government contract selectors and regulatory authorities will rely too much on means-oriented specifications and measures. Public organizations are notorious for evaluating performance according to inputs rather than outputs. In the case of correctional institutions, this often means such things as the development of elaborate inmate classification procedures (and the promotion of their developers whether or not they work), and a slavish adherence to a given inmate-to-officer ratio, even when there is no evidence that higher or lower ratios are associated with better or worse levels of institutional safety and programming.[31]

In sum, there is reason to worry that, as one public corrections official stated, "either the contractors will be allowed to run wild as they did in the old days, or we'll make the specifications, regulations, and monitoring so rigid that the firms will become as bureaucratized and inefficient as we are—killing the goose before he lays any eggs."

Historically, a good deal of serious thought has gone into the search for a contracting and monitoring system that achieves both accountability and flexibility. It was the desire to find an optimal path in regulating private incarcerational institutions that inspired Jeremy Bentham to write the famous *Panopticon* (1791). The same quest has recently led to several creative and well-reasoned proposals (e.g., the use of a fine system).[32] Only time and experimentation can tell us whether any of these proposals is the answer.

The privatizers claim that they will operate in accordance with the most stringent contemporary correctional standards. Some CCA officials, for example, boast that all of their facilities are accredited by the American Correctional Association (ACA). Although the boast is valid, it is also true that the accreditation process leaves much to be desired. Accredited facilities have been and are among the worst in the nation.[33] The deficiencies in the accreditation process can be and are being worked out.[34] Still, because the CCA and its competitors covet accreditation (if only as a rough and ready shield against litigation), they are prone to engage in what critics call "correctional creaming": assuming control of modern, lower-custody facilities whose populations are small and do not include serious offenders (e.g., juvenile centers), and staying away from institutions and programs that are more difficult to manage (e.g., most existing maximum-security prisons). I will return to this issue in the next section.

One wholly unchanged historical reality about U.S. prisons and jails is that those incarcerated in them come disproportionately from the lowest rungs of the socioeconomic ladder.[35] Criminologists and others may debate the relevant empirical and moral issues, but none denies the simple truth that this country's incarcerational institutions house large percentages of poor, dark-skinned persons. Nor does anyone deny that most of the rest of society is neither poor nor dark-skinned. Historically, racial and class prejudices and the low visibility of penal facilities have conspired to make the average U.S. citizen unconcerned about what happens inside prisons and jails. There is nothing about public ignorance and apathy that makes wretched prison and jail conditions inevitable, but if history is any guide, we must believe that societal pressures against inmate abuse and political corruption will be at low ebb whenever largely underclass populations of offenders are placed in nonpublic hands.

At the same time, the move to an increasingly high-technology, service-oriented, and computer-driven economy may rekindle the demand for the sorts of labor that ill-educated, uneducated, and easily exploitable convicts can provide—a computer terminal chain gang.[36] The sigh of relief that public officials may breathe after turning over all or part of their penal complex to private firms may presage a death rattle for inmates' legal and constitutional rights while exposing the state to greater liability risks.[37]

These and other such possibilities become less frightening in light of the single most important post-1960s change in the operating environment of prisons and jails: the increase of judicial intervention in penal affairs. Since 1970 the operations of dozens of correctional systems have been placed under court orders. There continues to be disagreement about the causes and consequences of judicial intervention in this area.[38] Most experts, however, agree that activist state and federal judges have become a permanent part of the correctional scene. Although I harbor some serious reservations about the judges' involvement,[39] it is impossible to deny that the courts can and do provide a salutary barrier against any repetition of the kinds of unmitigated administrative horrors that characterized the previous era of for-profit corrections. If anything, the courts may prove especially eager to hold the feet of the corrections corporations to their well-stoked judicial fires.

For those deciding whether the authority to administer prisons and jails ought to be delegated to private contractors, history is an ambivalent tutor counseling both openness and vigilance. This country's last experience with private corrections was hellish, but in the intervening decades much has changed. We can neither dismiss the possibility that the problems may recur, nor assert that this history is bound to repeat itself. We can, however, gain additional perspective on the wisdom of privatization by considering its political and administrative dimensions.

Politics: Prisons, Profits, and the Public Good

Historically, public preferences with regard to corrections have been multiple, vague, and contradictory. Different citizens and groups have placed different but hard to measure values on the ends of punishment, rehabilitation, deterrence, and incapacitation. There has been conflict over a lesser constellation of penal goals as well—jobs for prisoners without posing threats to free workers; more adequate prison programs and living space without imposing more taxes or opening more sites for construction; stern treatment without infringing on prisoners' rights; and social stigmatization without causing permanent alienation. Corrections has been, and continues to be, an inherently political "business" because people disagree, often violently, over what prisons, jails, and other postsentencing activities are for.[40]

The politics of corrections has never been played out in the sort of pluralistic universe that defines much of the rest of U.S. public policymaking, however.[41] Most of the time, it is the corrections commissioner and a handful of executive and legislative branch officials who set the correctional policy agenda, make decisions, and oversee their implementation. In certain jurisdictions, the officials who make corrections policy are influenced by certain outside (nongovernmental) persons and groups. They form what political scientists call "subgovernments": "clusters of individuals that effectively make most of the routine decisions in a given area of policy."[42] It is certainly true that since the 1960s, those who make and administer corrections policy have faced an expanding contingent of outside "coaches, customers, and critics"—prisoners' rights organizations, victims' rights organizations, judges, special masters, court-appointed monitors, and so on.[43] But it is also true that the coaches have remained relatively few, the customers virtually powerless, and the critics divided (liberals versus conservatives). In short, the politics of corrections supplies evidence for the existence of what one scholar has termed "the autonomy of the democratic state."[44]

The nonpluralistic nature of corrections policymaking would

seem to pose significant challenges and opportunities for the privatizers. On the one hand, it means that skillful lobbying and careful negotiating are necessary if they are to get their foot in the door; on the other hand, it means that they can probably wield a great deal of influence once they are on the inside. The second half of this political equation has not been ignored by either private corrections representatives or their opponents. The representatives insist that the firms can do better precisely because they are (or will be) almost completely insulated from political pressures and unencumbered by governmental red tape.[45] The opponents worry that the firms will influence corrections policy in ways that keep beds filled, prison and jail construction booming, less profitable alternatives to incarceration on the drawing board, and more offenders of all types under some form of state-mandated but privately administered supervision. Some opponents are haunted by the specter of a corrections version of the military-industrial complex.[46]

It is too soon to know whether the political dynamics of privatization will validate either the hopes of its supporters or the fears of its detractors. Already, however, it is obvious that the firms are steering clear of jurisdictions where the corrections policy subgovernments include strong labor unions. Over half of the contractors in existence in late 1986 were based in the South.[47] The Corrections Corporation of America, the acknowledged leader in the industry, is based in Nashville, Tennessee. It is part of the CCA's long-term corporate strategy to establish itself firmly in the South and the Southwest, and to make major inroads in Great Britain and France (where conservative governments are in control), before attempting to move into more politically complicated parts of the U.S. "prison market."[48] This strategy is by no means destined to succeed. For one thing, corrections policy subgovernments need not include labor unions to be inhospitable to private venturers. For example, after opening several impressive facilities in Tennessee, in late 1985 the CCA bid $225 million for the whole Tennessee prison system.[49] The bid was stymied mainly by a few key legislators.[50] Outside the South and the West, the firms have had little success. In Pennsylvania, the home of three firms, a one-year moratorium on privatization initiatives went into effect in 1986 and was extended in 1987.[51] Apart from affecting decisions about where to locate, a mix of political and financial considerations has led the firms to lock themselves out of "big house" prisons and jails and to engage in correctional creaming when they bid. Violence (including riots and gang warfare), racial tensions, and staff corruption are more common in the institutions that they leave to the public sector. Such problems may bring negative media attention, legislative inquiries, staff unrest, lawsuits, and judicial intervention. Naturally, the firms wish to avoid such problems. Among private corrections executives, there is great unease that one major blowup in a private facility resulting in a loss of life and extensive property damage could make financial backers panic and venture capital "dry up."[52] As a hedge against such politically debilitating threats to their financial and public relations positions, the firms have thus far scrupulously avoided bidding for control of the Atticas and Rikers Islands of the country, forsaking for strategic reasons an enormous part of the available market for their services.

The creaming strategy, however, may cause the firms to suffer political headaches just the same. For one thing, lower-custody facilities are not immune from the kinds of problems that the firms hope to avoid.[53] For another, political opponents such as the American Federation of State and County Municipal Employees (AFSCME) have zeroed in on this "unfair" attempt to leave public corrections workers with an unwanted monopoly on the worst prisons and jails.[54] Already, the Immigration and Naturalization Service has presided over private facilities that are uncrowded and well staffed in close proximity to public facilities that are overpopulated and understaffed. Eventually, such spectacles are bound to raise legal and other questions about the firms that redound to their political disadvantage. In navigating in search of smooth political waters, the firms may sail into a political storm.

The privatization of corrections has enjoyed political momentum as part of a broader effort, supported by the Reagan administration, to transfer public tasks to the private sector.[55] Whether the movement ultimately succeeds, stumbles, or dies politically, however, will depend largely on the firms' skills in bargaining, public advocacy, and propagandizing about the intrinsic virtues of private management. Comparative cost-effectiveness cannot be the firms' only selling point; opponents can almost always lodge a plausible challenge to the figures; and the firms may actually cost more than they promised.[56] Proponents of privatization initiatives in other areas have outlined strategies for meeting objections related to such potential political problems as unrealized cost savings, low quality, corruption, lack of control and accountability, and reduced services to the poor.[57] Most of these strategies, however, seem better suited to such things as the privatization of trash collection than to the privatization of corrections; and none of them meet the controversial moral and constitutional issues that continue to be raised about the private management of prisons and jails.[58]

In the final analysis, the political strength of the privatizers will depend on their ability to persuade skeptics and critics that prisons for profits are in the public interest. In other words, they must persuade enough people in scores of disparate political jurisdictions that to join a pro-privatization coalition is not to join what Madison termed a "faction"—a wholly self-interested group that acts contrary "to the rights of other citizens," or is at odds with "the permanent and aggregate interests of the community."[59] This is not to say that they must pose as altruists concerned only with the well-being of their clients and the future of corrections in the United States. Rather, it is to suggest that they must by their words and deeds persuade others that they will not reflexively put profits ahead of public safety or the inmates' civil rights, if only because it is not in their long-term political and financial interest to do so. In most respects, the CCA has shown signs of such political prudence. At this stage, however, its record and that of its competitors are too shallow to know whether for-profit corrections firms will further or frustrate the public good.

Administration: Public, Private, and Competent

Closely related to the historical and political questions surrounding private prison and jail management are questions about the administrative differences between public corrections agencies and private corrections firms.

There is evidence to suggest that private firms can produce and deliver more of a wide range of goods and services, and do it more cheaply, than public bureaucracies can.[60] But what do correctional agencies "produce and deliver"? Should we expect that what is apparently true for trash collection, air transport, and many other services must also be true for prisons and jails? Most claims that private corrections firms can outperform public corrections agencies rest on two sets of assumptions:[61] first, that significant differences exist between public and private management, that business firms are necessarily more efficient and innovative than government agencies, and that these advantages of private management are universal—they obtain whether the task is picking up garbage or locking up prisoners; second, that the public sector's administrative experience in corrections has been an unmitigated disaster: prisons and jails have been, and continue to be, horrible places horribly run.

In my judgment, both sets of assumptions are false. The former is the product of bad empirics, poor conceptualization, and lazy moralizing; the latter results from an inadequate appreciation of the reality that the performance of public corrections agencies has varied enormously and in ways that are clearly traceable to differences in public management practices. There is more than human caprice behind the fact that some tasks are in public rather than private hands; there are nontrivial reasons why we have both government and business, both politics and markets, both public agencies and private corporations, both MPAs and MBAs. In the public sector, the relationship between valued inputs (e.g., people, money) and desired outputs (e.g., less crime, better public health) is often unclear and may even be impossible to specify with any degree of precision; hence, "efficiency" (maximizing output for a given set of inputs or minimizing the inputs needed to achieve a given level of output) is harder to measure. The political and legal constraints on what work gets done, how, and by whom tend to be far greater in the public arena. "Sophisticated" management theories and techniques may or may not help in the private sector, but they are almost always more likely to come away limping when applied to public tasks. Some characteristics of certain public management tasks make them "impossible jobs"; corrections is a paradigm case.[62] Such verities about public versus private management have been discovered by successive generations of top-flight business executives who have entered government service only to find that the lessons of Wall Street have limited application in government.[63]

Nevertheless, suppose we wanted to make hard and fast evaluations of public versus private correctional management. What performance measures could we use? Most students of corrections would agree that there is no clear relationship between institutional penal practices, on the one hand, and rates of recidivism, on the other. Basically, prisons and jails "produce and deliver" an imprecise mix of incapacitation, deterrence, retribution, and rehabilitation—or so we tend to believe. It is quite difficult to specify the relationship between any of these ends and how penal facilities are managed. There are, however, at least three rough surrogate performance indexes that are related less ambiguously to managerial practices: order, amenity, and service.

By order I mean the absence of individual or group misconduct behind bars that threatens the safety of others; simply stated, it means no assaults, rapes, riots, suicides, or murders. By amenity I mean anything intended to increase the inmates' comfort—clean living quarters, good food, color television sets. By service I mean anything intended to enhance the inmates' lifetime prospects—programs in remedial reading, vocational training, work opportunities, and so on.[64] Measured accordingly, are prisons and jails simply wretched, or are some relatively safe, humane, treatment-oriented, and productive? There are extremist views on both sides of this question, but the available data suggest that public penal institutions have been, and continue to be, a terribly mixed bag: Some are clean, others filthy; some are orderly, others riotous; some offer many programs, others none at all. Some public corrections agencies have improved over time; others have gotten worse; still others have changed little if at all. One thing, however, seems clear: the quality of life inside prisons and jails depends mainly on the quality of penal management. Through more caring and more intelligent institutional management, prisons and jails can be improved even when budgets are tight, facilities are dilapidated, and inmate populations are large and dangerous.[65]

A truly remarkable but untold correctional success story is that of the federal Bureau of Prisons. Before the bureau was established by an act of Congress and signed into being by President Hoover on May 14, 1930, inmates in federal custody were subject to the arbitrary and often cruel treatment of whichever of seven federal wardens they happened to be assigned to. Inmates ate slop served from buckets and discipline was harsh. Under the bureau's first director, Sanford Bates (1930–1937), the situation began to improve. Under its second director, the dynamic James V. Bennett (1937–1964), an incredible number of positive innovations were made in the care and custody of prisoners. The bureau's third director, Myrl Alexander (1964–1970), consolidated these gains; its fourth director, Norman A. Carlson (1970–1987), issued policy directives, established recruitment and training programs, and instituted scores of other changes that made the bureau's facilities more safe, humane, and productive.[66] Since 1930 the record of the Bureau of Prisons confirms that good public correctional management is possible.[67] Other public corrections systems have also had talented executives, conscientious workers, a prudent penal management philosophy, favorable laws, political support, good community relations, and so on.[68] Under such administrative conditions, publicly managed prisons and jails have produced what most of us would probably consider to be acceptable (if far from ideal) levels of order, amenity, and service. The public sector has constructed, financed, and, most important for our purposes, operated many safe, clean, productive, and arguably cost-effective institutions and has administered them at a reasonable human and financial cost.

Absent such administrative conditions, however, publicly managed systems have done less well. In some places, prisons and jails have been run by oppressive, uncaring officials; in others, they have resembled states of nature where violent inmate predators rule; in still others, administrations have alternated between the poles of anarchy and tyranny under conditions that judges have found unconstitutional and average citizens would find disgusting and inhumane.

The crucial point, however, is that the administrative performance of public prisons and jails has not been uniformly bad, and there is no reason to suppose that the performance of private facilities would be uniformly good. To believe otherwise one would have to believe that there is something magical about the private sector. In the chapter one world of the economics textbooks, a world of perfect competition and ceteris paribus assumptions, the market is magic. In this fantasy world, it is certain that efficient market-driven organizations can give us whatever bundle of goods and service we demand, from widgets to more complex commodities. But in the real world, we see that organizations, public or private, tend to succeed when they combine good workers with sufficient resources under the right conditions, and tend to fail when they do not.

One novel argument for private prison and jail management is that it will somehow stimulate innovation and improve performance by increasing the repertoire of administrative strategies and structures being employed. Early in the privatization debate, for example, Peter Greenwood argued that "government is not going to give us better prisons, better programs, or better personnel. . . . [Private managers] would be free to innovate, to use the latest technology and management techniques as in any profit-motivated industry. . . . Why not give private enterprise a chance?"[69]

There are at least two basic flaws in this sort of pro-privatization argument. First, it is grounded in abject ignorance of the existing range of intersystem, intrasystem, and historical variations in correctional philosophies, practices, and outcomes. Second, it is based on highly rebuttable theoretical assumptions about the relationship between given organizational conditions and organizational innovations. For at least a generation, no agreement has been reached on which set of factors (e.g., organizational slack, loose structure), if any, is associated with either technical or managerial innovations (strategic and nonstrategic). One searches in vain through the books and journals (such as *Administrative Science Quarterly*) published in the last twenty-five years that would permit one to make the assumptions necessary to conclude that privatization will lead to the kinds of positive (or negative) management developments being forecast.

The core administrative issue here is not public versus private correctional management but the possibility of competent correctional management. There has been, and continues to be, variation in the performance of public sector corrections agencies. By probing the political, budgetary, and other conditions associated with better incarcerational and nonincarcerational institutions and programs, public managers can learn from each others' mistakes and successes; indeed, since 1980 they have begun to do so.[70] Rather than abandoning governmental stewardship of prisons and jails, why not give public administration a chance?

Government behind Bars: Who Ought to Administer Justice?

For the sake of argument, let us suppose that, contrary to all of the arguments being made against privatization, corrections corporations can operate institutions successfully on a wide scale—constructing, financing, and managing everything from small new community centers to massive old maximum-security prisons. Let us concede, without any qualifications, that private firms can indeed maximize services while minimizing costs in an abuse- and corruption-free environment, satisfying all political, legal, and other such constraints. In other words, we assume that private prisons and jails are eminently feasible. Must it then follow that they are desirable? Is the private operation of prisons and jails, however instrumental it may prove to be in reducing costs and bettering services, morally justifiable? Does the government's responsibility to govern end at the prison gates? Who ought to administer justice behind bars?

The answer to each of these questions depends in part on more general considerations. For example, where (or how) does one draw the line between "contractually deputized" private individuals and "duly authorized" public authorities? Since the authority wielded by public administrators is delegated to them by "the people," by what funny metaphysic does the extension of that authority "one more step" to private firms constitute any moral (or constitutional) problem whatsoever? The fact that "many different officials contribute in many different ways to decisions and policies in the modern state" gives rise to what has been aptly labeled "the problem of many hands"—the problem of sorting out and deciding who in government is responsible for political or policy outcomes.[71] The private management of prisons and jails brings into focus what may be termed "the problem of whose hands"—the problem of sorting out and deciding whether the moral responsibility for given communal functions ought to be lodged mainly or solely in the hands of government authorities.[72]

In my judgment, to continue to be legitimate and morally significant, the authority to govern those behind bars, to deprive citizens of their liberty, to coerce (and even kill) them, must remain in the hands of government authorities. Regardless of which penological theory is in vogue, the message "Those who abuse liberty shall live without it" is the philosophical brick and mortar of every correctional facility. That message ought to be conveyed by the offended community of law-abiding citizens, through its public agents, to the incarcerated individual. The administration of prisons and jails involves the legally sanctioned coercion of some citizens by others. This coercion is exercised in the name of the offended public. The badge of the arresting police officer, the robes of the judge, and the state patch of the corrections officer are symbols of the inherently public nature of crime and punishment.[73]

The moral implications of privatizing the administration of this central communal function—administering justice to those whose acts endanger the public welfare—can be illustrated by some analogous situations. Let us suppose that the issue is not who ought to administer justice to the community's offenders but who ought to administer rewards to the community's heroes? Consider the following hypothetical scenario. You have worked tirelessly on behalf of your fellow citizens. You have (pick your favorite) discovered a cure for cancer/negotiated successfully with the nation's friends and foes abroad/made a major contribution to the performing arts. For your good deeds, you are to receive the National Medal of Honor. The big day arrives. The crowd is assembled on the White House lawn. The Marine Band begins to play. You gaze into the crowd and notice that the distinguished-looking guests (and the "Marine" musicians) have little pins on their lapels that read "MCA" for Medals Corporation of America. The ceremony is grand. The crowd roars as your name is called and the "president" (better-looking than the real commander-in-chief) shakes your hand and embraces you. You know for a fact that by every tangible measure—the physical quality of your medal, the warmth of the presenter, the duration and intensity of the crowd's ovations, the sound of the music, and so forth—MCA gave you a ceremony that was far superior to the one you would have received had the government and its officials presided; moreover, MCA spent only one-third of what the government would have spent. Satisfied? Bothered? Why?

In scene one of the second scenario, a mother is driven crazy by her mischievous son who pulls his sister's hair, flushes the goldfish down the toilet, and then carves his initials on the new dining room table. "Just wait till your father gets home!" she yells. In scene two, in response to the same misdeeds the mother yells, "Just wait till Child Rearing Associates, Incorporated opens!" Assume that, whatever the favored method of child discipline, CRA's staff of child development experts can administer it better and more consistently than can the parents themselves—and the parents know it. Is there yet any reason to prefer the first scene to the second?

To bring matters closer to home, let us suppose that the CCA has proven that it can do everything the privatizers have promised and more. The corporation decides to branch out and changes its name to Criminal Justice Corporation of America. It provides a full range of criminal justice services—"cops, courts, and corrections." In an unguarded moment, a CJCA official boasts that "our firm can arrest 'em, try 'em, lock 'em up, and if need be fry 'em for less." Is there anything wrong with CJCA?

In each case, the relevant human collectivity abdicated its duty to reward or punish its members—the nation its heroes, the family unit its children, the community of law-abiding citizens its criminals. Implicit in the delegation of such responsibility is a denial of the group's reality and moral integrity. Ought not the nation express its gratitude directly through the agency of its elected and duly appointed public representatives? Ought not parents themselves administer loving discipline to their children? Is it not the community of law-abiding citizens that is offended by criminals and that must take them in hand?

In this connection, the opinions of New York State's Corrections Commissioner Thomas A. Coughlin III are interesting and revealing.[74] Coughlin argues on moral grounds against the private management of adult prisons and jails. He is not opposed in principle, to the private operation of juvenile facilities. He reasons that there is something inherently stigmatizing about being confined in publicly administered facilities. In his view, private institutions provide a way of "drawing heat" from the symbolic moral disapprobation that society heaps on criminals who "do time" in public institutions. He believes that many classes of juvenile offenders ought to be spared this moral condemnation; hence, he has no moral qualms about placing juveniles in private hands. At the same time, he believes that adult criminals deserve this moral disapproval and so it is the government itself, as the agent of the disapproving public, that ought to assume direct responsibility for the care and custody of persons in adult prisons and jails.

Whatever the specific merits or demerits of Coughlin's position, his views are evocative of a general question that is central to any properly constructed normative case for (or against) private prison and jail management: If "everything else is equal" (or, as I suggested at the beginning of this section, if every tangible advantage clearly belongs to private management), does it matter whether the corrections officer's patch reads "Corrections Corporation of America" or "State of Tennessee"? Where government behind bars is concerned, is management by private hands morally distinguishable from management by public hands?

To make symbolic differences the sum and substance of one's normative position on private prison and jail management (or any other issue) is to forsake moral reasoning for a species of mysticism. It is not unreasonable to doubt both the practical efficacy and the moral significance of what have been termed "institutional props of authority."[75] But it is not going too far in that direction to argue that such differences may matter in ways that make privatizing this particular communal function especially problematic and wholly resistant to facile moral judgments of any kind.

At a minimum, it can be said that, both in theory and in practice, the formulation and administration of criminal laws by recognized public authorities is one of the liberal state's most central and historic functions; indeed, in some formulations it is the liberal state's reason for being. In the opening chapter of

Locke's Second Treatise of Government, political power is defined as "a Right of making Laws with Penalties of Death, and consequently all less Penalties, for the Regulating and preserving of Property, and of employing the force of the Community, in the Execution of such Laws . . . and all this only for the Publick Good."[76] Criminal law is the one area where U.S. citizens have conceded to the state an almost unqualified right to act in the name of the polity, and hence one of the few areas where one can discern a conception of political community that is not a mere collage of individualistic and materialistic assumptions. It is not unreasonable to suggest that "employing the force of the Community" via private penal management undermines the moral writ of the community itself.

But what about the argument that the community's moral writ remains intact so long as the presentencing process remains in public hands? Returning to our earlier illustration, one might assert that the CJCA would be wrong but that the CCA is not. There are at least two problems with this position. First, it rests on the wholly untenable presumption that the administration of penal facilities involves no exercise of discretion by the administrators, at least none that would affect the duration of an inmate's stay or the basic conditions of confinement. There is, however, a mountain of empirical studies that show how much discretion is of necessity vested in those at every level—from the commissioner's office to the cell block—who run prisons and jails.[77] Any normative case for private penal management that hinges on a resurrection and acceptance of the thoroughly discredited notion of a politics-administration dichotomy is prima facie too weak to require a rebuttal.[78] Second, it is simply unclear how one can distinguish morally between private and public courts, and between private and public policing, and yet see no moral difference between private and public corrections. The moral logic required to accept a CCA while rejecting a CJCA would appear to be the same sort of moral quackery that one hears when the death penalty issue is raised and supporters of privatization declare that whereas corporations may "play jailer" (even for life), the government alone should "play executioner." Those who claim that a CCA is morally legitimate have no grounds on which to reject not only private police but also corporate judges, juries, and executioners as well. One can imagine the employees of a private corrections firm being put through some sort of "publicization" ritual in which they are instructed to raise their right hand, read the state constitution, and salute the governor. But so long as their organization remains private, the chain of delegated authority can be said to have a weak link.

There is no limit to the amount of hairsplitting that can occur in the endless discussions of such points. Though we have only scratched the surface of the moral issues, enough has been said, I hope, to suggest that serious moral and constitutional problems surround (and may militate against) the private management of prisons and jails.

Conclusion: A Better Corrections Alternative?

Privatization efforts have been motivated by the belief that public correctional institutions are too crowded, but the crowding problem is less acute than is commonly supposed.[79] Privatization initiatives have been offered as ways of tightening the reins on corrections budgets, yet spending on corrections remains a pittance compared with most other public expenditures, and the public sector has made innovations that promise to reduce the taxpayers' burden.[80] Privatization ventures are driven by the perception that public corrections managers have failed, but the public record is by no means consistently bleak and in some respects it is quite outstanding.[81] The problems of crowding, rising costs, and failed management are most real in the area of higher-custody prisons and jails, but at present the privatizers offer no help for these institutions.

In the 1960s a cadre of self-styled penal reformers shouted "Tear down the walls!"; in the 1980s, another cadre of self-styled penal reformers is shouting "Sell them!" We did not heed the former, and there is as yet no good practical or moral reason to heed the latter. When the privatizers boast that they will do better because they, unlike their public sector counterparts, will be immune from the administrative and financial woes caused by governmental red tape, they should be reminded that "one person's red tape may be another's treasured safeguard."[82] Even a cursory review of the historical, political, and administrative issues surrounding private prison and jail management raises grave doubts, and not a few fears, about the prospects of privatization in this area.

The central moral issues surrounding private prison and jail management have little to do with the profit motive of the privatizers and much to do with the propriety, in a constitutional democracy, of delegating the authority to administer criminal justice to nonpublic individuals and groups. Throughout much of U.S. history, government has allowed too many of the nation's prisons and jails to be ill-managed, undermanaged, or not managed at all. Especially in light of the progress that has been made in the last two decades, no self-respecting constitutional government would again abdicate its responsibility for protecting and guiding criminals in state custody.

The most promising corrections alternative is to focus on the nitty-gritty of governing penal institutions well with the human and financial resources available in the public sector, jurisdiction by jurisdiction. In jurisdictions where public corrections agencies have used their considerable discretion and exercised their coercive powers with common sense and compassion, prisons and jails have been relatively safe, clean, and cost-effective. But far too many institutions are still unsatisfactory, and more progress must be made in public corrections management. Private corrections firms like the CCA have run juvenile centers and other facilities admirably. But this country's prisons and jails are most likely to be improved if they are viewed not as a private enterprise to be administered in the pursuit of profit, but as a public trust to be administered on behalf of the community and in the name of civility and justice. The choice is between the scribbled promises of privatization and the unfulfilled duty to govern.

When Government Fails:
Going Private as a Last Resort
DOUGLAS C. MCDONALD

A few months ago, I received a telephone call from a civic official asking if I would come to his city and "audit" the local jail system for the board of county managers that runs the county government. The jails there hold several thousand inmates, which makes the agency larger than many state prison systems. The conditions of confinement in these facilities are notoriously bad. For the better part of a decade, the jails have been found by a federal court to be in violation of the Eighth Amendment's ban on "cruel and usual punishment," and there seems to be little likelihood that these conditions will be eliminated in the foreseeable future. Even though the board members have governing authority in this jurisdiction, they seemed powerless to find out what was going on in their jails, much less to reform them enough for the federal court to drop the lawsuit.

The problem stems in large part from the fact that jails are run not by the board or its appointed agents but by a sheriff who is an independently elected official. A popular political figure, he has been reelected many times and has managed to build the strong support of the governor and other important state officials. Insulated from having to take the heat for raising taxes or cutting other county services, the sheriff advocates consistently higher budgets for his agency and has no reason other than civic-mindedness to restrain his budget requests. At the time of their call to me, the county's managers were faced with the need to cut the government's budget because of falling tax revenues, but they could not get any realistic indication from the sheriff of how the cuts would affect his operations. Instead, the sheriff said simply that he would have to release prisoners onto the streets. Ignorant about what goes on inside the jails and afraid to call the sheriff's bluff, the board was hard pressed to ask him to accept budget cuts proportionate to those of other city agencies.

In these circumstances, might not contracting for a privately operated jail provide the means for more effective management and increased accountability? When the commissioners of Bay County, Florida, were in a similar situation, they contracted with the Corrections Corporation of America to take control of the county's jails. Within a short time, these facilities had been renovated and conditions improved so substantially that a lawsuit that had been filed against the county was dropped.[1] By taking responsibility for administering the jail out of the sheriff's hands and writing an explicit contract that set clear obligations, the country Board of Commissioners gained *more* direct and effective control over the jail than it had previously had, and performance improved dramatically.

Clearly, turning to private firms is not necessary, but consider the alternatives. One option is to compel local authorities to heed what John DiIulio calls their "duty to govern."[2] But how is this to be done? In the county to which I was being invited, as in many of the nation's nearly four thousand other counties, government responsibility is fragmented, so county managers have power to finance the jail but no authority to manage it. That job belongs to the sheriff, an independent political power with his own political base. Nor is there any local auditing authority in that county. That responsibility rests with the state auditor's office, which is distant and exercises little oversight of local affairs. The real issue, anyway, is not whether the public funds are being mismanaged in a legal sense but whether the local government is coherent and effective. Unfortunately, the connecting tissue among the various agencies—especially the institutional mechanisms for achieving accountability and control—and the elected officials is weakly developed. The failure of local governments to govern well is the principal reason persons demanding adequate correctional services have often had to go to the federal courts for help.

Even though the privatization of correctional services may be a means for raising the level of services and for strengthening accountability and control, it is being faulted on several grounds. They include questions about the propriety and constitutionality of privatization and doubts about whether the promised benefits really outweigh the risks.

The Constitutionality of Privatization

In 1989, a resolution was drafted by a committee of the American Bar Association urging jurisdictions to proceed "with extreme caution in considering possible authorization of contracts with private corporations or other private entities for the operation of prisons or jails.[3] Furthermore, in the report accompanying the proposed resolution, the committee argued that "there can be no doubt that an attempt to delegate total operational responsibility for a prison or jail would raise grave questions of constitutionality under both the federal Constitution and the constitutions of the fifty states. The more sweeping the delegation, the more doubtful would be its constitutionality."[4]

On this question of constitutionality, the resolution's authors seem, in my view, to be searching for life in an issue that has been dead for some time, at least at the federal level. As David Lawrence concluded in his review of private delegations, "Private exercise of federally delegated power is no longer a federal constitutional issue."[5] For fifty years, since *Carter* v. *Carter Coal Company*,[6] the courts have allowed the federal government to delegate broad powers to private actors. Nor has delegation by state and local governments been seen as a federal constitutional issue since the 1920s. For example, private bail bondsmen's powers to arrest and detain those for whom they posted bond have consistently been upheld.[7] Private security guards are also permitted to detain persons forcefully.[8]

Despite the fact that the U.S. Supreme Court has not been troubled by the delegation doctrine since 1948, Ira Robbins, the author of a report on which the ABA resolution was based, argues that the federal courts "might apply more stringent standards of review to delegations that affect liberty interests than they do to those that affect property interests."[9] This amounts to little more than a hope and a suggestion that the courts will do so, however. Bail bondsmen's powers certainly affect liberty interests, as do private security guards' powers, and the courts have not viewed this as raising a federal constitutional issue.

Although no case brought before the federal courts has challenged head on the unconstitutionality of privately administered imprisonment, judges have been presented with opportunities to rule against them and have not done so. For example, in a 1984 case[10] concerning the delegation of federal detention powers to a private firm, the U.S. District Court for the Southern District of Texas did not rule that it was illegal. This case was brought on behalf of twenty-six Colombian stowaways who were discovered aboard a ship docked in the port of Houston. Because stowaways are considered excludable aliens in usual circumstances, federal immigration rules prescribe that they be held on board ship until quick transfer out of the United States can be arranged. Given the large number of stowaways discovered on this ship, Paul

O'Neill of the U.S. Immigration and Naturalization Service granted Danner, Inc., a private security firm, the authority to hold them in temporary detention. The twenty-six aliens were confined in a cell designed for six persons, and after two days' they tried to escape. The Danner guards accidentally killed one individual and wounded another.

Attorneys acting on behalf of the aliens argued that the INS failed to oversee their detention, and that this detention amounted to punishment that violated the aliens' constitutional rights. The INS responded that it was not liable because the plaintiffs' detention arose from purely private acts. Challenging this, the plaintiffs' attorney declared that the Constitution does not permit the government to "retail out the detention of human beings." Chief Judge John Singleton agreed in part, holding that "detention . . . is the exclusive prerogative of the state," and that the private firm was providing a public function even though its employees were private individuals.[11] Because they had been delegated detention powers by the INS, they were state actors, and the INS was liable for their actions. The judge did not rule, however, that the federal government may not delegate that authority.

State laws regarding delegation by state governments are somewhat more confusing. There is no clear legal ban on the private delegation by correctional authorities in state constitutions. But in the absence of explicit prohibitions, state governments may, according to prevailing doctrine, take any action whatsoever as long as it does not contravene the U.S. Constitution. (The established doctrine holds that state constitutions are limitations on power rather than grants of power.)[12] Nonetheless, judges in state courts have ruled inconsistently on issues regarding private delegation of state powers.[13] To clarify this legal question, legislatures in several states have passed laws authorizing the delegation of correctional authority to private individuals or firms.[14]

Robbins recognizes that the private delegation of a state government's administrative powers is not barred by law, but then asserts that private incarceration is fundamentally different from other kinds of delegation, which he suggests may be grounds for finding private prison operations unconstitutional. The difference, in his view, is that incarcerating prisoners "is a power that states traditionally had to themselves," and "because this function is 'intrinsically governmental in nature,' the courts may distinguish private-prison operations on delegation grounds."[15] Robbins concludes that therefore, "privatization of incarceration may be neither constitutional nor wise."[16] The report to the ABA's House of Delegates concurred with Robbins's argument, asserting that "power over the conditions of confinement of individuals convicted of violating the criminal law is a core responsibility of government, one that cannot be left to the discretion of private parties."[17]

This argument against privatization glosses over the crucial distinction between the power to *impose* imprisonment and the power to *administer* it. The power to order incarceration, and the ultimate authority over the conditions under which prisoners are confined, rests with the public authorities. In this country, only governments have the legal authority to decide who is to be imprisoned and for how long. But this principle is not violated if the administration of the imprisonment sentence is delegated to a private firms. Moreover, private delegation does not mean that power over the conditions of confinement is necessarily "left to the discretion of private parties." Governments cannot abdicate their responsibilities. The courts have established in the *Medina* case and others that private imprisonment, undertaken on behalf of government agencies, constitutes "state action," and that governments retain the ultimate responsibility for what goes on in such institutions. Furthermore, these private facilities are required to comply with the same standards that apply to public ones.[18] Delegating administrative authority for imprisonment does not free private firms to do what they want with the persons they hold. They must conform to law and established standards.

Finally, it is true that the power to order persons to be imprisoned has been a governmental power for several centuries in the West, but it cannot be said that incarceration has been an "intrinsically governmental" function. Throughout earlier centuries, right up to the twentieth, imprisonment by private parties in Anglo-American societies was commonplace and considered legitimate. To be sure, the practices of private jailing and of leasing state prison convicts to private parties were abandoned because of the scandalous conditions in which inmates were being held. But the fact that private prisons existed at all, and in such abundance, testifies to the fact that incarceration has historically not been an "intrinsically governmental" function.[19] Moreover, there still exists a variety of private halfway houses, work release centers, other residential community correctional facilities for adult criminals, and secure facilities for juveniles, all of which involve the exercise of coercive detention power. The public monopoly of prison and jail administration is of recent vintage.

Whether it is wise for imprisonment to be administered by

private firms is another matter, however. This question turns not on constitutional considerations but on other values and principles, some of which are rooted in political philosophy, as well as on other, more mundane considerations, such as cost and efficiency.

On the Propriety of Privatization

The fundamental question is not whether privately administered imprisonment is acceptable in the legal sense, but whether it offends more deeply held principles. Commenting on the current vogue for privatizing a broad number of services that are now provided mostly by governments, Robert Kuttner points out that "in organized society, we counterpose certain public values to those of a pure market. Some things aren't supposed to be bought and sold. It is against the law to sell votes, although interest groups do try to buy influence. You are not supposed to buy love, although prostitutes merchandise sex. It is against the law to buy and sell people, although many babies are virtually purchased for adoptions. But such breaches of our stated values show that society holds dear things besides markets." Many social institutions that exist reflect not simply market values but civic values, and, he argues, it consequently "offends us, as citizens, to have the national symbols auctioned off to the highest bidder."[20]

In a similar vein, John DiIulio argues that the criminal law "is the one area where U.S. citizens have conceded to the state an almost unqualified right to act in the name of the polity, and hence one of the few where one can discern a conception of political community that is not a mere collage of individualistic and materialistic assumptions." To delegate responsibility for administering prisons to private individuals threatens to "undermine the moral writ of the community itself.[21] DiIulio argues further than the "administration of criminal laws by recognized public authorities is one of the liberal state's most central and historic functions," and quotes John Locke's assertion that political power itself is defined as "a Right of making laws . . . and of employing the force of the Community, in the execution of such laws . . . for the Publick Good."[22]

The moral superiority of public over private provision of imprisonment is therefore seen to rest, in these critics' eyes, on three arguments: 1) that it is offensive to involve private interests—especially those seeking profit—in punishment, 2) that the power to make and execute laws has traditionally been a central function of the liberal state, and 3) the legitimacy of the power to administer sanctions is eroded when it is done by a private rather than a public officer. ("Does it weaken [the court's] authority," Ira Robbins asks rhetorically, "—as well as the integrity of a system of *justice*—when an inmate looks at his keeper's uniform and, instead of encountering an emblem that reads 'Federal Bureau of Prisons' or 'State Department of Corrections,' he faces one that says 'Acme Corrections Company'?"[23]

With regard to the first argument, why is a well-run privately operated facility considered more offensive than a public facility in which conditions are substandard and the treatment unconstitutional? Should not the higher value be given to the quality of treatment and conditions than to the status of the keeper? The issue of profit seeking should not divert attention from what is important. If conditions and treatment are acceptable, it should not matter that private individuals have been rewarded for putting themselves and their capital at risk in a business to provide services. Why is this any less acceptable than relying on the market to provide medical services, upon which human lives often depend? The principal issue here should be whether the overall quality of service and level of provision is likely to be higher in a market-based, privately delivered system than in a government-run system. In the case of imprisonment, if market incentives can in fact be taken advantage of to raise the standard of services, why is that not acceptable?

The second argument, that imprisonment ought to be reserved to government because the administration of the criminal law has traditionally been a governmental function, is not a strong enough principle to justify a ban on private delegation of correctional administration. If this argument rests on the belief that the state possesses an exclusive right to administer punishment, then it runs counter to the assumptions on which our democratic system of government is based. One of the foundations of our political system is the notion, derived from theories of social contract, that all rights are individual and not collective. They reside ultimately in the people, and governments derive their rights by virtue of individuals entering into a social contract, delegating to government certain rights, including the right to punish on their behalf. One need not conclude, as philospher Robert Nozick has demonstrated, that the state's de facto monopoly on punitive powers means that the state has special *rights* that are not derived from popular (and individual) will.[24] Consequently, "the state does not *own* the right to punish," concludes Charles Logan in his argument on behalf of private prisons. "It merely *administers* it in trust, on behalf of the people and under the rule of law. Because the authority does not originate with the state, it does not attach inherently or uniquely to it, and can be passed along."[25]

DiIulio, for one, does not go so far as to assert that the power to sanction is (or must be) an exclusive right of the state. Instead, he raises what amounts to a utilitarian defense: that the sense of moral community, the glue that holds society together, will be weakened by having private agents rather than public ones administer correctional sanctions. This argument constitutes the third line of defense.

Viewed in this way, the issue is not really a moral one but an empirical one: Is the social cohesiveness of the larger community in fact lessened by such delegations of authority? Or, in the case of prisoners, is the perceived legitimacy of the sanction undercut by having "Acme Corrections Company" on the correctional officers' arm patch? With regard to the latter question, I suspect that one would find that the logo on the arm patch matters little to most inmates, because they know that they were sent to the institution by a judge acting on behalf of the state, and the larger community, for violating the laws of society. Moreover, their release will be decided by public parole authorities (in those states that have not yet abolished parole release) or judges rather than by private individuals. A great many inmates are already profoundly alienated from society and its laws. That jailers are employees of a private firms rather than employees of a distant, and nearly-alien, government authority probably matters little to such prisoners.

With respect to the question of whether the moral cohesiveness of the larger society will be affected, I cannot imagine that the state will be drained of authority by the delegation of operational responsibilities to private firms. These firms are clearly acting as agents of state power.

This is not an argument for the pervasive privatization of government responsibilities. Judicial and legislative functions should be public, especially those in the realm of criminal law. The risks of weakening the moral authority of the system of justice are more substantial if judicial or legislative decisions are made by private actors. If the responsibilities for making laws and for choosing sanctions are kept within the province of government, the tendency to distort their exercise in favor of private interests is restrained, though not always perfectly, and the rule of law is thereby advanced over the rule of private vengeance.

Running the institutions to which public judges send criminals is a different matter, however. The legitimacy of the state and of the criminal law is likely to be maintained by having public officers pass judgment in criminal cases, even though the place of punishment (or correction) may be operated by the Acme Corrections Company. If it is not, one should worry about the myriad of privately operated programs that exist throughout the adult and juvenile justice systems. Should such private involvement be proscribed? Or should one try to find a principled line between correctional programs that require incarceration and those that require less burdensome obligations? The search for such a line makes little sense. Many of the innovations in criminal corrections have been pioneered by private organizations, and to ban their involvement for the purpose of achieving consistency with a ban on privately operated prisons would be to throw the baby out with the bath water.

The matter of private imprisonment is undoubtedly complicated by the fact that correctional officials often exercise powers that seem similar to judicial ones. Prison or jail administrators in government-run facilities have generally been delegated the right to discipline inmates for violations of prison rules. Certain liberties can be taken away, and administrators may even place an inmate in solitary confinement—the "jail within the jail." Especially in those jurisdictions where release from prison or jail depends in any measure on good behavior, these disciplinary powers take on special significance; so does the fact that correctional officers have the authority to exercise force (including deadly force) against prisoners.

Although it is true that the deprivation of liberties in the prison or jail makes these administrative powers quite weighty, administrators in many institutional spheres exercise powers that have substantial impact on peoples' lives. What matters is that this administration is carried out in ways that conform with law and due process. The legitimacy of the activity depends not on the status of the actor (whether an employee of a public or a private organization) but on whether the act itself is lawful. Therefore, even the actions of public officials are illegitimate if they violate law or due process. This principle is well established.

Still, there remains the possibility that decisions regarding

prisoners' liberty will be affected illegitimately by private interests. If, for example, private correctional facilities are paid by
governments for housing prisoners, might there not be a pressure to keep these people from being released? By fabricating
disciplinary violations, and by lifting prisoners' credits against
their sentences for good behavior, could not private firms ma-
nipulate the demand for their services at the expense of prisoners? Such tendencies may indeed exist (although we have no
indication that they are given free rein), but one need not out-
law private correctional management altogether for this reason.
To counter whatever tendency may exist for such self-interested
distortions of the disciplinary process, governments may choose
to create a mechanism for reviewing decisions that affect prisoners' liberty, or even establish a process whereby the decisions
are made by public officials.

Does Privatization Weaken Public Control of Prisons and Jails?

At the root of much of the concern about delegating operational
responsibilities to private firms is the belief that such delegation weakens public control of correctional facilities. This is
based on several assumptions. Private facilities are assumed to
be less accountable and less responsive to governments because
a formal legal boundary separates the public sector from the
private sector. In public correctional facilities, an unbroken
chain of command is assumed to exist between the officer who
deals with inmates on a day-to-day basis and the highest elected public official in the jurisdiction. In private firms, no such
direct linkage exists. A legal barrier divides the governing entity and private correctional firms, and thus divide is bridged by
contractual agreements that have to be negotiated and then put
in writing. The barrier, the break that it makes in the administrative chain of command, and the rigidity of the contract that
bridges private firms and governments are assumed to increase
the difficulties in controlling prisons and jails. They are also
assumed to reduce the likelihood that private facilities will conform to legal and professional standards of performance.

The Prevalence of "Government Failure"

Unfortunately, control over public correctional facilities in many places is neither as direct nor as effective as the idealized model of the unbroken chain of command suggests. Nor do the incentives that prevail in many public correctional agencies engender good correctional administration and performance. Indeed, the performance of a very large number of prisons, and especially jails, is not only below professional correctional standards but also below the much lower floor of constitutionally acceptable standards. Only a dozen of the nation's approximately 3,500 jails and 21 percent of all state and federal prisons had been accredited by the Commission on Accreditation for Corrections as meeting established professional standards by 1986.[26] As of mid-1988, the prison systems in thirty-nine states, the District of Columbia, Puerto Rico, and the Virgin Islands were under federal court orders to remedy conditions of confinement that had been found to be violative of constitutional standards.[27] According to a survey administered in mid-1986, 27 percent of all jails holding 100 inmates or more—which, taken as a group, held about three-fourths of the nation's jail inmates at that time—were under court orders to reduce overcrowding or to improve other unconstitutional conditions of confinement.[28]

Although the causes of deficient prison and jail services are several, the provision of adequate services in many jurisdictions stems from what can be termed "government failure." Political and administrative controls over correctional administration are excessively fragmented; too many correctional agencies are insulated from the higher levels of government, which has given administrators room to wield broad discretionary powers; and administrators have resisted being held accountable for their performance. This is more true today with respect to local jails than for state prisons, because the control and accountability of prison officials have improved enormously during the past two decades. Prior to the 1960s, prisons were permitted much autonomy by state governments. Central control over wardens was weak, in part because wardens developed their own political constituencies in state legislatures. Oversight was nearly nonexistent. The result was that prisons often became little duchies, or perhaps more accurately, quasi plantations. The failure of these political and administrative systems not only to provide adequate services but to prevent appalling abuses was so profound that control had to come from outside—

from the federal courts. Under the pressures of litigation, and more recently, of rising costs, prison administration in most states has been brought under more effective state government control.[29] Improvement of jail administration has been much slower.

Especially in situations where the public correctional authority has successfully resisted being held accountable either to higher governing authorities or for meeting standards of performance, going outside government and delegating administrative authority to a private firm may increase rather than attenuate control. Opportunities for such improvement are most abundant at the local level, where administrative responsibilities are often more fragmented. State prison systems are now more tightly administered by central offices, which are administered, in turn, by commissioners who serve at the pleasure of governors. At the state level, privatization is less likely, as a consequence, to bring tighter administrative control (but still may be appealing for other reasons).

Incentives for Doing Good and Doing Bad

Critics worry that private interest in profits may prevail over the public interest in providing adequate services to inmates and to governments. "Cost-cutting measures will run rampant," according to a statement by the American Bar Association. "Conditions of confinement will be kept to the minimum that the law requires. . . . In short, the private sector is more interested in doing well than in doing good."[30] Although these assertions seem to some to express obvious truths, they ignore the incentives that exist to compel good performance by private firms and overestimate the efficacy of such incentives in public correctional agencies. Private firms may try to provide minimum or sub-standard services, but they do so at the risk of losing their contract. Moreover, governments may exert even more control over private facilities than over public ones through the device of the contract. Writing into the contract what shall be the required conditions of confinement gives the government power to compel adherence to those standards, perhaps more than public legislators or even governors have when services are provided by public agencies, simply because the government has the ability to sever the contract entirely or to award it to another competitor at the end of the contract period (which is more likely). The ability to replace middle managers, much less an entire department, is not available to most corrections commissioners in public systems. Commissioners in some states cannot replace even their chief deputies because of civil service protections. (Contracting in and of itself does not provide a governing body with strong control over the other party, however. Provisions for monitoring, for giving notice of inadequate performance, for developing plans to remedy such performance, and for termination need to be so written that the government's ability to terminate for cause is well protected.)

Laws regarding liability also create incentives for private firms to provide adequate and fair services. The federal courts have clearly established that private correctional firms are liable for monetary damages if inmates' rights are violated, whereas public officials acting on behalf of public authorities are not.[31] Private firms have to carry costly insurance against claims, and these costs go up with numerous or large claims. Private operators therefore face the possibility of being put out of business by lawsuits if they exploit inmates unfairly.

Exploiting inmates also increases tensions in prisons and jails, as well as the likelihood of riots, fires, and other "disturbances," none of which further the interests of private operators. This was emphasized by administrator of a private jail, who explained that it was in his short-term interest to provide adequate services to prisoners and to do so in a professional manner that they respected. The unrest generated if he were to do otherwise would make the jail a harder place in which to work and would increase staff turnover and associated costs.[32] Avoiding violence, riots, and bad morale among staff members is also in private firms' longer-term interest because their ability to stay in business depends upon whether they continue to please their clients—the governments with which they contract.

This suggests another structural difference in the incentives that operate in public agencies and in private markets. As Robert Dahl and Charles Lindblom have argued, a price system in which self-interested actors offer services to consumers is more likely to produce the performance sought than is provision by command-and-control systems in hierarchically structured public agencies. The penalties and rewards for bad and good performance are more automatic in a price system because they are intrinsic to it. In public agencies, the review of performance becomes a task that somebody has to be assigned to do. This does not imply that hierarchical supervision is always unsatisfactory. It simply suggests that a check on performance becomes a burden on some part of the hierarchy, whereas in a price system, much of the task is accomplished as a by-product of consumers' purchasing decisions—or, in the case we are concerned with here, the decisions about choosing from among contractors' bids.[33]

Can Private Correctional Firms Save the Taxpayer Money?

Whether these various incentives actually result in the provision of good services, and at a cost lower than that incurred by public correctional agencies, cannot be conclusively answered at this early stage of the industry's development. But whereas the critics are predisposed to say that the private firms will not be able to do so, the evidence to date suggests the opposite. The Corrections Corporation of America began making a modest profit in 1988, and its facilities have not been found deficient by observers. The jail in Bay County, Florida, is far and away a better institution under the CCA's authority than it was when the sheriff ran it. Similarly, the Santa Fe County Board of Commissioners is pleased that the spending for its jail was brought under control when the CCA resumed control of it.[34] Logan and McGriff's analysis of the firm's Silverdale Detention Center in Tennessee found that public operation would be more expensive, and there is no indication that service is poorer.[35] The Wackenhut Corporation's detention centers, which hold illegal aliens under contract with the Immigration and Naturalization Service, are not losing money. As my analysis in my first essay in this volume shows, the cost of detaining aliens in private detention centers has been, in most years, lower than the cost of detaining them in facilities operated directly by the government. Nor are the units of government that contract with these private firms reporting negatively about their experiences.[36]

John Donahue has argued that private jails and prisons are not likely to be more productive—and, consequently, less expensive to operate—than public facilities, because the primary tasks of correctional officers (watching, counting, and escorting prisoners) do not lend themselves to labor-saving technologies that help bring down costs.[37] This ignores, however, other methods of cost reduction. Private firms can lower their costs because they can more easily avoid some of the inefficiencies that governments impose upon themselves. For example, they can build facilities that are designed to require fewer persons to staff, whereas governments often prefer to renovate buildings that they already own, which frequently results in inefficient design constraints. (Labor costs represent approximately 80 percent of the total cost of a correctional facility over its lifetime; small efficiencies in staffing thus yield large savings over the long term.) Private firms are also able to avoid legal obstacles to efficient construction that exist in some states. In New York, for example, three statutes, collectively known as the Wicks Law, require the use of at least three contractors instead of one general contractor for new public buildings or renovations of public buildings that cost more than $50,000. Passed to favor labor unions and construction contractors, these laws add at least $100 million annually to New York City's construction bills.[38] Others states have laws requiring that supplies used in public facilities be purchased locally.

In making purchasing decisions, private correctional firms are also less likely to be swayed by electoral considerations. When jails are run by elected sheriffs, efficient administration and cost-efficiency may take a back seat to politics. By purchasing from local buyers, elected officials have a potent means of developing their political base.[39]

That private firms may be able to deliver prison services at a lower cost than public agencies should not be surprising, given the firms' experience of contracting for a variety of other services. In their review of current research on contracting, Robert Poole and Philip Fixler conclude: "On the whole, the empirical studies have found that contracting out tends to be less costly than governmental provision. These findings cover a number of distinct services and pertain to a variety of geographical areas. Therefore, it seems reasonable to conclude that the evidence in favor of contracting out is moderately strong."[40]

The Risks of Privatization: Monopoly and Entrenchment

Most of the benefits that may result from privatization do not derive simply from the fact that the provider is a private entity rather than a public one. These advantages stem principally from the existence of a market for correctional services that is competitive and not dominated by only a few firms. In a competitive market, governments have several firms from which to choose. To the extent that these firms compete with one another in offering the lowest price for their services, there will be a tendency toward cost control, and governments will be able to take advantage of this rivalry by picking the most cost-efficient provider. If governments have the option of canceling or not renewing a contract and signing up another provider, firms will be forced to perform effectively or risk going out of business. Moreover, a firm's performance will be measured not only against standards agreed upon in contracts but also against what the competition offers. If, on the other hand, monopoly conditions prevail because a single provider becomes entrenched in the jurisdiction, the governing entity will loose freedom of action and become excessively dependent upon the private provider, and the advantages of privatization may evaporate.

This raises three important questions. First, is a private imprisonment industry likely to be a competitive one? Second, what conditions are most conducive to competitiveness, and what steps can be taken to sustain it? Third, if monopolistic provision does occur, are there steps that the government can take to protect itself from the inherent risks while continuing to contract for prisons or jails?

At present, there are relatively few competitors in the private imprisonment industry, and some government Requests for Proposals have even gone begging for lack of interested bidders. There is, however, a potentially large market for private firms' services. If the experiment with four 500-bed privately operated prisons in Texas proves successful, nervousness about contracting for maximum-security facilities will probably abate, and more states may contract for facilities. Given the nearly relentless pressure to build and staff new prisons for a growing number of inmates, the prospect of contracting with private firms to operate these prisons at their own risk will probably become more appealing.

The accumulation of large capital assets by private firms may ultimately work to restrict competitiveness, however. Oliver Williamson has argued that when services are provided through contractual arrangements, competition among providers is severely constrained if the assets specific to a contractual relationship are substantial and not easily redeployed.[41] To the extent that such assets exist, the original contracting firm will have an advantage over other bidders, and parity among them will not exist. To take a hypothetical example, the Acme Corrections Corporation will thus have a significant competitive edge over all other firms when its contract comes to an end, simply because it already has a facility in place that has largely been paid for during the first contract period. With this barrier to entry and the limited competition that results from it, the number of suppliers that will be willing to offer their services, and that will be able to do so at a competitive price, will be fewer than in a market where no transaction-specific assets have been developed. Buyers will become more dependent upon the original contractor, will find it difficult to exit if its performance falls below the agreed-upon level, and may be faced with the prospect of having to create a new public correctional agency in the absence of a suitable private provider. In such circumstances, the power of the buyer is much reduced, the cost to the buyer of ending the contractual relationship increases, and the supplier's ability to exact higher fees for its services is consequently strengthened.

This suggests that if governments want to maximize the conditions for competitiveness in the private corrections industry and to protect themselves against the risk of contractor failure, they will be best served by owning the facilities and contracting only for their operation. Entry costs will thereby be reduced, permitting easier "hit and run" entry.[42] Contracting only for operations is an especially appropriate strategy, given the structure of the imprisonment market. County governments offer the largest potential market because approximately 3,500 counties have jails, compared with only fifty states, in almost all of which only one adult jail is supported. Because the purchasing decisions are made rarely (usually every few years), and because one firm can gain a nearly overwhelming edge over potential competitors by building a facility that it owns, a market in which physical plants, management, and labor are bought and sold in bundles is unlikely to remain competitive for very long.

Even if a sole provider becomes entrenched in a jurisdiction, a privately operated prison or jail may still be preferable to a re-created public agency. In such a situation, however, market mechanisms are less likely to regulate performance to the benefit of the buyer. To ensure adequate performance, governments might choose to build regulatory structures similar to those that regulate public utilities. This will raise the federal government's overall cost of providing correctional services (but such an arrangement may still be preferable, on balance, to public provision in some instances).

Private Ownership and Financing: Loosening Controls on Debt

The delegation of responsibility to operate prisons and jails is only one form that privatization has taken. The other is the privatization of ownership, which may or may not be accompanied by private operations. (A firm may build its own facility and then lease it to a government to operate.) This phenomenon raises issues that are different from those posed by the delegation of operating authority. The principal problem is that resorting to private ownership threatens to weaken the fiscal discipline of governments.

In the late 1970s and early 1980s, stimulated by the liberalized treatment of depreciation in the Economic Recovery Tax Act of 1981, bond underwriters and municipal finance officers at state and local levels began to devise new ways of financing capital projects of all kinds—fire trucks, computers, telecommunications systems, and various types of facilities including prisons. Conventional methods such as the issuance of general obligation bonds, backed by the full faith and credit of the government, were becoming less attractive and less feasible. Debt ceilings were being reached in many communities. Popular movements to limit government expenditure and debt stimulated legislation that made increasing debt more difficult; thus voters were increasingly unwilling to approve measures that meant going into debt further to build prisons. The conventional process was to request voter approval in scheduled elections, which often meant waiting years.

Faced with a rising tide of prisoners and badly overcrowded correctional facilities, finance officers at state and local levels have resorted to new "creative financing" methods to encourage construction of new correctional facilities. Owned by private corporations and financed through the corporate bond market, these facilities are then leased to governments for their use or sold to them on an installment basis—that is, through a lease-purchase arrangement, whereby government leases the facility from the private concern and then purchases it at the end of an agreed-upon period.[43] Because payments under leases are not legally considered debt payments but are operating costs, governments are able to acquire capital without going further into debt, at least in the strictly legal sense of the word.

Reliance on the creative financing of prisons and jails unduly relaxes the discipline on spending that conventional debt restrictions impose. Although the payment of lease fees is not legally considered debt, it is indeed a debt in reality. To make debt offerings sufficiently attractive to investors, the issuing entity—which is legally private but may have been created by governments specifically for the purpose of raising private capital, and is thus controlled entirely by government officials sitting on the board of directors, but may be operated entirely with no address except a post office box—extracts from governments restrictive promises that come approximate those in the agreements given to holders of general obligation bonds. Even though governments do not obligate future legislatures to appropriate funds for lease payments (which would constitute debt, officially defined), governments do enter into agreements specifying that if they cancel their leases, they cannot enter into another lease with another party for construction of a replacement facility. These "nonsubstitutability" agreements, coupled with the assurance that the project is essential (and therefore not likely to be canceled a few years later), have been viewed by the securities-rating industry being almost as safe as municipal bonds. (The risk to the investors is not quite as low as that of a general obligation bond debt instrument, however; investors are consequently paid a higher rate of return for bearing the higher risk.) If governments fail to appropriate funds needed to pay the leasing fees—payments that are then used by the private entity to pay dividends to private investors—investor confidence in the stability of these instruments will be shaken and perhaps destroyed.

If voters have confidence that public officials are managing mounting debt obligations well (including both legally defined debt and the quasi-debt obligations incurred through lease-purchase agreements), there is little reason for concern. The risk of creative financing in the correctional arena, however, is that the further loosening of restraints on government expenditure will exacerbate a negative dynamic that pervades in criminal justice policymaking. In promising to control crime through higher levels of imprisonment, but failing to produce the desired results, many legislatures have intended to throw ever-greater quantifies of resources in their efforts to find a cure. "As long as levels of crime are high enough to generate substantial anxiety, those who view increased imprisonment as a solution will continue to demand more prisons and will do so in terms that do not change markedly at any level of incarceration," observe Franklin Zimring and Gordon Hawkins in their analysis of costs and benefits of imprisonment. "Indeed, the more attenuated the link between the malady and the proposed remedy, the more insatiable will be the demand for more of the remedial measure."[44]

The only brake on this tendency is likely to be the pain of paying for such policies. By reducing the obstacles to incurring de facto debt, officials can promise to provide still higher levels of incarceration to present generations while obligating later generations of taxpayers to pay for them. "Buy now, pay later" plans are undoubtedly tempting to public officials who are caught in the bind of trying to placate vocal demands for services on one side and public resistance to higher taxes on the other. This is precisely why state constitutions require governments to win voters' approval of public debt increases.

Rather than trying to buy their way out of this bind (and thereby following a course that entails higher levels of *future* debt repayment and much larger expenditures to operate the additional prisons), a more prudent solution might be for public officials to balance available resources, the public's willingness to bear taxes, and alternative penal strategies that deliver just results without compromising public safety. Privatization of ownership and financing, and of facility operations, is not a desirable long-term solution to the current penal crisis. A more direct solution is for legislatures to devise sentencing policies that are geared to a fixed number of imprisonment cells, rather than allowing public officials to be free of resource constraints.[45]

Conclusion

The thorough privatization of prisons and jails in the United States is neither necessary nor desirable. Correctional facilities and agencies in many places are run well by governments and provide commendable levels and types of services. In many other places, however, they are not. When governments are not able or willing to attempt to overcome the obstacles to providing satisfactory penal services, contracting with the private sector to operate prisons, jails, or detention centers may be the most effective strategy for increasing the quality of those services (and, perhaps, for satisfying the courts' demands for improvements). These governmental deficiencies are probably more pervasive at the local levels of government, which is one reason a large number of the nation's approximately 3,500 jails are in such deplorable shape. If private firms are willing to take on the task of improving these facilities and operating them more humanely, and especially if they can do so at a cost that is equal to or lower than the costs of public correctional agencies, it seems reasonable that they should be permitted, and even encouraged, to do so.

Relying on private entities to finance and build penal facilities that are then leased to governments is less easily justified. The two principal reasons for doing so are to avoid holding a public referendum to get voters' authorization for increased public debt, and to provide a shortcut and thus avoid waiting for such referenda. Although there are frequently irrationalities in the various expressions of public will at the ballot box—the support of tough sentencing policies but an unwillingness to foot the bills for them—to avoid the limitations on public indebtedness altogether risks imposing obligations on future generations that are more burdensome than they need to be. Adopting a "buy now, pay now" approach will force voters to confront their contradictory wishes and seek some resolution, and elected officials will be pressed to show the way by developing more coherent sentencing and penal policies. Using privatization of ownership to dodge necessity to seek a the resolution makes only short-run sense; the costs in the long term are substantial.

Notes

Introduction

1. Corrections Corporation of America, "Proposal for State of Tennessee," Nashville, Sept. 1985. The news coverage of this event and its denouement was extensive. For a listing of nearly a hundred articles and reports on them, see Russ Immarigeon, "Privatizing Adult Imprisonment in the U.S.: A Bibliography," *Criminal Justice Abstracts* 19 (Mar. 1987):136–139.

2. For example, private correctional facilities have been or are being built in Colorado and New Mexico without the necessity of first obtaining a contract for the housing of prisoners with any public correctional authorities. See Judy Harrington, "Ault Private Prison Will Teach 'Real World Job Skills' to Cons," *Denver Post*, Jan. 10, 1987.

3. American Bar Association, Section on Criminal Justice, "Report to the House of Delegates," dated Feb. 1986. See the last essay in this volume for a discussion of the constitutionality question, and of further developments in the ABA's position regarding privatization.

4. Clifford D. Shearing and Phillip C. Stenning, "Modern Private Security: Its Growth and Implications," *Crime and Justice: An Annual Review of Research*, vol. 3 (Chicago: University of Chicago Press, 1981), pp. 193–245; William C. Cunningham and Todd H. Taylor, *The Hallcrest Report: Private Security and Police in America* (Portland, Oreg.: Chancellor Press, 1985); Marcia Chaiken and Jan Chaiken, *Public Policing—Privately Provided* (Washington, D.C.: National Institute of Justice, 1987).

5. The literature on privatization is growing rapidly. Readers may wish to begin with E. S. Savas, *Privatizing the Public Sector: How to Shrink Government* (Chatham, N.J.: Chatham House, 1982); Stuart Butler, *Privatizing Federal Spending: A Strategy to Eliminate the Deficit* (New York: Universe Books, 1985); the special volume edited by Janet Rothenberg-Pack, *Journal of Policy Analysis and Management*, vol. 6, no. 4 (Summer 1987); and Steve H. Hanke, ed., *Prospects for Privatization*.

Proceedings of the Academy of Political Science, 36, no. 3 (1987):61–73.

6. E. S. Savas estimates that by 1991, a total of 2,000 state enterprises in Western Europe will have been sold for roughly $130 billion. "Private Enterprise Is Profitable Enterprise," *New York Times,* Feb. 14, l988, sec. 3, p. 2.

7. Touche Ross, *Privatization in America: An Opinion Survey of City and County Governments on Their Use of Privatization and Their Infrastructure Needs* (Washington, D.C.: Touche Ross, 1987), p. 4.

8. Computed from data in Bureau of Justice Statistics, *Prisoners in l986* (Washington, D.C.: Department of Justice, 1987); and Bureau of Justice Statistics, *State and Federal Prisoners, 1925–85* (Washington, D.C.: Department of Justice, 1986).

9. Bureau of Justice Statistics, *Prisoners in 1986.*

10. Computed from data in Bureau of Justice Statistics, *Jail Inmates 1984* (Washington, D.C.: Department of Justice, l986).

11. Federal Bureau of Investigation, *Crime in the United States* (Washington, D.C.: Government Printing Office, 1986), p. 168. Estimates of increases over longer periods are complicated by changes in the numbers of agencies that were reporting arrests to the F.B.I.

12. Bureau of Justice Statistics, *Setting Prison Terms* (Washington, D.C.: Department of Justice, l983), p. 3.

13. Bureau of Justice Statistics, *Jail Inmates 1986* (Washington, D.C.: Department of Justice, 1987).

14. Bureau of Justice Statistics, *Prisoners in 1986,* p. 5.

15. Bureau of Justice Statistics, *Prisoners in State and Federal Institutions on December 31, 1983* (Washington, D.C.: Department of Justice, 1986), Table 16; National Coalition for Jail Reform, "Facts about America's Jails" (Washington, D.C., undated), p. 1.

16. National Coalition for Jail Reform, "Facts about America's Jails," p. 1; and computations from miscellaneous data in American Correctional Association, *Directory 1986* (College Park, Md.: ACA, 1986).

17. Private communication from a representative of the American Civil Liberties Union's National Prison Project, June 7, 1988.

18. *Corrections Compendium,* 1986. Another 1986 survey by the Bureau of Justice Statistics found that 27 percent of all jails holding at least 100 inmates—which as a group held about

three-quarters of the nation's jail inmates at that time—were under court orders to eliminate unconstitutional conditions. *Jail Inmates 1986,* Table 9 and p. 3.

19. Bureau of Justice Statistics, *Prisoners in 1985* (Washington, D.C.: Department of Justice, 1986), p. 6.

20. American Correctional Association, *1989 Juvenile and Adult Correctional Departments, Institutions, Agencies, and Paroling Authorities (Laurel, Md., 1989),* pp. x, xi.

21. Douglas C. McDonald, *The Cost of Corrections: In Search of the Bottom Line* (Washington, D.C.: National Institute of Corrections, 1989).

22. Whereas all state and local government expenditures combined rose at an average annual rate of 10.1 percent during this period, corrections costs grew 14.9 percent on average each year. Bureau of the Census, *Government Finances in 1984–1985,* series GF85, no. 5 (Washington, D.C.: Government Printing Office, 1986), Table B, p. xi.

23. Thomas R. Swartz, "A New Urban Crisis in the Making," *Challenge,* Sept.–Oct. 1987, pp. 35–37.

24. John Herbers, "The New Federalism: Unplanned, Innovative, and Here to Stay," *Governing,* Oct. 1987, p. 30.

25. Ibid.

26. Cited in Susan D. Grubb, "Huber Supports Justice Programs before House," *County News* (newspaper of the National Association of Counties), Oct. 5, 1987, p. 8.

27. Thomas F. Rich and Arnold I. Barnett, "Model-Based U.S. Prison Population Projections," *Public Administration Review* 45 (Nov. 1985):780–789.

28. Alfred Blumstein, Jacqueline Cohen, and Harold D. Miller, "Demographically Disaggregated Projections of Prison Populations," *Journal of Criminal Justice* 8 (1980):1–26.

29. Bureau of Justice Statistics, *Prisoners in 1985*, p. 1.

30. Ibid, p. 2.

31. Computed from data in Bureau of the Census, *Current Population Reports,* series P-25, no. 985, *Estimates of the Population of the United States, by Age, Sex, and Race: 1980 to 1985* (Washington, D.C.: Government Printing Office, 1986), Table 1.

32. A study of arrest trends in New York State found that the proportion of black males aged 16–19 arrested for a felony increased 23 percent between 1970 and 1984. Even more troubling was the increase in felony arrest rates of those with prior felony convictions on their record: about 150 percent for the 16–

19 age-group, and about 70 percent for those between the ages of 20 and 29. This latter trend is likely to have an especially strong effect on prison populations, because New York State laws require judges to impose mandatory prison sentences upon those persons convicted of a second felony. See David J. van Alstyne, *Demographically Disaggregated Male Felony Arrest Trends: New York State (1970–1984)* (Albany: New York State Division of Criminal Justice Services, 1986), pp. 62, 72.

33. For a statement of this view, see, for example, James K. Stewart (director of the National Institute of Justice), "Costly Prisons: Should the Public Monopoly Be Ended?" in Patrick B. McGuigan and Jon S. Pascale, eds., *Crime and Punishment in Modern America* (Washington, D.C.: Institute for Government and Politics, Free Congress Research and Education Foundation, 1986), pp. 365–388.

34. Touche Ross, *Privatization in America,* p. 5.

35. Press briefing by David F. Linowes (Washington, D.C.: Office of the Press Secretary, the White House, Sept. 3, 1987).

36. See Allen J. Beck, "Recidivism of Young Parolees," *Bureau of Justice Special Report* (Washington, D.C.: Department of Justice, 1987), which states that 69 percent of the young parolees in fourteen states were rearrested within six years of release from prison; Illinois Criminal Justice Information Authority, *The Pace of Recidivism in Illinois,* Research Bulletin no. 2 (1988), which reports a 60 percent rearrest rate; S. Klein and M. Caggiano, *The Prevalence, Predictability, and Policy Implications of Recidivism* (Santa Monica, Calif.: Rand Corporation, 1986), which reports rearrest rates of 76 percent, 60 percent, and 53 percent of released state prisoners in California, Texas, and Michigan, respectively; and Delaware Statistical Analysis Center, *Recidivism in Delaware—A Study of Rearrest after Release from Incarceration* (1984), which reports a 51 percent rearrest rate.

37. According to John Peterson, *Corrections and the Private Sector: A National Forum,* (Washington, D.C.: National Institute of Justice, 1988), less than half of all jail construction bond issues in recent years have been approved. Cited in Jan Chaiken and Stephen Mennemeyer, *Lease-Purchase Financing of Prison and Jail Construction* (Washington, D.C.: National Institute of Justice, 1987), p. 2.

38. See Chaiken and Mennemeier, *Lease-Purchase Financing,* p. 2.

39. Kenneth Schoen worries that they will. See "Private

Prison Operators," *New York Times,* Mar. 28, 1985. See also Martin Tolchin, "Experts Foresee Adverse Effects from Private Control of Prisons," *New York Times,* Sept. 17, 1985.

40. Camille G. Camp and George M. Camp, *Private Sector Involvement in Prison Services and Operations* (Washington, D.C.: National Institute of Corrections, 1984).

41. Criminal Justice Associates, *Private Sector Involvement in Prison-Based Businesses: A National Assessment* (Washington, D.C.: Government Printing Office, 1985).

42. Martin Tolchin, "Prisons for Profit: Nashville's CCA Claims Operations Aid Government," *The Tennessean,* Feb. 24, 1985.

The Good, the Bad, and the Ugly: Private Prisons in the 1980s

1. Author's interview with J. Clifford Todd.

2. As it happened, Todd entered the private prison business in 1986 by acquiring another institutional property—an attractive former Catholic seminary—because his plans for the hospital collapsed.

3. Bureau of Justice Statistics Special Reports, *Population Density in State Prisons* (Washington, D.C.: Department of Justice, 1986).

4. Legislative Research Council, Commonwealth of Massachusetts, *Prisons for Profit,* July 31, 1986, p. 8.

5. *Privatization: Toward More Effective Government,* Report of the President's Commission on Privatization (Washington, D.C., Mar. 1988).

6. Ted Gest, "Prisons for Profit: A Growing Business," *U.S. News and World Report,* July 2, 1984, pp. 45–46.

7. "The Best Judges Money Can Buy," *National Law Journal,* Dec. 12, 1987, p. 1; "Alternatives to Litigation Are Maturing," *National Law Journal,* May 12, 1986; James F. Henry and Jethro K. Lieberman, *The Manager's Guide to Resolving Legal Disputes* (New York: Harper and Row, 1986).

8. National Criminal Justice Statistics Associations, *Private Sector Involvement in Financing and Managing Correctional Facilities* (Washington, D.C.: National Criminal Justice Statistics Association, 1987), pp. 53–54.

9.   David Wecht, "Breaking the Code of Deference: Judicial Review of Private Prisons," *Yale Law Review* 96 (1987):815–816.

10.   David C. Anderson, *Crimes of Justice* (New York: Times Books, 1988), pp. 277–278; see also National Criminal Justice Statistics Association, *Private Sector Involvement,* pp. 5–6.

11.   Bureau of Justice Statistics, *Children in Custody: 1982/83 Census of Juvenile Detention and Correctional Facilities* (Washington, D.C.: Department of Justice, 1983).

12.   National Criminal Justice Statistics Association, *Private Sector Involvement,* p. 27.

13.   Legislative Research Council, *Prisons for Profit,* p. 48.

14.   J. Michael Keating, Jr., "Seeking Profit in Punishment: The Private Management of Correctional Institutions" (Washington, D.C.: American Federation of State, County, and Municipal Employees, undated monograph), p. 5.

15.   Ibid.

16.   Ibid., pp. 8–9.

17.   Joan Mullen, "Correction and the Private Sector," *Privatization Review* 1 (Fall 1985):12.

18.   Gillian M. Spooner and Carol S. Werner, "Privatization after the 1986 Tax Reform Act," *Privatization Review* 3 (Spring 1987):11–23.

19.   See, for example, competing articles by Charles H. Logan and by Edward Sagarin and Jess Maghan on the topic "Should States Opt for Private Prison?" *Hartford Courant,* Jan. 12, 1986, p. E1.

20.   House Committee on the Judiciary, *Privatization of Corrections: Hearings before the Subcommittee on Courts, Civil Liberties, and the Administration of Justice,* 99th Cong., 1st and 2d sess., Nov. 13, 1985, and Mar. 18, 1986.

21.   See, for example, National Institute of Justice, *Contracting for the Operation of Prisons and Jails* (Washington, D.C.: Department of Justice, Apr., 1987); Joint State Government Commission, *Report of the Private Prison Task Force* (Harrisburg: General Assembly of the Commonwealth of Pennsylvania, Mar. 1987); also Legislative Research Council, *Prisons for Profit.*

22.   Legislative Research Council, *Prisons for Profit,* p. 29.

23.   For the most recent prediction from the Corrections Corporation of America, see Erik Larson, "Captive Company," *Inc.,* June 1988, p. 88.

24.   National Institute of Justice, *Contracting,* p. 4.

25.   See also the New Mexico attorney general's opinion no.

83–5, Nov. 29, 1983. There it is argued that localities need state authorization before delegating power to private jailers. Shortly afterward, the state legislature approved two county jails as the focus of private, pilot projects.

26. House Committee on the Judiciary, *Privatization of Corrections*, 884; Legislative Research Council, *Prisons for Profit*, pp. 86–95.

27. Author's interview with Robert Schmidt, former supervisor of detention operations of the U.S. Immigration and Naturalization Service.

28. Ibid. For a fuller analysis of the costs of the detention of aliens, see McDonald's essay on the costs of operation in this volume (which reports different numbers).

29. House Committee on the Judiciary, *Privatization of Corrections*, p. 132.

30. Ibid.

31. Schmidt interview.

32. House Committee of the Judiciary, *Privatization of Corrections*, p. 133.

33. Schmidt interview.

34. For example, "Partners in Crime," *Forbes*, Feb. 11, 1985, p. 115; CBS's "60 Minutes," segment on topic "Crime Pays," Nov. 25, 1984.

35. Author's interview with Mark Neimeiser of AFSCME and Hedy Weinberg, executive director, Tennessee Civil Liberties Union.

36. Kem E. Morgan, "Waiting to Vote on CCA's Prisoner Rate Could Have Saved the County Some Money," *Chattanooga Times*, Aug. 21, 1986, p. B2.

37. Interview with Hubert L. McCullough.

38. Interview with George Zoley.

39. Interview with Joseph Fenton.

40. Terry Bivens, "Can Prisons for Profit Work?" *Philadelphia Inquirer Magazine*, Aug. 3, 1986, p. 14.

41. Ibid.

42. Ibid.

43. Interview with William G. Babcock.

44. Interview with Cheryl Roberts.

45. Interview with Clifford Todd.

46. Interview with Mary Beth Smith.

47. Legislative Research Council, *Prisons for Profit*, p. 98.

48. Ibid., p. 100.

49. Interview with Nancy Rodriguez.

50. Much of the rich detail about the situation in Bay County comes from an unpublished memorandum prepared in June 1987 by David Gonzalez, a correspondent for *Newsweek* magazine based in Miami.

51. Minutes of the Bay County Board of County Commissioners meeting, Jan. 22, 1985.

52. Bay County board meeting minutes, Jan. 31, 1985.

53. Bay County board meeting minutes, May 7, 1985.

54. Interview with Charles Thomas by David Gonzalez.

British Penal Policy
and the Idea of Prison Privatization

1. Sixteen items were listed by the Treasury in 1988, with estimated proceeds for 1986–1987 of £4,400 million. *The Government's Expenditure Plans, 1988–89 to 1990–91,* Cm. 228-i (1988), pp. 55–56.

2. Stuart M. Butler, "Changing the Political Dynamics of Government," in Steve H. Hanke, ed., *Prospects for Privatization. Proceedings of the Academy of Political Science* 36, no. 3 (1987):13.

3. Paul Starr, "The Limits of Privatization," in ibid., p. 125.

4. There are three separate prison systems within the United Kingdom. The Scottish system shares many of the pressing problems of those of England and Wales. In Northern Ireland, there have been twenty years of large-scale expansion, dating from the resumption of the "troubles"; yet the prison population, uniquely within the United Kingdom, has since 1980 declined and stabilized. Unless otherwise stated, the data cited in this essay refer to England and Wales.

5. *Report of the Commissioners of Prisons for the Year 1960,* Cmnd. 1467 (1961); and *Prison Statistics, England and Wales 1988* Cm. 825 (1989).

6. Council of Europe, *Prison Information Bulletin,* Strasbourg, December 1988, p. 22.

7. See note 5.

8. *Criminal Statistics for England and Wales, 1986,* Cm. 233 (1987).

9. *The Government's Expenditure Plans, 1988–89 to 1990–91,* Cm. 288-ii p. 197. The figure for 1979–1980 is from *The Government's Expenditure Plans, 1980–81 to 1983–84,* Cmnd. 7841 (1980).

10. *The Government's Reply to the Third Report from the Home Affairs Committee,* session 1986–1987, *State and Use of Prisons,* Cm. 263 (1987), pp. 1–3.

11. *Report on the work of the Prison Service 1986/87,* Cm. 246 (1987) 8. Overcrowding is represented by a bar chart and, in a break from previous practice, no figures were published. The peak overcrowding total (i.e., number of persons held in cells designed for single-person use) of 19,054 for 1986–1987 was supplied to the author by the Home Office in January 1988.

12. The use of police cells to hold prisoners on a contract basis with the Prison Department greatly increased during the mid-1980s. The first pledge by a home secretary to end this practice was made in 1984. It was repeated by his successor in 1987 but it was not until 1989 overcrowding that the practice largely ceased following the unexpected reduction in the prison population between 1988 and 1990.

13. National Audit Office, report by the comptroller and auditor general, *Home Office and Property Services Agency: Programme for the Provision of Prison Places,* H.C. 135 (1985), p. 6.

14. See Andrew Rutherford, *Prisons and the Process of Justice* (Oxford: Oxford University Press, 1986), pp. 97–101; Roy D. King and Rod Morgan, *The Future of the Prison System* (Farnborough: Gower, 1980), pp. 114–121.

15. *Prisons Briefing Paper,* Dec. 1987, p. 1.

16. *The Government's Reply to the Third Report from the Home Affairs Committee,* p. 10.

17. Sir Brian Cubbon, speech to the Australian Bicentennial International Congress on Corrective Services, New South Wales, Jan. 24, 1988.

18. *The Omega Justice Report* (London: Adam Smith Institute, 1984).

19. Sean McConville and J. E. Hall Williams, *Crime and Punishment: A Radical Rethink* (London: Tawney Society, 1985).

20. *Twenty-fifth Report from the Committee of Public Accounts,* session 1985–1986, *Prison Building Programme,* H.C. 248 (1986), p. 8.

21. *Contract Provision of Prisons, Fourth Report of the Home Affairs Committee,* H.C. 291 (1987). The prisons were a local jail and annex in Panama City, Florida, and a youth institution in Memphis, Tennessee, both run by the Corrections Corporation of America.

22. Ibid.

23. The institutions were the Hidden Valley Ranch in California, run by Eclectic Communications Inc.; the Houston Processing Center, operated on behalf of the U.S. Immigration and Naturalization Service by the Corrections Corporation of America; and the Silverdale facility in Chattanooga, Tennessee, run by the Corrections Corporation of America. Association representatives also visited a private juvenile facility that held contracts with state and federal agencies.

24. *Third Report from the Home Affairs Committee,* session 1986–1987, *State and Use of Prisons, Proceedings,* H.C. 35-ii (1987), p. 103.

25. Ibid., pp. 111–112.

26. Ibid., p. 94.

27. Ibid., pp. 68–69.

28. Ibid., pp. 22–23.

29. Peter Young, *The Prison Cell* (London: Adam Smith Institute, 1987), p. 2.

30. Ibid., p. 39.

31. Maxwell Taylor and Ken Pease, "Privatising Prisons," unpublished paper, 1987. *The Independent* prefaced a summary of the paper as follows: "Privatisation of prisons has won its first public commitment of support from the liberal wing of the penal reform lobby, giving crucial new authority to the campaign" (Mar. 5, 1987).

32. *The Independent,* Sept. 14, 1987.

33. *The Independent,* Nov. 18, 1987. This observation echoes sentiments expressed by Ted Nissen, founder and president of Behavioral Systems Southwest: "We don't just take any old chowderhead who wants to get into the system . . . we turn away five for every one we accept." *The Guardian,* Mar. 3, 1987.

34. *Private Sector Involvement in the Remand System,* CM. 434, 1988, pp. 8–9.

35. *New Builder* 21, 15 Feb. 1990, p. 6. The article was headed, "Government's private prisons plan shelved."

36. When an offense has been committed or is suspected, the individual is detained in a Prison Department facility. In 1986 the average number of persons held in the prison system daily under the Immigration Act of 1971 was 132. *Prison Statistics, England and Wales 1986,* Cm. 210 (1987), pp. 18–19.

37. *Parliamentary Debates* (H.C.) 5th ser., vol. 805 (Nov. 5, 1970), col. 415.

38. *Parl. Deb.* (H.C.), 5th ser., 952 (June 20, 1978):111–112.

39. *Parl. Deb.* (H.C.), 6th ser., 44 (June 30, 1983):107.

40. *Fifteenth Report from the Expenditure Committee,* session 1977–1978, *The Reduction of Pressure on the Prison System, Proceedings,* H.C. 662-ii, (1978) p. 506.

41. Ibid., p. 507.

42. Ibid., pp. 507–508.

43. *Fifteenth Report from the Expenditure Committee,* session 1977–1978, *The Reduction of Pressure on the Prison System, Report,* (H.C.) 662-i, (1978) p. xlviii.

44. *The Reduction of Pressure on the Prison System. Observations on the Fifteenth Report from the Expenditure Committee,* Cmnd. 7948 (1980), p. 11.

45. Report by H.M. Chief Inspector of Prisons, *Detention Centre Harmondsworth,* Home Office, December 1988.

46. *Sixth Report from the Immigration and Nationality Department of the Home Office,* session 1984–1985, H.C. 277 (1985), p. 109. Similar figures were given two years later in a Written Answer. *Parl. Deb.* (H.C.), 6th ser., 76 (Mar. 30, 1987):343.

47. Stephanie d'Orey, *Immigration Prisoners: A Forgotten Minority* (London: Runnymede Trust, 1984), pp. 33–34.

48. *Parl. Deb.* (H.C.), 6th ser., 40 (Apr. 14, 1983): 221.

49. Prison Reform Trust and Joint Committee for the Welfare of Immigrants, *Immigration Prisoners Project* (1985), p. 3. For a less favorable assessment, see Penny Green, *Private Sector Involvement in the Immigration Detention Centre* (London: Howard League for Penal Reform, 1989).

50. *Report of the Departmental Committee on Prisons,* Home Office, C. 7702 (1895), p. 401.

51. *Howard Journal* 2 (1922):48–49.

52. Julius Carlebach, *Caring for Children in Trouble* (London: Routledge and Kegan Paul, 1970), pp. 162–163.

53. *Children in the Care of Local Authorities, Year Ending 31 March 1985,* Department of Health and Social Security, 1987.

54. Paul Lerman, *Deinstitutionalization and the Welfare State* (New Brunswick, N.J.: Rutgers University Press, 1982), p. 150.

55. Carlebach, *Caring for Children in Trouble*, p. 112.

56. Gordon Rose, *Schools for Young Offenders* (London: Tavistock, 1967), pp. 227–230.

57. Gillian Stewart and Norman Tutt, *Children in Custody* (Aldershot: Avebury, 1987), p. 215.

58. Young, *The Prison Cell*, p. 4.

59. *Fourth Report from the Home Affairs Committee*, p. v.

60. Ibid., p. vi.

61. *Third Report from the Home Affairs Committee*, p. 24.

62. In 1982 the Home Office announced that consideration was being given to drawing up a set of minimum standards for prisons. This proposal was abandoned in 1984. *Parl. Deb.* (H.C.)., 6th ser., 58 (Apr. 12, 1984):311. The argument for minimum standards was pursued by the Home Affairs Committee in 1987. *Third Report from the Home Affairs Committee*, pp. vi–viii. The approach was again rejected by the Home Office. *The Government's Reply to the Third Report from the Home Affairs Committee*, pp. 4–5. See also Silvia Casale, *Minimum Standards for Prison Establishments* (London: National Association for the Care and Resettlement of Offenders, 1984); and Vivien Stern, *Bricks of Shame: Britain's Prisons* (London: Penguin Books, 1987) pp. 219–242.

63. *Third Report from the Home Affairs Committee*, p. viii.

64. *Fourth Report from the Home Affairs Committee*, p. vii.

65. Stephen Shaw, quoted in *The Law Magazine* 18 (Jan. 22, 1988): 21.

66. *Fourth Report from the Home Affairs Committee*, p. vi.

67. Starr, "The Limits of Privatization," p. 134.

68. *Fourth Report from the Home Affairs Committee*, p. vii.

69. For example, the evidence of Howard League for Penal Reform in, *Third Report from the Home Affairs Committee*, p. 95. An expanded role for the voluntary sector (and perhaps commercial sector) is evisaged by the government. See especially, *Supervision and Punishment in the Community*, Cm 966 (1990).

70. Andrew Rutherford, *Growing Out of Crime* (London: Penguin Books, 1986), pp. 136–147.

71. Preliminary findings of a national survey concerning these new noncustodial arrangements for juvenile offenders indicate that half of the statutory social services departments mentioned

problems of controlling a voluntary agency, and in one-third of the cases reference was made to the voluntary sector's ability to innovate. Only one-fifth of the statutory agencies saw no advantages in using voluntary agencies. Institute of Criminology, Cambridge University, *Intermediate Treatment Evaluation Project,* Research Bulletin no. 2 (1986), pp. 9–10.

72.   Lord Windlesham, *The Times,* July 8, 1987; see also Lord Windlesham, *Response to Crime* (Oxford: Clarendon Press, 1987), pp. 246–247. In a subsequent article, Lord Windlesham appears to qualify his proposal by stating that he did not "envisage full management contracts" but a scheme of "limited delegation . . . namely the appointment of Home Office managers and the employment of private sector companies to supply operational staff under contract." Windlesham, "Punishment and Prevention: The Inappropriate Prisoners," *Criminal Law Review,* Mar. 1988, p. 149. At the time of these publications Lord Windlesham was chairman of the Parole Board and a former Conservative minister in the Home Office.

73.   John Irwin, *The Jail: Managing the Underclass in American Society* (Berkeley: University of California Press, 1985), p. 45.

74.   Phil Hornsby, *Profit from Punishment* (London: Prison Officers' Association, 1987).

75.   *Evidence by the Home Office to the Inquiry into the United Kingdom Prison Services* 2 (1979):124–125.

76.   Arthur de Frisching, quoted in Rutherford, *Prisons and the Process of Justice,* p. 86.

77.   *Report of the Inquiry into the United Kingdom Prison Services,* Cmnd. 7673 (1979), p. 119.

78.   *Report of an Inquiry by Her Majesty's Chief Inspector of Prisons for England and Wales into the Disturbances in Prison Service Establishments in England between 29 April and 2 May 1986,* H.C. 42 (1987), p. 106. The chief inspector noted that "the P.O.A. instructed its members not to respond to governors' calls for help, even to avert the kind of real emergency which was the subject of a Full Alert" (p. 107).

79.   *Third Report from the Home Affairs Committee,* p. 103.

80.   *Report by the Comptroller and Auditor General, Home Office and Property Services Agency: Programmes for the Provision of Prison Places,* National Audit Office, H.C. 135 (1985); *Twenty-fifth Report from the Committee of Public Accounts.*

81.   There has been speculation that the government will fol-

low France in opting for a "mixed system" of this sort. In December 1987 the French government contracted with the private sector to provide laundries and catering in new prisons. *The Law Magazine* 18 (Jan. 22, 1988):12.

82. In addition to envisaging a much wider role for the voluntary sector in delivering supervision schemes for offenders in the community, the government turned to the commercial sector for its experimental electronic tagging of persons on bail in August 1989. See *Crime, Justice and Protecting the Public, The Government's Proposals for Legislation,* Cm 965 (1990), pp. 22–23.

83. Sean McConville, *A History of English Prison Administration,* vol. 1, *1750–1877* (London: Routledge and Kegan Paul, 1981), p. 11.

84. For an assessment of the hands off stance of British courts on prison conditions see Genevra Richardson, "Judicial Intervention in Prison Life," in Mike Maguire, Jon Vagg, and Rod Norgan., eds., *Accountability and Prisons: Opening Up a Closed World* (London: Tavistock, 1985), pp. 46–60.

85. *Criminal Statistics for England and Wales, 1988.* A slight decline, however, occurred during 1988.

86. *Prison Statistics, England and Wales 1988.* Cm. 825 (1989).

87. William Whitelaw, *Parl. Deb.,* H.C. 6th ser., 21 (Mar. 25, 1982):1122.

88. *Third Report from the Treasury and Civil Service Committee,* session 1985–1986, *The Government's Expenditure Plans, 1986–87 to 1988–89,* H.C. 192 (1986), p. 149.

89. *Punishment, Custody and the Community,* Cm 424 (1988).

90. *Crime, Justice and Protecting the Public, The Government's Proposals for Legislation,* Cm 965 (1990).

91. Andrew Rutherford, "The English Penal Crisis: Paradox and Possibilities," in Roger Rideout and Jeffrey Jowen, eds., *Current Legal Problems 1988,* (London: Stevens, 1988), pp. 93–133.

Private Time:
The Political Economy of Private Prison Finance

I am deeply indebted to a number of individuals who have helped me develop my thinking about privatization and about what accountability in government should mean. Since these are the central themes in this essay, those parties should all claim any credit they would like for anything they agree with in this essay, and I (and, I assume, the readers) are grateful for the many errors that might have appeared here that their intervention has eliminated. I am particularly grateful for the support of the Vera Institute of Justice and the National Center for State Courts, and for the comments of members of the study team. This essay has been improved appreciably by the extensive comments of Douglas McDonald and several anonymous reviewers. Jack Donahue, Michael O'Hare, and Robert Leone have been especially helpful in getting me to focus productively on what is special about private action under public aegis. No one has stepped forward to share the guilt for any remaining errors, so it rests with me.

1. John D. Donahue reviews this argument in detail in his book, *The Privatization Decision: Public Ends, Private Means* (New York: Basic Books, 1989). He finds it difficult to understand the supposed difference between public and private behavior.

2. Under some models of privatization—for example, when a private company takes complete responsibility for the operation of a prison facility—both public officials and the private management company may have an interest in involving the managing organization in the design and planning process. Thus, further progress in other aspects of privatization may eventually lead us to reexamine the involvement of private interests in the planning and construction phase.

3. The debt-related procedures are not, of course, the only points in the process where enemies of a project can assert their opposition; there is a considerable array of options for influencing public decisions. For example, they can appear at hearings on site selection or appropriations, petition legislative committees, or demand public hearings by executive agencies.

4. It is also not obvious that the incentives are *wrong*. If the punishment is intended to be the denial of liberty alone, not incarceration in an undesirable residential arrangement, then a bargain between providers and inmates that keeps costs down and keeps inmates from being exploited seems better for everyone. It may not be what some taxpayers had in mind, but it is not clear what taxpayers as a group want.

5. John J. DiIulio discusses this issue extensively in his essay in this volume.

The Costs of Operating
Public and Private Correctional Facilities

I am grateful to Todd Clear, Barbara Greenberg, Barry Mahoney, David Nee, Kenneth Schoen, and Michael Smith for their comments on earlier versions of this essay. I owe a special debt to Robert Schmidt, who was chief of detention operations for the U.S. Immigration and Naturalization Service when I began work on this study. He provided a great deal of the data on the detention centers operated either by the U.S. Immigration and Naturalization Service or by firms under contract. The responsibility for the accuracy of the figures and calculations in this essay is, of course, mine alone.

1.   Martin Tolchin, "Private Concern Makes Offer to Run Tennessee's Prisons," *New York Times,* Sept. 13, 1985.

2.   Kenneth Schoen, of the Edna McConnell Clark Foundation, made this observation in a conversation with me during 1986.

3.   John Peterson, *Corrections and the Private Sector: A National Forum* (Washington, D.C.: National Institute of Justice, 1988), p. 78.

4.   Keon S. Chi, "Private Contractor Work Release Centers: The Illinois Experience," *Innovations* (Lexington, Ky.: Council of State Governments, 1982).

5.   Ibid., p. 6.

6.   Ibid.

7.   Aaron A. Brown, Roy E. Gerard, Roberta L. Howard, Wallace A. Kennedy, Robert B. Levinson, Carol A. Sell, Paul A. Skelton, Jr., and Herbert C. Quay, *Private Sector Operation of a Correctional Institution: A Study of the Jack and Ruth Eckerd Youth Development Center, Okeechobee, Florida* (Washington, D.C.: National Institute of Corrections, 1985).

8.   John Donahue, *Prisons for Profit: Public Justice, Private Interests* (Washington, D.C.: Economic Policy Institute, 1988), pp. 12–13.

9.   *Report on a Study of Issues Related to the Potential Operation of Private Prisons in Pennsylvania,* (Harrisburg, Pa.: Legislative Budget and Finance Committee, a Joint Committee of the General Assembly, Oct. 1985), p. 63.

10.   Public agencies usually report the entire amount spent for capital equipment in the year the purchase was made, whereas private firms spread the costs across several accounting years because the value of the asset is consumed during subsequent

years. For a fuller discussion of the problems of understanding public corrections costs, see my essay, *The Cost of Corrections: In Search of the Bottom Line* (Washington, D.C.: National Institute of Corrections, 1989). Also see Gail S. Funke and Billy L. Wayson, *What Price Justice? A Handbook for the Analysis of Criminal Justice Costs,* (Washington, D.C.: National Institute of Justice, 1989); and Todd Clear, Patricia Harris, and Albert Record, "Managing the Cost of Corrections," *Prison Journal* 62 (1982). Examples of attempts to establish the true costs of several different types of correctional services are given in Douglas C. McDonald, *The Price of Punishment: Public Spending for Corrections in New York* (Boulder, Colo.: Westview Press, 1980).

11.   Charles H. Logan and Bill W. McGriff, "Comparing Costs of Public and Private Prisons: A Case Study," *NIJ Reports,* no. 216 (Sept.–Oct. 1989), pp. 2–8. This study revises and extends an analysis presented in Logan's "Proprietary Prisons," in Lynne Goodstein and Doris L. MacKenzie, eds., *The American Prison: Issues in Research and Policy* (New York: Plenum Press, 1989).

12.   Corrections Corporation of America, "Fact Sheet: Silverdale Detention Center" (undated and unpublished). For descriptions of the facility, see also the CCA's "Silverdale Detention Center Milestones, Oct. 15, 1984–Oct. 15, 1985" (unpublished); and Mark Northern, "Pros and Cons—Turning Silverdale into Gold," *Chattanooga Life & Leisure,* Apr. 1986, pp. 24–25, 40.

13.   Logan and McGriff, "Comparing Costs," p. 7.

14.   National Criminal Justice Association, *Private Sector Involvement in Financing and Managing Correctional Activities,* (Washington, D.C.: National Criminal Justice Association, 1987), p. 18.

15.   "Comparison of Privately and Publicly Operated Corrections Facilities in Kentucky and Massachusetts" (Washington, D.C.: The Urban Institute, August 1989).

16.   Ibid., pp. ES 6–7.

17.   Ibid., p. ES–7.

18.   Computed from CADM524 reports of INS expenditures.

19.   Ibid.

20.   Computed from staff/days billed to the INS during fiscal year 1988, provided by Jack Luvender and George Sourk, U.S. Immigration and Naturalization Service, 1990.

21.   These skeptical views were expressed by John Donahue, of Harvard's Kennedy School of Government, in a newpaper re-

port by Jean DuBail, "State Private-Prison Bids Falter," *Sun-Sentinel* [Delray Beach, Florida], Feb. 21, 1990.

22.   Author interview with Robert Schmidt, former head of detention operations for INS, 1988.

23.   Telephone interview with Schmidt, November 1989. At the time of the interview, Schmidt was a consultant to Wackenhut Corporation's correctional services division.

24.   CADM524 reports.

25.   "Cost-cutting measures will run rampant," according to one of the American Bar Association's statements. "Conditions of confinement will be kept to the minimum that the law requires. . . . In short, the private sector is more interested in doing well than in doing good." American Bar Association's Criminal Justice Section, "Report to the House of Delegates," Feb. 13, 1989, p. 4.

26.   Telephone interview with Michael Mattice, contracts officer for the INS, March 1989.

27.   All salary figures from Robert Schmidt, including estimates of private firm's fringe benefit rates. Estimates of government employee fringe benefit and retirement rates computed by the author.

28.   Schmidt, 1989 interview.

29.   Telephone interview with Jack Luvender, INS, Detention and Deportation unit, March 1990.

30.   This average is not adjusted by adding the additional off-budget costs discussed above.

31.   See Aric Press's essay in this volume.

32.   OMB circular no. A–76 (rev.), *Performance of Commercial Activities,* part 4: *Cost Comparison Handbook* (Washington, D.C.: Office of Management and Budget, 1983) pp. iv–16.

33.   According to CADM524, costs other than personal service charges constituted 33 percent of the average per diem cost of INS facilities during that year. I have arbitrarily assumed that half of these expenses were for materials and supplies.

34.   This estimate assumes that the only asset is the cost of replacing a detention center ($20,000 per inmate), which is undoubtedly a basic cost that does not include either much of the equipment added to the basic plant or the various supplies housed with it. The 0.05 percent estimate is from OMB circular A-76, p. iv-23.

35.   Computed on a straight-line depreciation basis. If one assumed a seventy-five-year life of the building, the amortized

capital expenditure would equal 2.4 percent of the reported operating cost. Because detention centers, unlike warehouses, take a great deal of wear and tear, assuming a useful fifty-year life is probably more realistic. I am also assuming here that the centers have no residual value at the end of their useful life.

The Privatization of Imprisonment: A Managerial Perspective

The authors are grateful for research support provided by the Edna McConnell Clark Foundation, the Florence V. Burden Foundation, the Pew Foundation, and the Executive Education Programs in National Security at Harvard University's John F. Kennedy School of Government. Our conclusions are our own.

1.   The American Bar Association summarizes this point in its policy statement on privatization: "The private sector, advocates claim, can save the taxpayers money. It can build facilities faster and cheaper than the public sector can, and it can operate them more economically and more efficiently." Testimony of Robert Evans; see House Committee on the Judiciary, *Privatization of Corrections: Hearings before the Subcommittee on Courts, Civil Liberties, and the Administration of Justice,* 99th Cong., 1st and 2d sess., Nov. 13, 1985, and Mar. 18, 1986, p. 113. Although not himself a proponent of privatization, Edward Koren of the American Civil Liberties Union has expressed this "no worse" position of privatization advocates quite well. When testifying about the effect of privatization on civil liberties, he stated, "prisoners must not be placed in any worse situation in terms of their treatment care, and legal status than those prisoners confined to public institutions." Ibid., p. 5. Among the proponents of privatization at these hearings was Richard Crane of the Corrections Corporation of America. In his list of the advantages of privatization at the beginning of his testimony, all benefits related to lower costs. Ibid., pp. 31–35.

2.   Mocking the privatization concept with a clear reference to the notion of prison privatization as a dichotomous choice, Dave Kelly, president of the Council of Prison Locals, American Federation of Government Employees, stated before a congressional committee: "If the committee decides that the function of punishment is an appropriate realm for the profit incentive, we hope that it recommends to the states to privatize all the punishment functions. We have not seen a cost estimate on the

death penalty. But whatever it is, we know of entrepreneurs who will do it for less. We see them every day in cell blocks across the country." Ibid., p. 18.

3. Jacqueline M. Moore provides a good discussion of how privatizing prison health services can improve managerial focus in "Privatization of Prison Health Services," *Privatization Review* (Fall 1986):12.

4. An alternative approach is to try to identify what elements of production determine the intrinsic publicness or privateness of an activity. In his essay, John DiIulio, Jr., for example, argues that the central issue in prison privatization is who manages the prison and by what authority. He contends that prison management is an intrinsically public activity for two reasons. First, only the state can legitimately balance competing notions of the proper role and function of prison systems. Second, private administration of punishment diminishes the symbolic importance of the punitive act. Privatizing prison management, in essence, undermines the notion that crime and society's response to it are inherently public acts. DiIulio suggests that the question of privatizing prison functions other than management is important, but is not central to the philosophical debate. Although we neither endorse nor reject DiIulio's conclusions, we believe that his approach provides an important insight: The privatization of a production function should be seen as an incremental process and not a wholesale volleying of enterprises (in this case prisons) back and forth across the public-private boundary.

5. At the extreme, so long as labor is freely supplied and not conscripted or enslaved, there will always be a "private" component of any publicly produced good or service.

6. A 1982 survey of 1,433 cities and 347 counties conducted by the International City Management Association made this point clear. Of thirty different public services, only four were considered "solely public" by 75 percent or more of the respondents: snow plowing, code enforcement, payroll, and secretarial services. Two services directly related to the state power of taxation, assessment and delinquent tax collection, were considered solely public by only 54 percent and 59 percent of the respondents, respectively. Mental health facilities, which involve incarceration, rehabilitation and physical restraint, were deemed solely public by only 13 percent of the respondents. International City Management Association, *Alternative Approaches for Delivering Public Services,* Urban Data Service Report, vol. 14, no. 10 (Oct. 1983).

7.   Typical of the current approach is E. S. Savas's *Privatization: The Key to Better Government* (Chatham, N.J.: Chatham House, 1987). Savas provides an interesting and valuable discussion of the various consumer services that can be supplied by the public and private sectors (pp. 35–57), and generic strategies for the efficent delivery of these services (pp. 58–92). Savas fails, however, to suggest how public managers and elected officials might assess proposals to privatize particular elements of the production chain. Such analysis would enable public officials to draw public-private boundaries that allow optimal managerial performance, in ways that extend the public agenda where consensus exists, and that effectively balance competing interpretations of the public interest where it does not. Savas opts instead for a prescription, made explicit in the title: where possible, privatize.

8.   See Robert A. Leone, *Who Profits?* (New York: Basic Books, 1986) p. 32.

9.   A survey limited to fifty-four state correctional agencies revealed that fifty-two of them had at least one contract with the private sector. Camille G. Camp and George M. Camp, *Private Sector Involvement in Prison Services and Operations* (Washington, D.C.: National Institute of Corrections, 1984).

10.   The National Fire Protection Association and the Underwriters' Laboratory are two common examples of private organizations whose decisions (the *National Electrical Code* and product "listings," respectively) have the force of law in many jurisdictions.

11.   The Electric Power Research Institute, the major research arm of the electricity industry, is funded by such a taxlike charge; the semiconductor industry's share of the (now moribund) Sematech project would have been financed in a similar fashion.

12.   John J. DiIulio, Jr., *Governing Prisons: A Comparative Study of Correctional Management* (New York: Free Press, 1987) p. 237.

13.   James W. Culliton, *Make or Buy: A Consideration of the Problems Fundamental to a Decision Whether to Manufacture or Buy Materials, Accessory Equipment, Fabricating Parts, and Supplies,* Harvard University Graduate School of Business Administration, Business Research Studies, vol. 24, no. 4 (Dec. 1942).

14.   Even these deliberations can take on a larger political significance, as in the case of "domestic content" legislation regarding automobiles.

15. William Rosenau (under the direction of Robert A. Leone), "Mess and Maintenance at Marine Boot Camp" (Cambridge, Mass.: John F. Kennedy School of Government, Harvard University, 1987), case no. C96-87-792.0. This case is discussed in Michael O'Hare, *The Productive Environment* (forthcoming).

16. Indeed, as evidence of this, the editor of this volume advised that the term "prison guard" be replaced by "correctional officer." This concern with title and image and the possible conveyance of stereotypes illustrates the manner in which even informal norms of expression and behavior shape organizations.

17. DiIulio, in his essay in this volume, addresses the significance that attaches to symbols that clarify the boundaries of the corrections function: "The badge of the arresting policeman, the robes of the judge, and the state patch of the corrections officer are symbols of the inherently public nature of crime and punishment." Boundary clarification, however, has more than symbolic meaning. The literature on manufacturing focus suggests that the production function should be organized in ways that advance the strategic purposes of the firm—which may well be symbolic—rather than simply aiming for lowest unit cost, based on often elusive economies of scale. Techniques for developing proper focus include physically dividing space in a production facility along product lines, segregating production facilities by manufacturing process, and developing separate production facilities as a means of supporting products whose manufacture requires incompatible work cultures within the same organization (i.e., custom work versus standard production runs). See, for example, Robert H. Hayes and Roger W. Schmenner, "How Should You Organize Manufacturing?" *Harvard Business Review* (Jan.–Feb. 1978), pp. 105–111; Roger Schmenner, "Before You Build a Big Factory," *Harvard Business Review* (July–Aug. 1976), pp. 100–104; Roger Schmenner, *Production/Operations Management: Concepts and Situations,* 3d ed. (Menlo Park, Calif.: Science Research Associates, 1987), pp. 693–699; Wickham Skinner, "The Focused Factory," *Harvard Business Review,* May–June 1974, pp. 113–121. With respect to prisons, the literature on manufacturing focus suggests that managers would gain more from experimentation with different forms of correctional facilities targeted at different needs than from a strategy aimed at cost reduction through wholesale privatization of state prison systems, utilizing a single supplier.

18. An example of the latter case is W. L. Gore & Associates, which has one job classification: associate. The organization, which manufactures Gore Tex waterproof fabric, claims that job

titles inhibit communication and effective job performance. Similarly, the company's recently deceased founder believed strongly that production could not be effectively managed in units of more than two hundred people. The company's philosophy is described in Tom Peters and Nancy Austin, *A Passion for Excellence* (New York: Warner Books, 1985) pp. 239–240. A more exhaustive description of the firm and its "lattice" management structure is contained in a memo from Vieve Gore to "the Associates" entitled "The Lattice Organization—a Philosophy of Enterprise," May 7, 1976.

19. Prisoner quarrels over management performance have periodically erupted in violence. An uprising at Rikers Island in New York in early 1988 was incited by issues including abuse by guards, the quality of food, and the temperature of the cells. "Hundreds of Prisoners Take over 12 Dormitories on Rikers I.," *New York Times*, Feb. 19, 1988, p. B1; "Rikers Island Warning Signals," editorial, *New York Times*, Feb. 20, 1988, p. 26. This type of uprising prompts us to ask two questions. First, would the riot have had different social, legal, and moral implications had it taken place under private watch? Second, much of the privatization debate revolves around whether guarding is intrinsically different from providing food, laundry, and health services. Knowing whether it is in the minds of the prisoners, and to what extent, seems crucial to evaluating the strategic benefits and liabilities of privatizing this aspect of the incarceration function.

20. See the *Boston Globe:* "Wilson Wants Drivers to Be City Employees" (Sept. 25, 1987), p. 1; "Flynn Backs Idea to Hire Drivers" (Sept. 26, 1987), p. 1; "Putting the Children First," editorial (Sept. 29, 1987), p. 18.

21. In many markets, the short-run disequilibria that inevitably exist have created a whole industry of arbitrageurs whose role is to exploit, and thus eliminate, these disequilibriums. The process of continuously redrawing the public and private boundaries in an industry is analogous.

22. Stephanie Gould (directed by Philip B. Heymann), "Jerome Miller and the Department of Youth Services (A), (B) and Part (B) sequel," Harvard University, John F. Kennedy School of Government, Teaching Cases C14-76-101.0, C14-76-102.0, C14-76-102.1. This case is discussed in Michael O'Hare, *The Productive Environment* (forthcoming).

23. We respectfully acknowledge the existence of differences of opinion on this point. Edward Koren of the American Civil Lib-

erties Union has testified that "from a civil liberties perspective it is irrelevant whether the correctional officer carrying a truncheon on the tier is wearing a badge with a star or a badge with a dollar sign." *Privatization of Corrections: Hearings,* , p. 6. Ironically, this statement is followed by Koren's enumeration of the ways private and public guards *are* different.

24. Telephone interview by Douglas McDonald with William Hutcherson, Legal Division, Tennessee Department of Correction, March 1990.

Public over Private: Monitoring the Performance of Privately Operated Prisons and Jails

1. For a discussion of the symbolic issues involved, see the last two essays in this volume, by John J. DiIulio, Jr., and by Douglas McDonald.

2. Essay by John J. DiIulio, Jr. in this volume.

3. The classic prison cases for these trend-setting judges were, respectively, *Pugh* v. *Locke,* 406 F. Supp. 318 (M.D. Ala. 1976) (Judge Johnson); *Landman* v. *Royster,* 354 F. Supp. 1302 (E.D. Va. 1973) (Judge Merhige); *Palmigiano* v. *Garrahy,* 443 F. Supp. 956 (D.R.I. 1977) (Judge Pettine); and *Ruiz* v. *Estelle,* 503 F. Supp. 1265 (S.D. Tex. 1980) (Judge Justice).

4. For a broad and competent analysis of monitoring, evaluation, and quality control issues in human services, see Valerie J. Bradley, *Assessing and Enhancing the Quality of Services: A Guide for the Human Services Field,* (Boston: Human Services Research Institute, 1984).

5. Essay by John J. DiIulio, Jr., in this volume.

6. See, for example, *Monroe* v. *Pape,* 365 U.S. 167 (1961), which spelled out requirements for establishing the jurisdiction of Federal courts; and *Cooper* v. *Pate,* 378 U.S. 546 (1964), which early dealt the "hands off" doctrine a mortal blow.

7. See Alvin Bronstein, "The Legal Implications of Privatization," *National Prison Project Journal,* no. 2 (Winter 1984), pp. 1–2.

8. Florida, for example, has a particularly elaborate correctional code; see *Florida Statutes Annotated* (St. Paul, Minn.: West Publishing Co., 1987), chap. 944.

9. Judith C. Hackett, Harry P. Hatry, Robert B. Levinson, Joan Allen, Keon Chi, and Edward D. Feigenbaum, "Issues in Contracting for the Private Operation of Prisons and Jails" (Washington, D.C.: Council of State Governments and the Urban Institute, 1987), chap. 6. These authors were impressed by the monitoring process of the Massachusetts Department of Youth Services and rated it the best they reviewed. For an earlier detailed review of that department's procedures for monitoring accountability, see J. Michael Keating, Jr., *Public Ends and Private Means: Accountability among Private Providers of Public Social Services* (Washington, D.C.: National Institute for Dispute Resolution, 1985), Report no. 2.

10. *Florida Statutes Annotated,* chap. 944, sec. 105.

11. Marc R. Levinson, "Special Masters: Engineers of Court-Ordered Reform," *Corrections Magazine* no. 4 (Aug., 1982):6.

12. A case involving only discipline in a correctional facility is *Powell* v. *Ward,* 487 F. Supp. 917 (S.D.N.Y. 1980).

13. The largest omnibus correctional suit to date, with or without a master, is *Ruiz* v. *Estelle,* 503 F. Supp. 1265 (S.D. Tex. 1980), which involved all state-operated correctional facilities in Texas.

14. Ibid.

15. House Committee on the Judiciary, *Privatization of Corrections: Hearings before the Subcommittee on Courts, Civil Liberties, and the Administration of Justice,* 99th Cong., 1st and 2d sess., Nov. 13, 1985, and Mar. 18, 1986, pp. 64–65. Reported here is the testimony of Richard G. Crane, vice-president for legal affairs of the CCA.

16. David D. Dillingham and Linda R. Singer, *Complaint Procedures in Prisons and Jails: An Examination of Recent Experience* (Washington, D.C.: National Institute of Corrections, 1980), p. 15.

17. *Annotated California Codes: Welfare & Institutional Code,* sec. 1766.5 (St. Paul, Minn.: West Publishing Co.).

18. Dillingham and Singer, *Complaint Procedures in Prisons and Jails,* pp. 5–6.

19. Hackett et al., *Final Report,* p. 11.

The Duty to Govern:
A Critical Perspective on the
Private Management of Prisons and Jails

1.   The literature on the history of penal reform in the United States is vast. The best one-volume survey of the subject is Blake McKelvey, *American Prisons: A History of Good Intentions* (Montclair, N.J.: Patterson-Smith, 1977). David J. Rothman has written two indispensable books about the birth and development of U.S. penal institutions: *The Discovery of the Asylum: Social Order and Disorder in the New Republic* (Boston: Little, Brown, 1971); and *Conscience and Convenience: The Asylum and Its Alternatives in Progressive America* (Boston: Little, Brown, 1980).

2.   The observations in this paragraph are based largely on two sources: (1) personal interviews with some two dozen persons directly involved in the privatization debate, including the executives of leading private corrections firms, penal reform organizations, and associations of corrections professionals; and (2) information gathered in the course of a four-month workshop on the privatization of corrections that brought together federal, state, and local actors representing the entire spectrum of opinion on the issue. For a concise summary of the workshop's proceedings and its findings, see Lynne J. Davidson et al., "Report of the Policy Workshop on the Privatization of Corrections" (Woodrow Wilson School of Public and International Affairs, Princeton University, July 1987).

3.   For a concise statement of these questions as they pertain to private management, construction, and finance, see John J. Di-Iulio, Jr., "Private Prisons," in *Crime File,* ed. Michael Tonry (Washington, D.C.: National Institute of Justice, 1987), p. 5. As of this writing, the single most comprehensive bibliography on the privatization of corrections is Russ Immarigeon, "Privatizing Adult Imprisonment in the U.S.: A Bibliography," *Criminal Justice Abstracts* 19 (Mar. 1987):123–139. In the 1980s some large-scale research projects examined the privatization of airlines, public works, urban mass transit, and other activities; a few of these studies adopted a cross-national perspective. Although the privatization of corrections is not been considered in these studies, they provide valuable frameworks for analysis. For example, see Steve H. Hanke, ed., *Prospects for Privatization. Proceedings of the American Academy of Political Science,* vol. 36, no. 3 (1987). Among the essays in that volume that are

of special interest to students of the privatization of corrections is Paul Starr, "The Limits of Privatization," pp. 124–137.

4.   To date, virtually all of the arguments over the morality of privatization have centered on the private administration of prisons and jails. So far as I know, nobody has lodged serious moral objections to private prison and jail construction. Certain private financing arrangements have been challenged as "undemocratic" because they enable politicians to build facilities without gaining voters' approval of bond issues; see Jan Elvin, "A Civil Liberties View of Private Prisons," in *Prison Journal* 65, no. 2 (Autumn–Winter 1985), esp. pp. 51–52. The same basic objection to certain private financing arrangements has been raised in dozens of other articles. There are, however, ways of involving the private sector in the finance of correctional activities that would answer this objection. For a brief overview of private financing arrangements, see Lawrence Shubnell and William Cobbs, "Creative Capital Financing: A Primer for State and Local Governments," in *Alternative Financing of Jail Construction* (Boulder, Colo.: National Institute of Corrections, 1983), pp. 16–26.

5.   A simple diagram in which public $= X$ and private $= Y$ may help to illustrate this point.

	1	2	3	4	5	6	7	8
Administration	X	X	X	X	Y	Y	Y	Y
Finance	X	X	Y	Y	X	X	Y	Y
Construction[a]	X	Y	Y	X	Y	X	X	Y

[a]In the case of probation, parole, and nonincarcerational programs, construction may be construed broadly as any plant and equipment used routinely—cars, monitoring devices, and so on.

6.   One such exception is Joan Mullen, Kent Chabotar, and Deborah Carrow, *The Privatization of Corrections* (Washington, D.C.: National Institute of Justice, 1985). Mullen and her colleagues make a decent if not completely successful attempt to outline the moral issues surrounding privatization in light of historical, administrative, financial, political, legal, and constitutional concerns.

7.   Academics have committed this mistake too, but it is largely the error of correctional policymakers and practitioners. For an interesting example, see the statement on private involvement in corrections in Charlotte A. Nesbitt, ed., *Public Policy for Corrections: A Handbook for Decisionmakers* (College Park, Md.: American Correctional Association, 1986), pp. 50–

53. Here it is tacitly assumed that, although "government has the ultimate authority for corrections," the moral standing of private management is totally unproblematic so long as it conforms to "professional standards" and contributes in tangible ways to the "effectiveness and efficiency" of correctional operations.

8. This mistake has commonly been made by academic opponents of privatization, including at least one extraordinarily learned student of moral and political philosophy; see Michael Walzer, "Hold the Justice," *New Republic,* Apr. 8, 1985, pp. 10–12. The preoccupation with profits can be found in works by less learned (and less disinterested) parties as well; for example, see the American Federation of State, County, and Municipal Employees, ed., *Does Crime Pay? An Examination of Prisons for Profit* (Washington, D.C.: AFSCME, 1985). Although I concede that the profit motive of the firms raises many significant questions of both a practical (Will they cut corners to the detriment of the inmates and work to "keep beds filled"?) and a moral (Is their aim ever just to profit from the misfortunes of criminals and their victims?) nature, I doubt that these questions are the central ones. For one thing, there have been, and continue to be, nonprofit, nonpublic corrections enterprises (e.g., the Florida School for Boys in Okeechobee run by the Jack and Ruth Eckerd Foundation). As I shall suggest, a properly constructed moral case for (or against) private management would not turn on whether the private contractor reaps huge profits, obtains moderate profits, or does it for free. By analogy, if we reason that it is morally wrong (or right) for married men to have sex with women other than their wives, then it matters little (if at all) whether the cheating is done with high-priced call girls, cheap prostitutes, unpaid whores, or the girl next door.

9. At root, it is the fact that the privatization of corrections raises such questions that distinguishes it from most other privatization ventures. In this light, it is impossible to disagree with Paul Starr when he writes: "In adjusting the public-private balance, we need to be attentive, sphere by sphere, to the special practical and moral considerations that arise in each. No single remedy is appropriate to the vastly different problems that distinguish collecting taxes from collecting trash, running schools from running railroads, managing prisons from managing shipyards" ("The Limits of Privatization," p. 136).

10. There are, however, some noteworthy exceptions; for example, see David H. Bayley, *Patterns of Policing: A Comparative International Analysis* (New Brunswick, N.J.: Rutgers

University Press, 1985); as well as his earlier work, *The Police and Political Development in India* (Princeton, N.J.: Princeton University Press, 1969). Also see Stuart Nagel et al., eds., *The Political Science of Criminal Justice* (Springfield, Ill.: Charles C. Thomas, 1983). This title promises more than is delivered, but the volume stands out as one of the few efforts of its kind. Also see the following papers, delivered at the 1987 annual meeting of the American Political Science Association (APSA): Ethan A. Nadelmann, "Constitutionalism and Drug Enforcement: The Radical Sound of Common Sense"; Candace McCoy, "Constitutional Tort Litigation: Controlling the Police?"; and John J. DiIulio, Jr., "The Prison as a Constitutional Regime: A Theoretical Perspective on Administrative Change in American Penal Organizations, 1930–1986." These papers were delivered before a panel on "Constitutionalism and the Administration of Criminal Justice," one of the few such panels in the APSA's recent history.

11. Alexander Hamilton et al., *The Federalist Papers,* ed. Clinton Rossiter (New York: Vintage, 1961), No. 20, p. 138.

12. Ibid., No. 6, p. 57.

13. For an essay outlining the "science of politics" practiced by the Founding Fathers, see Austin Ranney, "'The Divine Science': Political Engineering in American Culture," *American Political Science Review* 70, no. 1 (Mar. 1976):140–148. Ranney posits a basic continuity between the political science of the Founding Fathers and the political science of our own day; the latter, in his view, has simply improved upon the "primitive methods" of the former. In contrast, I see the Founding Fathers' brand of political science—historical, philosophical, genuinely empirical, concerned with the ends of constitutional government and how best to achieve them—as different from (and in most ways superior to) the political science of today.

14. Gustave de Beaumont and Alexis de Tocqueville, *On the Penitentiary System in the United States, and its Application in France; with an Appendix on Penal Colonies, and also, Statistical Notes,* trans. Francis Lieber (Philadelphia: Carey, Lea and Blanchard, 1833), p. 35.

15. Ibid.

16. Ibid., p. 36.

17. There are several reliable histories of the Texas prison system. An overview is provided by R. Craig Copeland, "The Evolution of the Texas Department of Corrections (TDC)," masters thesis, Criminal Justice Center, Sam Houston State University,

August 1980. For an official history, see *Texas Department of Corrections: 30 Years of Progress* (Huntsville: Texas Department of Corrections, 1974). The Texas prison archives, located at the Sam Houston State University Criminal Justice Center in Huntsville, Texas, contain what is perhaps the most complete (but as yet relatively unmined) collection of historical and other data on a single penal system that is to be found anywhere in the country.

18. Remnants of this contract-lease system were still in place in 1947 when the first director of the modern Texas Department of Corrections, O. B. Ellis, assumed office. By 1962, when Ellis was succeeded by George Beto, no traces of the system remained.

19. As Paul Keve has noted, leasing the labor of prisoners was "a temptation to prison administrators everywhere as they desperately faced postwar shortages of resources at the same time that their prisons were overcrowded or . . . destroyed by military action." See Keve, *The History of Corrections in Virginia* (Charlottesville: University of Virginia Press, 1986), esp. pp. 70–81. One of the least well studied periods in U.S. penal history is the Civil War. By most estimates, during the war the Confederacy took around 200,000 prisoners of war; the Union took more than twice as many (about 460,000). Nevertheless, before, during, and after the war the South had much greater administrative problems. As E. Merton Coulter observed, it was not until late 1864 that the Confederacy developed a unified system for handling its prisoners; this system failed. See Coulter, *The Confederate States of America, 1861–1865* (Baton Rouge: Louisiana State University Press, 1950), pp. 470–481.

20. The best single-volume history of the Louisiana penal system is Mark T. Carelton, *Politics and Punishment: The History of the Louisiana State Penal System* (Baton Rouge: Louisiana State University Press, 1971). Carelton's tale of the miseries inflicted on convicts by the ruthless, cynical, and politically adept Jones is chilling.

21. From Carelton's account (ibid.), it appears that the political abuses grew worse through the first half of the twentieth century and persisted in one form or another into the 1960s.

22. George W. Donaghey, "Why I Could Not Pardon the Contract Lease System," *Annals of the American Academy of Political and Social Science,* 46 (Mar. 1913):22–34. Like many leading opponents of the contract system, Donaghey assumed that all would be well once the state resumed control: "When the state is the only party in interest and the only one to be

satisfied, there could arise no condition under which convicts would be underfed, badly treated or overworked" (p. 27). Unfortunately, the history of public penal administration in Arkansas from the 1920s through the early 1970s proved Donaghey to be wrong.

23. Keve, *History of Corrections,* pp. 80–81.

24. Ibid., p. 80.

25. For example, California's penal system began with a private contract that led to inmate abuses and financial misdeeds, resulting in the dismissal of San Quentin's first warden. Michigan's Marquette prison was partially privatized in the 1920s, but private involvement ended when it became clear that the contractors were insufficiently interested in such matters as contraband control and inmate health. The history of corrections in Kentucky is punctuated by privatization efforts. Founded in 1799, the Kentucky State Penitentiary was leased to an entrepreneur in 1825. The contractors, who often failed to pay the state the required annual rent, became a powerful political lobby and were able to defeat successive legislative proposals calling for the public administration of the prisons well into the 1930s. In the early 1980s Kentucky's Corrections Cabinet studied a plan to place the state's five penal farms in the hands of a private agricultural concern; the plan was rejected. Unfortunately, because there is no comprehensive history of private sector involvement in U.S. corrections, one is forced to rely on a wide range of disparate primary and secondary sources. There are, however, several single-volume records of historical documents that can serve as a fair guide to some of these materials; for example, see Sol Chaneles, *Prisons and Prisoners: Historical Documents* (New York: Hayworth Press, 1985).

26. In his 1984 speech before the American Correctional Association, Federal District Judge William Wayne Justice observed that few judicial decisions "go beyond the standards that you as a profession have recognized and approved for the operation of correctional institutions." See "Address of the Honorable William Wayne Justice Presented before the 144th Congress of the American Correctional Association," San Antonio, Texas, Aug. 20, 1984, p. 10.

27. See "Private Venture Contractors" (College Park, Md.: American Correctional Association, Sept. 1986).

28. I am indebted to Dr. George Beto of Sam Houston State University for directing me to this document. The Texas prison archives (see note 18) contain many other such documents.

29.   Hamilton et al., *The Federalist Papers,* No. 48, p. 308.

30.   Representatives of the Prison Officers' Association of Great Britain have commented on the lack of adequate oversight at certain privately administered county facilities in the United States. See "Memorandum Submitted by the Prison Officers' Association" to the House Affairs Select Committee of the House of Commons, Feb. 11, 1987. Following their tour of the Corrections Corporation of America's Silverdale prison, located in Chattanooga, Tennessee, the Prison Officers' Association representatives reported:

> We saw evidence of inmates being cruelly treated. . . . The operation was overseen by an official of the County which was party to the contract with Corrections Corporation of America. The effectiveness of this official was in our view negated by the fact that he was in permanent residence at the prison since it opened. This official told us that . . . none of his colleagues in the County Government really knew what his role was. He also admitted to us that he often toured the country to address authorities interested in privatising their prisons and was a keen advocate of the system. (P. 100)

In June 1987, however, I myself visited two of CCA's juvenile facilities located in Shelby County, Tennessee (the Shelby Training Center and the Tall Trees facility). I was quite impressed by how clean, orderly, and treatment-oriented these facilities were; indeed, they were the most well run juvenile operations I had ever seen. I was also favorably impressed by the county official (an officer of the local court) who had oversight responsibility for these facilities. He seemed to be very much on top of what the CCA was doing.

31.   A notable exception in this regard is the federal Bureau of Prisons. Since 1980, the bureau has been struggling to revise its policy directives and auditing procedures so that there is more emphasis on performance.

32.   James Theodore Gentry, "The Panopticon Revisited: The Problem of Monitoring Private Prisons," *Yale Law Journal,* vol. 96 (1986). Gentry claims that by "setting goals instead of operating standards, the fine system encourages innovation and reduces the need for centralized direction of prisons" (p. 357).

33.   For example, see Stephen Gettinger, "Accreditation on Trial," *Corrections Magazine* 8, no. 1 (Feb. 1982):6–21. Since 1982 I have been inside recently accredited facilities that were, by any reasonable measure, disorderly and dirty.

34. Among other things, the American Correctional Association has reduced the time between accreditations from three years to one year.

35. For an impassioned if less than well reasoned discussion of this fact, see Jeffrey Reiman, *The Rich Get Richer and the Poor Get Prison* (New York: Wiley, 1979). Also see Jerold Auerbach, *Unequal Justice* (New York: Oxford University Press, 1976).

36. Inmates are now being employed by manufacturers of shoes, lamps, and other items for retail sale. In one Arizona prerelease center for women, inmates have been worked as telephone operators handling hotel reservations. The Control Data Corporation has hired Minnesota inmates to assemble computer parts. In Florida, prison industries have been run by a private, nonprofit organization called Prison Rehabilitative Industries and Diversified Enterprises (PRIDE) that sells office furniture and dozens of other items to public agencies. PRIDE has paid inmates less than $2.00 per hour. In most cases, however, inmates are paid salaries at or near the minimum wage. Generally, they receive no extra pay for weekends or holidays. As of this writing, no serious problems such as sweatshop conditions have been reported. For an overview, see Camille G. Camp and George M. Camp, *Private Sector Involvement in Prison Services and Operations* (Washington, D.C.: National Institute of Corrections, 1984); and their "Private Sector Involvement in Prison Services and Operations," in AFSCME, *Does Crime Pay?* pp. 23–30. Also see James Hirsch, "What's New in Private Prisons," *New York Times,* Apr. 26, 1987, p. F17.

37. The state's liability may increase because, by delegating its incarceration function, the state may lose its defense of sovereign immunity in ordinary-negligence actions.

38. For an overview, see John J. DiIulio, Jr., "Prison Discipline and Prison Reform," *Public Interest,* no. 89 (Fall 1987), pp. 71–90; also see J. Thomas et al., "Issues and Misconceptions in Prisoner Litigation: A Critical Review," *Criminology* 24, no. 4 (1986):775–797.

39. DiIulio, "Prison Discipline."

40. The conception of politics used here is taken from Edward C. Banfield, "Note on Conceptual Scheme," in Martin Meyerson and Edward C. Banfield, *Politics, Planning, and the Public Interest* (New York: Free Press, 1955), pp. 303–329. As Banfield observed, when "there is a conflict, real or apparent, between the ends of different actors (or within the end-system of a single actor) and not all of the conflicting ends can be realized, an is-

sue exists and the actors whose ends conflict are the parties to the issue. . . . Politics is the activity (negotiation, argument, discussion, application of force, persuasion, etc.) by which an issue is agitated or settled."

41. See, for example, Richard A. Berk and Peter Rossi, *Prison Reform and State Elites* (Cambridge, Mass.: Ballinger, 1970); Nagel et al., *Political Science of Criminal Justice;* Barbara Lavin, "Political Theory and Correctional Politics," paper presented at the 1983 meeting of the American Political Science Association; Julia Gordon, "Under Lock and Key: Correctional Policymaking in Massachusetts," senior honors thesis, Harvard University, 1985. Also see the study of juvenile deinstitutionalization by George W. Downs, *Bureaucracy, Policy, and Innovation* (Lexington, Mass.: Lexington Books, 1976).

42. Randall B. Ripley and Grace A. Franklin, *Congress, the Bureaucracy, and Public Policy* (Homewood, Ill.: Dorsey Press, 1976), p. 5. In Michigan and California, for example, labor unions representing correctional officers have influenced corrections policy. See John J. DiIulio, Jr., *Governing Prisons: A Comparative Study of Correctional Management* (New York: Free Press, 1987).

43. Richard A. McGee, *Prisons and Politics* (Lexington, Mass.: Lexington Books, 1981).

44. Eric Nordlinger, *On the Autonomy of the Democratic State* (Cambridge, Mass.: Harvard University Press, 1981). Sociologists have implied that because the days of the autocratic warden are gone in most jurisdictions, because prisoners now enjoy institutionalized legal protection, and because groups have been mobilized to exert influence on what corrections officials do, the politics of corrections has changed fundamentally; see James B. Jacobs, *Stateville: The Penitentiary in Mass Society* (Chicago: University of Chicago Press, 1977). But as the prison has entered "mass society," the politics of corrections has remained essentially nonpluralistic. It would be interesting to know what general features of corrections make it relatively resistant to the pluralistic gravity of politics in the United States, and to make systematic comparisons among other substantive policy areas (preferably outside of criminal justice, e.g., national security policy) where the state appears to be relatively autonomous, in order to see whether any patterns emerge.

45. Among others, T. Don Hutto, formerly vice-president of the Corrections Corporation of America, now head of its international division, has stressed this point. He did so at the Wood-

row Wilson School Workshop on the Privatization of Corrections
(see note 2), and earlier in his comments at a national forum on
the issue. See *Corrections and the Private Sector: A National
Forum,* (Washington, D.C.: National Institute of Justice, 1985).
It is worth noting here that Hutto is also a high-ranking official
with the American Correctional Association. He was recently
awarded the ACA's Cass Medal for outstanding service to the
corrections profession.

46.   Such fears have been raised in dozens of essays and reports. They have also been raised in key public hearings. For
example, see House Committee on the Judiciary; *Privatization
of Corrections: Hearings before the Subcommittee on Courts,
Civil Liberties, and the Administration of Justice,* 99th Cong.,
1st and 2d sess., Nov. 13, 1985, and Mar. 18, 1986.

47.   See note 28.

48.   See note 2. This same point was made by CCA president
Thomas Beasley in a discussion with the author and Thomas A.
Coughlin III, commissioner of the New York State Department
of Correctional Services, Dec. 4, 1986.

49.   Corrections Corporation of America, "Proposal for State of
Tennessee," Nashville, Sept. 1985. This proposal is far less detailed than one might expect. It consists mainly of descriptive
material about the CCA's philosophy, the credentials of its staff,
and its past successes.

50.   See note 2; also see Bruce Dobie, "CCA Officials Meet to
Discuss Strategy Following Defeat," *Nashville Banner,* Mar. 12,
1986, p. C14.

51.   Strong lobbying efforts were made on both sides. For a fair
overview of the controversy, see Terry Bivens, "Can Prisons for
Profits Work?" *Philadelphia Inquirer Magazine,* Aug. 3, 1986.
In April of 1987, a bipartisan legislative task force voted 4–1 to
extend the ban. Officials of the Pennsylvania Prison Society, the
nation's oldest penal reform group, had argued vigorously that
it was morally wrong for the state to delegate its authority to
punish to for-profit organizations. To the surprise of many, this
argument was at the center of the debate.

52.   This worry has been expressed by Doctor R. Crants of the
Corrections Corporation of America; see note 2.

53.   For example, in 1986 the Corrections Corporation of America suffered an onslaught of negative media publicity when a
riot occurred at its Silverdale facility, a 360-bed prison (in Chattanooga, Tennessee,) for both male and female prisoners serving
seven years or less. The riot followed inmate protests for better

food, more adequate recreation, and improved treatment. The prison staff was too small and too inexperienced (so critics charged) to respond to the situation. A police special weapons and tactics (SWAT) team was called in to take control. When asked about the incident, a ranking corrections officer at a public jail for adults located in another Tennessee county expressed the widespread belief that "these rent-a-cop prisons can't even handle the easy cases."

54.   AFSCME, *Does Crime Pay?*

55.   For a comprehensive overview of this effort, see Fred L. Smith, Jr., "Privatization at the Federal Level," in Hanke, *Prospects for Privatization,* pp. 179–189. Also see Martin Tolchin, "U.S. Pressing Plan to Contract Work: Idea Is Private Enterprise Can Do Better Job," *New York Times,* Mar. 11, 1986; and the series of five articles on private corrections by Tolchin that appeared in the same newspaper in Feb. 1985.

56.   See Martin Tolchin, "Privately Operated Prison in Tennessee Reports $200,000 in Cost Overruns," *New York Times,* May 21, 1985.

57.   For example, see Philip E. Fixler and Robert W. Poole, Jr., "Status of State and Local Privatization," in Hancke, *Prospects for Privatizations,* pp. 164–178.

58.   By the same token, Fixler and Poole's advice (ibid.) is less applicable to private policing.

59.   Hamilton et al., *The Federalist Papers,* No. 10, p. 78.

60.   For a lively and critical review of the literature on public sector performance versus private sector performance, see George W. Downs and Patrick Larkey, *The Search for Government Efficiency: From Hubris to Helplessness* (New York: Random House, 1986). Also see Hanke, *Prospects for Privatization.*

61.   At this point, perhaps I should remind the reader of my own assumption, stated in the Introduction, that the empirical data and analyses necessary to address the claims of superior administrative performance by private contractors do not now exist.

62.   The notion of "impossible jobs" is being explored by a group of scholars working under the auspices of Vanderbilt University's Institute for Public Policy Studies. For an overview, see two papers presented at the Oct, 29, 1987, meeting of the Academy of Public Policy Analysis and Management: Erwin Hargrove, "Impossible Jobs"; John J. DiIulio, Jr, "Managing a Barbed Wire Bureaucracy: The Impossible Job of the Correc-

tions Commissioner." Like the typical contemporary police chief, welfare director, and mental health commissioner, the typical contemporary corrections commissioner has an "impossible job" in the sense that stated legal goals and public expectations about their achievement cannot be met because ends conflict, requisite technologies are not available, and bureaucratic authority is fragmented. Since 1973,the average tenure of corrections commissioners has been about three years.

63. For an interesting example, see W. Michael Blumenthal, "Candid Reflections of a Businessman in Washington," *Fortune,* Jan. 29, 1987, pp. 36–49. Also see Downs and Larkey, *Search for Government Efficiency;* and Hal G. Rainey et al., "Comparing Public and Private Organizations," *Public Administration Review* 36 (1976):233–244.

64. For a discussion of the measurement of prison order, amenity, and service, see DiIulio, *Governing Prisons,* esp. chap. 2.

65. Ibid. Also see Robert Johnson, *Hard Time: Understanding and Reforming the Prison* (Monterey, Calif.: Brooks-Cole, 1987).

66. For a fuller discussion of prison improvements, see John J. DiIulio, Jr., "Federal Experience Shows Prisons Are Not Hopeless," *Philadelphia Inquirer,* Feb. 23, 1987. I am in the early stages of research, supported in part by the National Institute of Corrections, on the subject of the politics and administration of the federal Bureau of Prisons, 1930–1987.

67. See John J. DiIulio, Jr., *Barbed Wire Bureaucracy: Leadership and Administration in the Federal Bureau of Prisons, 1930–1990* (New York: Oxford University Press, forthcoming). 99th Cong., 1st sess., June 26, 1985.

68. Although none of these systems is (or was) perfect, some examples include the California Department of Corrections under Richard A. McGee (1944–1967); the Texas Department of Corrections under George Beto (1962–1972); the Michigan Department of Corrections under Perry M. Johnson (1972–1984); the South Carolina Department of Corrections under William Leeke (1968–1987); and the New Jersey Department of Corrections under William Fauver (1973 to present).

69. Peter Greenwood, "Let Private Enterprise Run the Prisons," *Los Angeles Times,* May 11, 1981.

70. The National Institute of Corrections has done much to stimulate this development. See the proceedings of the NIC-sponsored meeting of new and veteran corrections commissioners, San Francisco, Calif., Oct. 29–31, 1987.

71. Dennis F. Thompson, "Moral Responsibility of Public Officials: The Problem of Many Hands," *American Political Science Review,* 74, no. 4 (Dec. 1980):905–916.

72. As should be obvious, an exhaustive preliminary effort could be made to define the competing epistemological and other assumptions that might support the various approaches to these questions, or merely to highlight the competing theories of criminal sanctioning—utilitarian, neoutilitarian, retributivist, and so on. This essay is not the place for such important philosophical gymnastics. In what follows, therefore, I shall take a more direct approach, beginning with a series of assertions and then attempting to support them with various arguments and illustrations. Readers will not miss the communitarian and nonconsequentialist presuppositions that support my basic argument. My chief presupposition is Kantian: "Penal justice (jusitia punitivia), because it is based on arguments about punishability that are moral (quia peccatum est), must be sharply distinguished from that kind of punishment that is purely pragmatic and utilitarian (ne peccetur) and that is grounded on what experience has shown to be the most effective means of preventing crime." Immanuel Kant, *The Metaphysical Elements of Justice* (part 1 of the *Metaphysics of Morals*), trans. John Ladd (Indianapolis: Bobbs-Merrill, 1965), p. 132.

73. That these symbols are not empty is presupposed in a wide body of public laws. James S. Kakalik and Sorrel Wildhorn, who conducted a thorough 1977 survey of private policing in the United States, observed that both "private citizens and private security personnel are generally prohibited from wearing badges or uniforms that might be confused with those worn by public police." Some states (e.g., California) go well beyond simple regulations proscribing impersonation and forbid private police from doing anything that might "create the impression that they are acting under government authority." Other states (e.g., New York) prohibit private investigators from "owning, exhibiting, or displaying a shield or badge in the performance of his duties." In every jurisdiction, a private police officer, unless deputized, "has no greater authority to assert powers of arrest than does a private citizen"; the fact that undeputized private police officers often wear uniforms and carry guns has given rise to all kinds of problems. See James S. Kakalik and Sorrel Wildhorn, *The Private Police: Security and Danger* (New York: Crane Russak, 1977), pp. 331–340, 474–476.

74. Discussion with the author, Dec. 4, 1986.

75.   The term is from R. M. MacIver, *The Web of Government* (New York: Free Press, 1965), p. 34. In chapter 3, MacIver defends the idea that the "web of government" is spun largely through "myths of authority" in which symbols are crucial.

76.   John Locke, *Two Treatises of Government*, ed. Peter Laslett (New York: New American Library, 1965), p. 308. The reader may need to be reminded that by "Property" Locke meant life, liberty, and the material fruits of one's labor.

77.   For an overview, see DiIulio, *Governing Prisons*.

78.   A very good discussion of the politics-administration dichotomy and the moral implications of its demise is found in John Rohr, *Ethics for Bureaucrats: An Essay on Law and Values* (New York: Marcel Dekker, 1978).

79.   See the Bureau of Justice Statistics Special Report, *Population Density in State Prisons* (Washington, D.C.: National Institute of Justice, Dec. 1986); also see George M. Camp, *The Management of Crowded Prisons* (New York: Criminal Justice Institute, 1978).

80.   In 1986, the cost of corrections was the fastest growing part of many state budgets. Yet, in 1986 less than a penny of every dollar of total government expenditures (federal, state, and local) went to corrections. As a category of federal spending, "Justice" ranked last or (depending on how one calculates the figure for "Space Research and Technology") next to last, and corrections costs were the smallest part of the national law enforcement budget. In scores of jurisdictions, money-saving penal reforms (e.g., intensive supervision programs) have been implemented or are on the horizon. For an overview, see John J. DiIulio, Jr., "True Penal Reform Can Save Money," *Wall Street Journal*, Sept. 28, 1987.

81.   DiIulio, *Governing Prisons*.

82.   Herbert Kaufman, *Red Tape: Its Origins, Uses, and Abuses* (Washington, D.C.: Brookings Institution, 1977), esp. chap. 2.

When Government Fails: Going Private as a Last Resort

1.   See Aric Press's essay in this volume for the Bay County story.

2.   See his essay in this volume.

3. American Bar Association, Criminal Justice Section, "Report to the House of Delegates," Feb. 13, 1989.

4. "Report to the House of Delegates," p. 3.

5. David Lawrence, "Private Exercise of Governmental Power," *Indiana Law Journal* 61 (1986):649.

6. 298 U.S. 238 (1936).

7. *Corpus Juris Secundum,* vol. 8, section 87 (St. Paul, Minn.: West Publishing Company).

8. For an excellent discussion of the bases of private security forces' exercise of power, see Clifford D. Shearing and Phillip C. Stenning, "Modern Private Security: Its Growth and Implications," *Crime and Justice: An Annual Review of Research,* vol. 3 (Chicago: University of Chicago Press, 1981), pp. 193–245.

9. Ira Robbins, *The Legal Dimensions of Private Incarceration* (Washington, D.C.: American Bar Association, 1988), p. 34.

10. *Medina* v. *O'Neill,* 589 F. Supp. 1028 (1984).

11. Craig Becker and Amy Dru Stanley, "The Downside of Private Prisons," *The Nation,* June 15, 1985.

12. Lawrence, "Private Exercise of Governmental Power," p. 658.

13. Ibid., p. 651.

14. For example, Colorado, Florida, Massachusetts, Montana, New Mexico, Oklahoma, Tennessee, Texas, and Utah. National Criminal Justice Association, *Private Sector Involvement in Financing and Managing Correctional Facilities* (Washington, D.C.: National Criminal Justice Statistics Association, 1987), Exhibit 1.

15. Robbins, *Legal Dimensions,* p. 43.

16. Ibid., p. x.

17. "Report to the House of Delegates," p. 3.

18. *Medina* v. *O'Neill* and *Ancata* v. *Prison Health Services, Inc.,* 769 F.2d 700, 702 (11th Cir. 1985).

19. See John DiIulio's essay in this volume for a discussion of incarceration in the United States. Also see Michael Sherman and Gordon Hawkins, *The Prison: Policy and Practice* (Chicago: University of Chicago Press, 1976).

20. Robert Kuttner, "The Private Market Can't Always Solve Public Problems," *Business Week,* Mar. 10, 1986, p. 14.

21. See his essay in this volume.

22. John Locke, *Two Treatises of Government,* ed. Peter Laslett (New York: New American Library, 1965), p. 308.

23. Ira Robbins, "Privatization of Corrections: Defining the Issues," *Judicature* 69 (Apr.–May 1986):331.

24. Robert Nozick, *Anarchy, State, and Utopia* (New York: Basic Books, 1974), chap. 5 and 6.

25. Charles H. Logan, "Propriety of Private Prisons," in Lynn Goodstein and Doris L. MacKenzie, eds., *The American Prison: Issues in Research and Policy* (New York: Plenum Press, 1989).

26. National Coalition for Jail Reform, "Facts about America's Jails" (Washington, D.C., undated); and computations from miscellaneous data in American Correctional Association, *Directory 1986* (College Park, Md.: ACA, 1986).

27. Letter from Alvin Bronstein of the National Prison Project, June 7, 1988.

28. Bureau of Justice Statistics, *Jail Inmates 1986* (Washington, D.C.: Department of Justice, 1987), Table 9 and p. 3.

29. See James B. Jacobs, *Stateville: The Penitentiary in Mass Society* (Chicago: University of Chicago Press, 1977), for an excellent history of the administrative evolution of corrections, reflected by the case of one institution. For a discussion of the changes in legal rights accorded inmates, see Alvin J. Bronstein, "Offender Rights Litigation: Historical and Future Developments," in Ira P. Robbins, ed., *Prisoners' Rights Sourcebook*, Vol. 2 (New York: Clark Boardman, 1980), pp. 9–28.

30. Criminal Justice Section, American Bar Association, "Report to the House of Delegates," 1986, p. 4. (This was the first of such reports, recommending a moratorium on privatization until the legal issues could be developed.)

31. *Medina* v. *O'Neill.*

32. Author's interview with the administrator of the Correctional Corporation of America's detention facility in Santa Fe, New Mexico, May 1987.

33. Robert A. Dahl and Charles E. Lindblom, *Politics, Economics, and Welfare* (New York: Harper and Row Torchbooks, 1953).

34. See Aric Press's essay in this volume for discussions of both of these jails.

35. Charles H. Logan and Bill W. McGriff, "Comparing Costs of Public and Private Prisons: A Case Study," *NIJ Reports* no. 216 (Sept.-Oct. 1969). For a discussion of this comparison, see my essay in this volume.

36. Judith C. Hackett, Harry P. Hatry, Robert B. Levinson, Joan Allen, Keon Chi, and Edward D. Feigenbaum, "Issues in

Contracting for the Private Operation of Prisons and Jails," (Washington, D.C.: Council of State Governments and the Urban Institute, 1987), p. 141.

37. John Donahue, *Prisons for Profit: Public Justice, Private Interests* (Washington, D.C.: Economic Policy Institute, 1988).

38. Selwyn Rabb, "Wicks Law Blocks School Construction Plans," *New York Times,* Jan. 1, 1988.

39. I am indebted to Professor Charles Thomas of the University of Florida, and an expert on privatization, for this observation.

40. Robert W. Poole, Jr., and Philip E. Fixler, Jr., "Privatization of Public-Sector Services in Practice: Experience and Potential," in *Journal of Policy Analysis and Management* 6 (1987):615. For similar reviews see, for example, Stephen Moore, "Contracting Out: A Painless Alternative to the Budget Cutter's Knife," in Steve H. Hanke, ed., *Prospects for Privatization (Proceedings of the Academy of Political Science,* 36, no. 3 (1987):61–73.

41. Oliver E. Williamson, "What Is Transaction Cost Economics?" Working Paper no. 1014 (New Haven, Conn.: Institution for Social and Policy Studies, Yale University, May 1984).

42. The phrase is Williamson's, ibid., note 7.

43. Jan Chaiken and Stephen Mennemeyer, *Lease-Purchase Financing of Prison and Jail Construction* (Washington, D.C.: National Institute of Justice, 1987); Kent John Chabotar, "Financing Alternatives for Prison and Jail Construction," *Government Finance Review,* Aug. 1985; A. John Vogt and Lisa A. Cole, "Types of Leases and Identifying Characteristics of Tax-Exempt Leases," in A. John Vogt et al., *A Guide to Municipal Leasing* (Washington, D.C.: Municipal Finance Officers Association, Government Finance Research Center, 1985).

44. Franklin Zimring and Gordon Hawkins, "The New Mathematics of Imprisonment," Working Paper no. 8 (Berkeley: Earl Warren Legal Institute, University of California School of Law, undated), p. 21.

45. For example, Minnesota's sentencing guidelines explicitly take into account the prison resources that are available; the guidelines direct judges to reserve imprisonment for those convicted of violent crimes rather than property crimes, even repetitive property crimes. See, for example, Dale G. Parent, *Structuring Criminal Sentences: The Evolution of Minnesota's Sentencing Guidelines* (Stoneham, Mass.: Butterworths, 1988).

Contributors

John J. DiIulio is an Associate Professor of Politics and Public Affairs at Princeton University. He spent the 1988–89 academic year on leave from Princeton as a John M. Olin Faculty Fellow and Guest Scholar at the Brookings Institution. At Princeton, he teaches in the Woodrow Wilson School of Public and International Affairs, and the Politics Department. He chairs the Woodrow Wilson School's domestic and urban policy graduate program. He is the author of *Governing Prisons: A Comparative Study of Correctional Management* (Free Press, 1987); *No Escape: The Future of American Corrections* (Basic Books, forthcoming); *Barbed Wire Bureaucracy: Administration in the Federal Bureau of Prisons* (Oxford, forthcoming); (editor) *Courts, Corrections, and the Constitution* (Oxford, forthcoming); and of numerous articles published in scholarly journals and leading magazines and newspapers. He has done consulting work for the National Institute of Justice, the National Institute of Corrections, the New York City Board of Corrections, and other agencies.

J. Michael Keating, Jr., is a partner and director of Alternative Dispute Resolution Services for the Providence, Rhode Island, law firm of Tillinghast, Collins & Graham. A graduate of Holy Cross College (B.A.), New York University (M.A.), and the Georgetown University Law Center (J.D.), Keating is a monitor for federal courts in prison and jail cases in Georgia, Massachusetts, Rhode Island, and Texas. Keating is also a nationally known mediator and arbitrator. He has written extensively about alternative dispute resolution and corrections.

Herman B. Leonard is the George F. Baker, Jr., Professor of Public Sector Financial Management at Harvard University's John F. Kennedy School of Government. His research interests include public finance and public financial management; his teaching closely parallels those interests in focusing on policy analysis, finance, and financial management and controls. Professor Leonard was a member of both the Governor's Council on Economic Policy of the state of Alaska and the Governor's

Advisory Council on Infrastructure of the state of Massachusetts. He currently serves as chairman of the Massachusetts
Governor's Task Force on Tuition Prepayment Plans, and was a
member of the National Academy of Sciences Committee on National Urban Policy, its Committee on the Superconducting
Super Collider, and the Senate Budget Committee's Private
Sector Advisory Committee on Infrastructure. He is currently a
member of the Massachusetts Health and Educational Facilities
Authority.

Robert A. Leone, a professor of operations management at the
School of Management, Boston University, is a principal of Put-
nam, Hayes and Bartlett, Inc., in Cambridge. He has also
taught at the John F. Kennedy School of Government and the
Harvard Business School, and has been a senior economist at
the Council of Economic Advisors, as well as a research associate at the National Bureau of Economic Analysis. He has acted
as a consultant to numerous public and private organizations on
issues relating to strategic operations management, competitive
analysis, and regulatory impact assessment; his clients have
ranged from regional telephone and utility companies to federal
agencies and trade associations. Among his books and articles is
Who Profits: Winners, Losers, and Government Regulation, published in 1985 by Basic Books.

Douglas C. McDonald is a senior social scientist in the Law
and Public Policy Division of Abt Associates Inc. in Cambridge,
Massachusetts. He was a senior research associate at the Vera
Institute of Justice in New York City. He has written several
books, articles, and reports on a variety of criminal justice matters. Among them are *Punishment without Walls: Community
Service Sentences in New York City* (Rutgers University Press,
1986), *The Price of Punishment: Public Spending for Corrections
in New York* (Westview Press, 1980), and *Privatize Federal
Prison Hospitals? A Feasibility Study* (Abt Associates, 1990) for
the National Institute of Justice and the Office of Management
and Budget.

Michael O'Hare is a lecturer in Public Policy at Harvard's
John F. Kennedy School of Government. An engineer and architect, he has written extensively on public management, public
finance, environmental and energy policy, regulation, and planning and design. He is the author of over forty publications,
including *Facility Siting and Public Opposition* (Van Nostrand

Reinhold, 1983). Formerly, he was Massachusetts' assistant secretary of environmental affairs for policy.

Aric Press is a senior editor at *Newsweek*. Before assuming his editorial duties in 1988, he was for eight years the magazine's chief writer on legal affairs. Press has covered a wide variety of issues and stories, both domestic and international. He is also an attorney and a member of the New York bar.

Andrew Rutherford is director of the Institute of Criminal Justice and a senior lecturer in the faculty of law in the University of Southampton, England. He worked in the English prison system for ten years and for a slightly shorter period taught and researched in various academic and public policy centers in the United States. The author of *Prisons and the Process of Justice* (Oxford University Press, 1986), he is chairman of the Howard League for Penal Reform.

Marc Zegans is currently executive director of the Innovations in State and Local Government Program at Harvard's John F. Kennedy School of Government, where he is pursuing his doctorate. He has been an adviser to Boston's Mayor Raymond Flynn and has worked for the city government in New York. His research concerns innovations in state and local government and public sector marketing.

Index